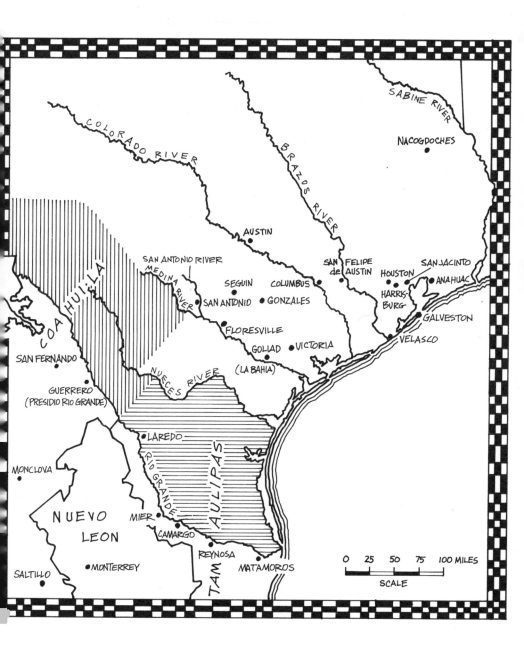

SABINE RIVER

COLORADO RIVER

BRAZOS RIVER

NACOGDOCHES

AUSTIN

SAN ANTONIO RIVER

MEDINA RIVER

SEGUIN

SAN ANTONIO

COLUMBUS

SAN FELIPE de AUSTIN

SAN JACINTO

HOUSTON

ANAHUAC

HARRIS-BURG

GONZALES

GALVESTON

FLORESVILLE

GOLIAD

VICTORIA

VELASCO

(LA BAHIA)

COAHUILA

SAN FERNANDO

NUECES RIVER

GUERRERO
(PRESIDIO RIO GRANDE)

LAREDO

MONCLOVA

RIO GRANDE

TAMAULIPAS

NUEVO
LEON

MIER

CAMARGO

SALTILLO

MONTERREY

REYNOSA

MATAMOROS

0   25   50   75   100 MILES

SCALE

A REVOLUTION REMEMBERED

The Memoirs and Selected Correspondence of

JUAN N. SEGUÍN

Para Gloria Cadena,
Con aprecio,

Jesús F. de la Teja
12/6/91

Portrait of Juan N. Seguín by Jefferson Wright, 1838.
Courtesy of the Texas State Library, Austin, Texas.

A REVOLUTION REMEMBERED

The Memoirs and Selected Correspondence of

JUAN N. SEGUÍN

edited by Jesús F. de la Teja

State House Press
Austin • Texas
1991

Library of Congress Cataloging-in-Publication Data

Seguín, Juan Nepomuceno, 1806-1890.
[Selections. English. 1991]
A revolution remembered : the memoirs and selected correspondence of
Juan N. Seguín / edited by Jesús F. de la Teja.
p. cm.
Includes bibliographical references and index.
ISBN 0-938349-68-6 (hardcover : alk. paper)
ISBN 0-938349-69-4 (ltd. ed. : alk. paper)
1. Seguín, Juan Nepomuceno, 1806-1890. 2. Soldiers—Texas—Biography.
3. Politicians—Texas—Biography. 4. Texas—History—Revolution,
1835-1836. 5. Texas—History—Republic, 1836-1846.
I. Teja, Jesús F. de la, 1956- .
II. Title.
F390.S465 1991
976.4'0099—dc20

91—23838

Printed in the United States of America

STATE HOUSE PRESS
P.O. Box 15247 • Austin, Texas 78761

Endpaper maps by Charles Shaw

Table of Contents

LIST OF ILLUSTRATIONS:

Preface

Juan Nepomuceno Seguín has been the subject of, or a central character in, several historical works, including a university master's thesis, a motion picture and a comic book. All rely on Seguín's own brief memoirs as a central source of information. Yet the memoirs themselves have never been critically analyzed nor annotated, and few other documents concerning Seguín have been published.

Juan claims to have written the memoirs, which appeared in 1858, in response to critics who insisted that he betrayed the Texan cause in 1842. While many of these attacks were verbal, some appeared in the press. Henderson Yoakum's *History of Texas* (1855), the first major history of Texas to include an accusation of treason against Seguín, may well have relied on these published allegations as source material. Yet, despite the accusations, Juan continued to find a significant measure of acceptance in an increasingly Anglo-American San Antonio. During the 1850s he served as a justice of the peace, election precinct chairman, and co-founder of the Democratic Party in Bexar County. Obviously, the judgment of a majority of his neighbors was favorable to him.

The memoirs served Seguín's political agenda. Narrowly focused on his military and political actions, with the exception of the pathos-filled account of his family's misfortunes during the Texas War of Independence, Seguín's memoirs shy away from other controversial topics such as his land speculation and his activities during his residency in Mexico after the Woll Expedition. He intended the memoirs to demonstrate his innocence of the allegations of treason which, although frequently vented in public forums, were never formalized in judicial charges. In the memoirs Seguín portrayed himself as a loyal champion of the Texas cause, a patriot whose innocent actions were twisted into treasonous ones by his personal enemies.

Juan Seguín's case exemplifies the various possible perspectives of "betrayal" and "loyalty." From the viewpoint of Mexican authorities who fought against Texas independence, Juan was a traitor to Mexico. From the Anglo Texans' point of view he became a traitor to Texas when he fled to Mexico in April 1842, returning in the fall with Adrián Woll's invasion forces. For many Texans the label of traitor was reinforced by Seguín's service to Mexico during the Mexican War.

Yet Seguín had a right to feel betrayed. Having defended the land of his birth against Mexico City, he was subsequently confronted by newcomers who treated him as if he were an alien in Texas. He felt himself "a foreigner in my native land." Ignorant, intolerant, greedy, misunderstanding the subtleties of border politics, a group of Anglo-American adventurers accused, judged and sentenced him for treason without allowing him the benefit of a defense. When Seguín called for help among those with whom he had served in the Army of the Republic and the Texas Congress, he found no support. Is it surprising, then, that Seguín fled to Mexico? Bitter, hounded and dispossessed, it is not hard to imagine that he might have taken up arms—albeit reluctantly according to his memoirs—against a Texas that not only spurned him but actively sought to destroy him.

All this is not to say that Seguín was beyond reproach. He made mistakes along the way, and with them a number of political enemies. Some of his economic activities, including speculation in land grants, also proved politically and economically compromising. At a time when the distinction between Tejano and Mexican was non-existent for Anglo Americans, Juan moved and acted too independently, perhaps even too arrogantly, to suit the tastes of some.

By the time he died Juan was an all-but-forgotten minor character in Texas history books. Biographers of Houston, Lamar, Rusk and Johnston completely ignored Seguín's associations with them. Most writers of historical accounts of the Texas War of Independence found it difficult to deal with Juan and discussed him ambivalently. But sympathizers emerged among Tejano and revisionist Anglo writers. In his 1936 book aimed at highlighting Tejano contributions to Texas independence, *Viva Tejas: The Story of the Mexican-born Patriots of the Republic of Texas,* Rubén Rendón Lozano portrayed

Juan as a hero. Other publications soon appeared and Seguín's reputation improved enough that a World War II cargo ship was named in his honor. In 1949 Ida Vernon wrote a more extensive account of Juan's activities in which she analyzes and defends his departure for Mexico. On the other hand, historian Joseph Nance's 1963 book *After San Jacinto*, while agreeing that Juan was wrongly treated, does accuse him of poor judgment.

The most revisionist view of Juan Seguín appears in Jesús S. Treviño's 1979 film *Seguín*. An overtly Chicano political statement, it portrays Juan as more democratic than the slave-owning Anglo Americans and more conscious than his fellow Bexareños of the threat the Anglo Americans posed to Tejanos. The film contains an anachronistic consciousness that detracts from the movie's effort to focus attention on the Tejano contribution to Texas history. Writing about the film in his article "Remembering the Alamo," Don Graham cites the following example: "Juan Seguín is portrayed as a strong proponent of women's rights, a bit of feminist wish-fulfillment by a post-sixties director."[1]

Enough evidence survives, much of it presented in the following pages, to suggest that, as with life in general, Juan Seguín's case is not cast in black and white. Seguín served Texas at the same time that he served himself. How many public figures can say otherwise? He led troops into battle, but was quick to recognize insurmountable odds and counsel retreat. Juan was a versatile man—statesman, soldier, businessman, politician—but foremost, he was a survivor.

I originally conceived of the present work as an essay on Juan Seguín and the San Antonio area during the period covered by Seguín's memoirs, with an annotated and edited version of the memoirs. It soon became apparent, however, that a large body of documentation existed in Texas and elsewhere that shed considerable light on parts of the memoirs. Publication of the documents would serve two purposes: first, they would supplement the memoirs in more decisive

---

[1]Don Graham, "Remembering the Alamo: The Story of the Texas Revolution in Popular Culture," SWHQ 89 (1985): 63.

terms than I ever could hope to achieve; and second, they would illustrate the possibilities for original research on early Tejano leaders.

This book is, however, neither a biography of Juan Seguín nor a collection of all his writings. A biography requires a comprehensive treatment of the subject's life, and this I have not attempted. Seguín lived almost a third of his life in Mexico, including his self-imposed exile 1842-1848 and his last two decades. He fought on the Mexican side in the Mexican War, retired to Nuevo Laredo in 1870, and was buried there in 1890. His years in Mexico remain a large void in our knowledge of Seguín. Although he was a family man whose children included prominent ranchers and a mayor of Nuevo Laredo, we know little about his personal life. Consequently, a considerable amount of research remains to be done, particularly in the Mexican archives, to tell Seguín's complete story. I do, however, present a general overview of Seguín's life in the biographical essay which precedes the edited memoirs.

The book is thus divided into three parts. First is my essay "The Making of a Tejano," which focuses not just on Juan but also on his father, Erasmo, who played an important political role during the Mexican period of Texas history (1821-1836). The second part of the book consists of the edited memoirs, which have been annotated to clarify and to correct the text. The third and last part of *A Revolution Remembered* consists of seventy-three appendices, chosen as representative of Juan's activities with relation to the period covered in the memoirs, 1834 to 1842.

Having chosen the memoirs as the book's centerpiece, it was natural to leave out many documents that might otherwise have been included. Among the types of records not included are: Juan's correspondence with his father, Erasmo Seguín, during the latter's stay in Mexico City as Texas representative to the Constituent Congress of 1823; the many orders, communications and reports signed by Juan as *jefe político, alcalde,* judge, mayor, justice of the peace and county judge beginning in 1834; most records of his land transactions and other economic activities; and documents about his activities in Mexico between 1842 and 1848 and during his later life.

The writings chosen, although they span the years 1833 to 1890, are illustrative of Seguín's political, military and economic activities in Texas during the eight years covered by the memoirs. Many of the documents are published for the first time and are first-time translations. I felt it important to make the material intelligible to as wide an audience as possible, and this could best be done in English. For a number of documents, most notably the memoirs themselves, the original Spanish was not available for consultation. In some instances I have noted that the text seems unclear, and for minor and obvious errors I have corrected the text myself. My goal has been to let Seguín and his correspondents tell as much of the story as possible.

My greatest debt of gratitude is owed to Tom Munnerlyn, Debbie Brothers and Erik Mason of State House Press. They have been patient with me, while at the same time supportive of the direction I was taking with the book. Their principal concern has been for my satisfaction with the contents. Therefore, all that is good about this work is in some way the product of their efforts.

Texas can boast of some first-rate avocational historians, and I have been fortunate to profit from my association with a number of them. In some respects this book got its start from Jack Jackson. By sharing the exhaustive research material he gathered in preparing his comic book treatment of Seguín, Jack gave me a considerable head start. When he found out that I was working on Seguín, Tom Lindley, an avocational historian of the Texas War of Independence, kept his eye open for anything that might be of use to me. Not only has he brought useful sources to my attention, he has shared a number of valuable insights on the period and some of its characters.

A number of individuals have helped on particular aspects of the work. Tom Cutrer, currently writing a biography of Ben Mc-Culloch, informed me of the Texan efforts to capture Juan Seguín during the Mexican War. Kevin R. Young, of the IMAX Theater in San Antonio, helped me with my questions regarding the spoils taken at the Battle of San Jacinto. Steve Hardin, a Texas military historian, has answered a number of questions. The Albert Sidney

Johnston documents came to me through the efforts of Ricki Janicek, a Tulane historian. It was Texas Supreme Court Chief Justice Tom Phillips who located Juan Seguín's resignation in the Texas State Archives, after I and staff members had lost hope of finding it. Lisa Shippee Lambert, Head of Special Collections, Rosenberg Library, Galveston, helped me with the Seguín material in the Samuel May Williams Papers. Brother Bob Wright, OMI, was extremely gracious in sharing Juan Seguín's previously unknown report on the San Antonio and La Bahía priests. Both Arnoldo De León and Carolina Castillo-Crimm read the manuscript and made valuable suggestions.

Among the institutions from which the documents for this collection were gathered, five stand out. As always, the staff of the Barker Texas History Center consistently provided useful and friendly service. The staff of the Texas State Archives came to the rescue more than once when I got lost in the maze of early Texas government records. Mike Zilligen, former archivist at the Catholic Archives of Texas, brought a large collection of Sam Houston material there to my attention. In San Antonio I was ably helped by the staff of the Daughters of the Republic of Texas Library, particularly by the late Bernice Strong, and by John O. Leal, of the Spanish Archives of the Bexar County Clerk's Office.

Lastly, I would like to thank my family. I have not shouldered the entire burden of preparing this work. I have all too often shooed my children, Eduardo and Julia, away from my study and told them I had no time to play with them. My wife, Maggie, has had to tend to the children, entertain herself, and pick up some of the slack. Yet she has been encouraging and patient and has willingly read and commented on the bits and pieces I have given her. I hope this work is in some measure worthy of them.

Explanatory Note

In the edited memoirs, first names have been added where Seguín introduced individuals only by their surnames. In some instances, complete names have been added where Seguín mentioned individuals only by their titles. The grammar and spelling in the edited memoirs have been altered to reflect more proper usage and to improve clarity. The memoirs in their original form, as translated and published in 1858, have been reproduced as appendix 1. In the notes and biographical essay, the term "Tejano" applies to the native Spanish-speaking population of Texas.

In the appendices the often erratic grammar, spelling and punctuation in English language originals have not been altered. Exceptions: the dates on letters have been standardized at the top of the document; the names of the writer and the addressee have been given even when not stated in the original; where the item was a copy, it has been presented in the same form as an original; formal indication of the rubric following a signature has been omitted.

The following abbreviations are used throughout the book:

AP   *The Austin Papers.* Eugene C. Barker, ed. 3 vols. I and II, Washington, D.C., Government Printing Office 1924, 1928; III, Austin, University of Texas Press, 1927.

BA   Bexar Archives, Barker Texas History Center, the University of Texas at Austin.

BC   Bexar County Clerk's Office, San Antonio.

BHC   Eugene C. Barker Texas History Center, the University of Texas at Austin.

DRT   Daughters of the Republic of Texas Research Library,
        San Antonio.

GLO   Texas General Land Office, Austin.

SF   San Fernando Parish Records, San Antonio Diocese
        Archives, San Antonio.

SWHQ   *Southwestern Historical Quarterly.*

TSL   Texas State Library and Archives, Austin.

TU   Howard Tilton Memorial Library, Tulane University,
        New Orleans, Louisiana.

The Making Of A Tejano

On November 3, 1806, seven-day-old Juan Nepomuceno Seguín was baptized by Father José Clemente de Arocha in San Antonio's parish church. He was the third generation Seguín to be baptized there, preceded by his father, Juan José María Erasmo on June 2, 1782, and his grandfather, José Santiago on June 8, 1754.[1]

Juan Seguín's ancestors had helped found San Antonio and make the settlement of Texas permanent. Pedro Ocón y Trillo, his paternal great-great-grandfather, was a soldier in San Antonio during the mid-1720s when he married Ignacia Flores Valdés, who was most likely a daughter of one of the other soldiers. After retiring from the military, Pedro moved to Saltillo for a time, but then returned to Béxar. From humble origins he rose to become one of the prominent members of the community, serving as alderman in the town council during the 1760s. His economic pursuits included both farming and ranching.[2]

Juan's paternal great-grandfather, Bartolomé Seguín, arrived in San Antonio in the late 1740s. Bartolomé, or Bartolo as this Seguín was often called, was a carpenter by trade but also did some farming. Bartolo must have been very successful at his trade. Aside from doing all the carpentry work on the large Veramendi home (which stood until the beginning of the twentieth century), he also participated in public works projects and did a number of estate appraisals. A sure sign of his success was his marriage to Luisa Ocón y Trillo, alderman Pedro's daughter, sometime in the early 1750s.[3]

There are abundant signs of Bartolo's prosperity. In 1772 he received a grant of land to build a carpenter's shop near his lot on the north side of town, and he purchased a small but expensive plot of land near the military plaza. In 1776 he became one of the grantees in the new farm and irrigation works constructed on the north side of town. He served in the 1777, 1782 and 1786 town councils and was an officer for one of the town's religious feasts. He outlived three wives, Luisa Ocón y Trillo, Manuela Martínez and Bernarda Guerrero, and died in 1791, age seventy or so.[4]

Bartolo's only son by his first marriage, Santiago Seguín, was Juan's grandfather. It was he who began the ranching tradition in the Seguín family. Instead of following his father into carpentry, Santiago appears to have devoted himself from an early age to agricultural pursuits. An heir through his mother to Pedro Ocón y Trillo's property, Santiago's share included livestock and farmland in the town's vicinity. He also did some business hauling stone for construction projects, and possibly operated as a muleteer.[5]

It was as a stockman, however, that Santiago made his mark. At the end of the 1770s and during the following decade Santiago was one of San Antonio's principal cattle exporters, driving herds into Coahuila on various occasions. It was also his ranching activities that first brought Santiago into contact with the law. In 1778 Governor Barón de Ripperdá arrested him and a large group of Bexareños for stealing cattle from the pastures of Mission Espíritu Santo. However, being a young man—he was twenty-four at the time—with only a minor role in the case, he was quickly dropped from the proceedings. His herds, which usually included both his own branded cattle and mavericks, numbered in the hundreds despite his never owning his own ranch land, for he kept his herd in the area along Cibolo Creek known as Rancho San Bartolo, along with the herds of two or three families to which he was related.[6]

As the son of one of the town's prominent citizens, Santiago could expect to marry well and to follow his father into political life. In July 1778 the twenty-four year old Santiago married María Guadalupe Fuentes, sister of the parish priest, Pedro Fuentes y Fernández. By 1784, before attaining his thirtieth birthday, he was a member of San Antonio's town council, in which he served again in 1787.[7]

Santiago's good fortune was not to last, however. Although he did not run afoul of the provincial authorities after his 1778 arrest, Santiago did embark on a militant course regarding local preroga- tives. In 1787 he signed a memorial presented to Governor Rafael Martínez Pacheco accusing former governor Domingo Cabello of conspiracy to defraud the citizenry of their cattle. Three years later he participated in an unauthorized citizens' meeting which discussed how to ask the governor for payment of services rendered in constructing the town jail. Although he was listed in the 1793 census, Santiago did not contribute to the construction of a new barracks that year because he was "not residing in the province." Such conduct might have contributed to Governor Manuel Muñoz's rejection, for what he called "scandalous behavior," of Santiago's election as alderman to the town council of 1795. The following year, town alderman Manuel Berbán brought charges of assault against Santiago, who was found guilty by the town council. Although the matter was dropped at the governor's request, it seems Santiago's time in Béxar was marked.[8]

Sometime after this last run-in with the law, Santiago took his family to Saltillo. The reasons for the move are not known. Perhaps he felt San Antonio had nothing to offer him but trouble; perhaps his brother-in-law, Father Fuentes, who had become parish priest in Saltillo, offered him some incentive to move. Whatever the case, Santiago appears to have been equally uncomfortable in Saltillo and returned to Béxar, for in 1803 Father Fuentes requested that the Béxar authorities force Santiago to return to the family in Saltillo.[9]

The Seguín name in San Antonio was carried on by Juan José María Erasmo de Jesús, the third of Santiago's seven children. Born toward the end of the eighteenth century, Erasmo was destined to play a role in the political upheavals that shook Texas from the Mexican War of Independence until Texas gained her own independence. Respected even by his enemies, Erasmo held office under three separate governments—Spanish Crown, Mexican Republic, and Texas Republic.

Beginning at an early age, Erasmo showed the same streak of independent thinking that had marked his forebears. Intent on making his fortune in his birthplace, at age twenty-one he remained behind when his father was forced to return to Saltillo in 1803. An opportunity for advancement presented itself after Francisco Xavier Galván vacated the position of postmaster. Erasmo's bond for the vacant post, guaranteed by merchants from both Saltillo and San Antonio, already described the young Erasmo as a merchant. The position, which he took up early in 1807, proved lucrative and, with two or three interruptions, he occupied it for nearly thirty years.[10]

At the same time he was starting his public career, Erasmo was also starting his family. During a visit to La Bahía (now Goliad) he met his future wife, María Josefa Becerra, daughter of a noncommissioned officer of the garrison there. Despite her humble military background, María Josefa was a woman of considerable accomplishment. She could read and write, and Erasmo trusted her with the family's business interests in his absence. They had three children: Juan Nepomuceno, born 1806; Tomás, born in 1807 but who did not survive infancy; and María Leonides, born 1809.[11]

By the time the Mexican War of Independence erupted in 1810, Erasmo had successfully diversified into ranching. Sometime after 1800 he had gained control of the five leagues of land that made up the former ranch of Mission San Antonio de Valero. The twenty-two thousand acre ranch, named La Mora, had belonged to the Mission until 1793 when the mission was closed. By 1810 Erasmo had more than five hundred head of cattle, over twenty horses, and a mule-breeding herd of mares and a jackass. He also had five ranch hands working for him, three of them married.[12]

The war brought to a halt Erasmo's social and economic success. Destined by talent and economic success to play an important political role in early nineteenth century Texas, Erasmo found himself at age twenty-eight caught up in the struggle for independence although, at least in the early stages, he was unwilling to challenge the established order. In January 1811, when a mutiny of the garrison against its royalist officers occurred, Erasmo, already among the town's "most important citizens,"[13] took an active part in the counterrevolt. He convinced many of his friends and other Bexareños to oppose the insurgents and served on the governing council which ran the town until royalist officers returned. He also traveled to Nacogdoches with fifty soldiers and twenty militiamen to help reinstate the royalist commander there. [14] Clearly Erasmo was no hot-head; local interests required a realistic appraisal of the province's weakness in the face of Crown strength and Indian menace.

On the side of law-and-order during the first revolutionary episode, Erasmo's position was more compromised during a subsequent rebellion, the so-called Gutiérrez-Magee Expedition, the following year. While on a business trip to Louisiana, Erasmo found himself, according to his own account, coerced into providing a letter of recommendation for an involved revolutionary, José Álvarez de Toledo, who was on his way to Texas. For this rather ambiguous role—there was no evidence of his revolutionary activities other than the letter—Erasmo found himself labeled a traitor to the king. His property was confiscated, his house turned into a school, and his family left homeless. Arrested upon his return from Louisiana, he refused to accept the general amnesty offered to most Tejanos and preferred to prove his innocence before a court.

Conditions were so bad in Béxar that he asked for and received permission to take his family to Saltillo, where he might earn a living. There is some doubt as to whether or not Erasmo actually left San Antonio after receiving permission to do so, but in any case, by 1818 he had cleared himself of the charges and was in San Antonio, where much damage had been done to his interests. Although the government returned his house and ranch, he apparently never recovered almost $8,000 in other property.[15]

Despite the reverses of the revolutionary decade, Erasmo quickly began to rebuild his fortune following Mexican independence. In the summer of 1820, he was elected *alcalde* of San Antonio, one of the many municipal offices he was to hold over the course of the next two decades. During the 1820s he farmed, with some difficulty, the irrigated land originally granted to his grandfather in 1776. In 1822 he regained the position of postmaster, and he was appointed quartermaster for Béxar in 1825, a post he held for a decade. These activities, along with several commercial ventures, made him one of San Antonio's most respected and prosperous citizens by 1830.[16]

In the early 1830s, Erasmo added to his ranch holdings a nine thousand acre tract near present-day Floresville.[17] Here, a day's ride from San Antonio, he built a fortified compound known as Casa Blanca. Doctor John Charles Beales, traveling through the area in February 1834, described Erasmo's ranch thus:

> The Rancho of Don Erasmo Seguin is admirably situated
> on a rising ground, about 200 paces from the river San

Antonio, and well surrounded by woods. They have
made a species of fortification as a precaution against the
Indians. It consists of a square, palisadoed [*sic*] round,
with the houses of the families residing there forming the
sides of the square. They have also three pieces of brass
cannon, but not yet mounted. This may be made a beauti-
ful place, but it is as yet in its infancy, having been planted
only two years. It consists of two *sitios* of very fertile land.
They have begun to sow cotton, which thrives very well:
I procured a small quantity as a specimen.[18]

Along with his economic interests, Erasmo quickly rebuilt his political standing. In February of 1821 he received an important commission that was to change not only the course of his family's history
but that of Texas as well: Governor Antonio Martínez sent Seguín
as his emissary to Moses Austin with word that the latter's plan to
bring three hundred Anglo-American families into Texas had been
approved.[19] Austin had visited San Antonio in December of 1820
to present his colonization plan to the government. After a brief
visit, he set out for the United States border but contracted
pneumonia on the journey. He departed Natchitoches, Louisiana,
for his home in Missouri in late February at about the same time
Erasmo left San Antonio on his mission. Although they never met,
Erasmo did manage to get Governor Martínez's message to Austin
by the time the latter reached Herculaneum in late March.[20]

Erasmo waited in vain for Austin's arrival at Natchitoches from
late March until July 1, 1821, when not Moses but, rather, his son
Stephen arrived. Entrusted by his father to begin preparations for
the colony, Stephen had decided to return to Texas with Erasmo
when word arrived of Moses's death. Not bashful about taking on
responsibility, Erasmo counseled the young Anglo American that
"this most unhappy event will not retard the progress of the settlement."[21] With those words of encouragement, Stephen took it upon
himself to complete his father's project. Thus, Erasmo Seguín and
Stephen Austin jointly helped open a new page in Texas history.

The Seguín-Austin relationship flourished throughout the next
fifteen years. As a member of the Tejano elite, Erasmo perceived in

Austin, and the Anglo Americans he represented, an unprecedented opportunity for Texas to rise from the depths of the poverty and backwardness in which the Mexican War of Independence had left the province. For Austin, Erasmo was a valuable source of information, advice, and support for his plans.[22] His respect for the Tejano was such that in proposing a plan for the settlement of all of Texas, Austin suggested himself and Seguín as the competent authorities to execute it:

> It can be said in our favor that Dn. Erasmo is Mexican by birth, that he is a man whose talents and enlightenment enable him to carry out a matter of such interest, that he merits the public's trust, and that he is much esteemed among the North Americans . . . .[23]

Austin had good reason to be impressed and beholden to Erasmo. Not only had Seguín been a valuable collaborator in helping to establish Austin's colony, he had also served Austin well in personal matters. When Stephen's younger brother James arrived in Texas, Stephen had him go to San Antonio where he could learn Spanish quickly. The Seguín family took in the young James, not only on this first trip but on subsequent travels as well.[24] Writing from San Antonio in August 1826, while on his way to Saltillo, James informed Stephen that Erasmo's son, Juan, was on his way to New Orleans on business:

> I wish you to be *very particular* in yr attentions to *Juan for my sake* for I am certainly *indebted* to his family for innumerable favors—[should] he want a new supply of provisions furnish him with the best let it cost what it may—Also he will want letters of recomendation [*sic*] to persons in New Orleans which I wish you to furnish him with . . . .[25]

Stephen also felt indebted to the Seguín family. Writing in 1833 to his secretary and partner, Samuel May Williams, regarding Erasmo's efforts to become a cotton planter, Austin stated:

> I owe something to Don Erasmo—he refused to receive pay for the time my brother staid here, and I have always

staid here in my visits to Bexar and he never would receive
pay—he has planted cotton and wants a gin. I wish you
to make arrangements to get one for him on my account—
not of the largest size, a strong gin of the common kind
would suit him better than any other for it would be easier
to keep in order. I wish you to write to him on the
subject.[26]

The relationship was not just personal, however, for it had its
financial and political sides as well. Erasmo's business ties with
Austin, and even with Austin's secretary and associate Samuel
Williams, developed during the course of the 1820s. Both Austin
and Williams contracted debts to him, with an agreement at one
point that Austin would pay off his account in cattle. Erasmo, in
return, relied upon his friends for help in collecting other debts.
Business arrangements went so far as to include Austin's attempts
to acquire a league of land for Erasmo in his colony—although that
effort fell through[27]—and Seguín's promise of support in obtaining
for Williams a position at the Galveston customhouse when it
opened.[28]

Erasmo's most important political service, for both Tejano and
Anglo-American Texas, came during the Constituent Congress of
1823-1824, called in Mexico City to make the country a constitutional democracy. As Austin told his colonists in attempting to raise
funds for Erasmo's expenses: "I will vouch for Don Erasmo Seguin
our deputy that he will use every exertion possible on his part to
secure us all the privileges and liberties practable [sic]."[29] Just as
Erasmo made his intentions clear to Austin soon after arriving in
Mexico City: "I consider myself one of [your] colonists as you have
set aside the land that I requested,"[30] he made his sentiments known
to his wife: "I have no money, but I am not hungry. And were I
hungry, I would not ask for help from my Province, for she is more
fit to receive [help] than to give [it]."[31]

For the underdeveloped Texas province there was a handful of
important issues to occupy Erasmo's attention. Foremost was the
province's status within the nascent federal system proposed by the
delegates to the Constituent Congress. It was clear that Texas had

neither the population nor the economic resources to form a state on its own, but the alternatives were not desirable: union with one or more neighboring provinces or territorial status under the direct control of Mexico City. Erasmo, on his arrival in the capital in December 1823, advocated territorial status, arguing that only Mexico City could muster the resources necessary to help Texas rise above its backwardness. In contrast, union with Coahuila offered only the status of department within that state, the political domination of Texas by Monclova or Saltillo, and the payment of taxes for the expenses of the whole state and for the establishment of schools in the capital. "The residents of Coahuila will not supply us with the money necessary to overcome our difficulties," he argued, "or to protect our lives and property."[32]

By April 1824 Erasmo had changed his mind regarding the question of with which government Texas should join its fortunes. In a letter to the Baron of Bastrop, Erasmo was pessimistic regarding the national government's political stability: "The [situation] is bad, very bad. Every day the number of conspiracies increases, and everyone is out to undo the government's orders." With Nuevo León successfully pressing its case for separate statehood and the other frontier provinces considering Texas "a burden," Erasmo found only the Coahuilans "disposed to shelter and help us—to a point." Under the circumstances he felt the Tejanos should accept Coahuila's offer, "although it provides us little comfort because they have nothing to give us," rather than to become a separate territory under Mexico City's control.[33] The congressional decree of May 7, 1824, made official the union of Texas and Coahuila, and created the poorest state in the Mexican union. Erasmo did succeed in obtaining a clause in the decree of union giving Texas the right to inform the national government once Texas determined it could sustain a state government of its own.

As for immigration, Erasmo seems to have been ambivalent. In January 1824 he informed Austin and Bastrop that he was opposed to open immigration for a number of reasons he wished to keep to himself, yet he worked hard on the colonization committee to get a national colonization law that was as flexible as possible. As it turned out, the National Colonization Law of August 18, 1824, left most of the prerogatives in the hands of the individual states. Most importantly, it allowed the state governments to establish the terms of colonization contracts with empresarios.[34]

Two issues with the potential to affect immigration, to which Austin drew Erasmo's attention, were those of slavery and religion. On the former, Erasmo assured Austin that he would do all that he could to protect the colonists' interests:

> In regard to the slaves, I will say everything that occurs to me in favor of that colony when the subject is discussed, whether about those [slaves] that may be brought by the colonists or those who are born in our territory; keeping in mind the observations you have made to me on the matter because of the benefits that may result to those inhabitants, on whose behalf I am so interested.[35]

Erasmo's arguments, if his correspondence with Austin is to be trusted, consisted of asserting that the introduction of slaves permitted the immigration of men of means who would foster Texas's growth, rather than poor ones who would do nothing to further the state's progress. Erasmo warned, however, that congress did not wish "to listen to such appeals." On the contrary, congress was "electrified by consideration of the unhappiness of that part of humanity."[36]

Erasmo's sentiments, which were shared by other prominent Bexareños, were understandable. Not only did he have an interest in the success of the Anglo-American colony, he was himself the owner of a slave, albeit one who was a domestic servant. Erasmo continued to provide Austin with help on the matter at the state level, helping to fend off the abolition of slavery in Texas for a number of years.[37]

As for the role of the Catholic Church in retarding Anglo-American immigration, Erasmo reassured Austin that it would not be a factor, claiming as early as March 1824 that even under the Spanish government *de facto* religious tolerance had been the practice in Texas. He did, however, admit that he was not as confident regarding worship in public, since the law calling for the reorganization of the government required that there be no religion other than the Roman Catholic. His sentiments proved accurate, for he reported near the end of the summer that one deputy's attempt to include a provision in the colonization law that all immigrants be Roman Catholics had failed unanimously with the exception of the sponsor.[38]

After his return from Mexico City, Erasmo busied himself with local matters. But as the political situation between Texas and Mexico worsened between 1832 and 1835, he appears to have taken a back seat to his son. Thus, when Austin traveled to San Antonio in May 1833, in search of support from the Tejanos for formal separation from Coahuila, and informed Erasmo that he had been chosen, along with Austin and James Miller, to petition the national congress on the matter, the aging Tejano declined the offer. Erasmo did, however, support Austin and was the only Bexareño "in favor of memorializing the General Congress for the separation."[39]

The elder Seguín continued to serve as postmaster and quartermaster, which no doubt gave him access to much sensitive information. As late as August 1835, before General Martín Perfecto de Cos' arrival, Don Erasmo in his capacity as quartermaster inspected the Morelos Battalion recently arrived from Matamoros.[40] Late in October 1835, Cos removed Erasmo from his post and ordered him to leave San Antonio after humiliating him "and others of the most respectable citizens" with threats of forcing them "to sweep the public square."[41] Early the following year, about a month before Santa Anna reached Béxar, Don Erasmo led the Seguín clan to refuge in East Texas for the duration of the hostilities.

The Texas War of Independence proved disastrous to Erasmo's economic interests. His Casa Blanca became a source of supply to the Texans for beef cattle and grain along with horses and mules which he provided willingly. Abandoning the ranch, Erasmo lost a great part of his sheep flock on the way to Nacogdoches. The return to Casa Blanca at the end of 1836 was no consolation, the ranch having been destroyed in his absence. In 1840 the Congress of the Republic agreed to reimburse Erasmo $3,004 for the supplies he had furnished.

Nearing the end of his public life, Erasmo faced still another rebuilding of his private fortunes. Although he served briefly as a

Republic-era magistrate in San Antonio, long enough to take the
testimony of some of Béxar's oldest residents with regard to the
routes of the Camino Real during a county boundary investiga-
tion,[42] it was clear that, at age fifty-six and facing a language barrier
and economic hard times, he had to leave public service and devote
himself to his personal interests. For the last twenty years of his life,
Erasmo seems to have experienced considerable economic success.
In 1840 he still controlled over fifteen thousand acres of land, owned
three town lots in San Antonio, and had acquired 130 head of cattle,
the second largest herd recorded in the Bexar County tax rolls for
that year. Despite the vicissitudes of the previous decade, Erasmo
also retained ownership of a domestic slave. In the first and only
United States census in which Erasmo appears, that of 1850, the
singular recuperative abilities of the sixty-eight-year-old are evident
in his stated worth of $8,000.[43]

Even these years were not without turmoil, however. In 1842,
Erasmo, along with other Tejano ranchers, faced a series of cattle
losses to rustlers. The *Telegraph and Texas Register* reported in
June of that year:

> We have been informed that some thieving volunteers,
> lately drove off nearly a thousand head of cattle towards
> the Colorado-belonging to citizens of Bexar. Messrs.
> Navarro, Flores, Erasmo Seguin, and others, who have
> ever been faithful to our cause, have suffered greatly.
> Shame on the men who claim the name of soldiers, and
> act the part of thieves, by robbing their own country-
> men![44]

In addition to the economic reverses caused by the rustlers, Erasmo
had to deal with the social and political consequences of his son
Juan's activities. Between 1842 and 1848 Juan was in the service of
Mexico, and even Erasmo's reputation came into question after his
son participated in the 1842 Woll Expedition against Texas. Thomas
Jefferson Green, a military figure during the Republic, implied that
Erasmo had betrayed the disastrous Somervell and Mier military
expeditions in the fall of 1842: "I have the evidence of Captain
Fitzgerald, and Messrs. Van Ness and Hancock, the three Santa Fe

prisoners . . . that Don Erasmo Seguin . . . then at San Antonia [*sic*], was in daily correspondence with the enemy while our army was marching upon the Rio Grande."[45]

For the most part, however, the judgment of contemporaries and posterity has been positive. Mary A. Maverick, one of San Antonio's early Anglo-American settlers, described Erasmo in her memoirs as "a cultivated and enlightened man, who had befriended Stephen F. Austin in a Mexican dungeon, had been friendly to the Americans, and was much esteemed by all."[46] Dr. Cupples, interviewed for a popular history of San Antonio in 1890, recalled Erasmo from the 1840s when the young Englishman had come to Texas as part of the Castro Colony. "Señor Erasmo Seguin," Cupples reminisced, was "a perfect and courtly old Spanish gentleman."[47] More recently, historian Joseph Nance, in assessing Erasmo's role in Texas history, described him as "one of the truest friends Texas ever had."[48]

Sadly, his passing was not widely observed. The November 14, 1857, issue of the San Antonio *Ledger* buried his obituary in the first column of page three. Under the heading "DIED" appeared the following simple notice:

> On the 30th ult., at his rancho, on the San Antonio River, Don Erasmo Seguin, well known to all old Texans.

Don Erasmo's son, Juan Nepomuceno Seguín, had been born in a sparsely settled land during very unsettled times. The political and social changes sweeping Mexico and the United States made Texas a crossroads of revolution and an object of desire. The Louisiana Purchase in 1803 brought the United States and Spain together along the Texas border, which the United States now claimed to be the Rio Grande. In Madrid, Paris and Washington, Texas took on a political importance it had not had for almost a century. In its new role as buffer between the ever-expanding Anglo Americans and the rich mines of New Spain, Texas became the destination of royalist troops intent on protecting the frontier, of Spanish and French refugees from Anglo-American Louisiana, and of filibusters from the United States.

The changes for Texas were profound. The military units that streamed into Texas expanded the population of the province by half. Many entrepreneurs, agriculturalists, and artisans who chose not to live in Anglo-American Louisiana settled in Texas, where opportunities for cheap and plentiful land, for contraband, and for work seemed to be expanding; the Crown founded new settlements on the banks of the San Marcos and Trinity rivers and stationed a cavalry detachment near Galveston Bay. A new royal order calling for a port at Matagorda Bay also contributed to the growing optimism that Texas would finally become a true gem in Spain's imperial crown.

Most of the change occurred against the backdrop of the Napoleonic Wars. Spain, fighting first against and then with the French, had the links to its New World empire severed several times. In 1808, after the forced abdications of the Spanish Bourbons Charles IV and Ferdinand VII in favor of Napoleon's brother Joseph, the stage was set for the empire's dissolution. In the fall of 1810 rebellion erupted in New Spain when the parish priest of Dolores, Father Miguel Hidalgo y Costilla, incited the locals to overthrow the Spanish authorities.

Despite its isolated place within the viceroyalty, Texas was not immune from the upheaval. In January 1811 a retired military officer, Juan de las Casas, originally from Nuevo Santander (present day Tamaulipas), led San Antonio's garrisons in a rebellion against the governor, managed to extend his revolt to the other Texas communities at La Bahía and Nacogdoches, and established himself as Father Hidalgo's representative and governor of the province. The so-called Casas Rebellion was short-lived and was quickly reversed by the local elite in Béxar. Texas proved much less fortunate when the next convulsion took place. In the fall of 1812 a large force of Anglo Americans and Mexicans under command of Augustus Magee and José Bernardo Gutiérrez de Lara, a native of Guerrero, Tamaulipas, who had been sent to the United States to seek assistance for the Hidalgo revolt, invaded Texas and captured all the settlements. The invaders, along with many Tejanos who had joined their ranks, were finally ousted in the summer of 1813 after a pitched battle near the banks of the Medina River and pursuit to the

Louisiana border. Subsequently, the Long Expedition in 1819 managed to capture Nacogdoches before being ousted by royalist forces sent from San Antonio.

The destruction caused during the Gutiérrez-Magee and Long Expeditions left Texas in a condition reminiscent of the worst days of Indian hostilities during the previous century. San Marcos de Neve, Santísima Trinidad de Salcedo, and Nacogdoches were abandoned. Béxar suffered a considerable decline in its population and became the object of repeated Indian depredations; fields and ranches were deserted, property confiscated. If man-made disasters were not enough, San Antonio also suffered a catastrophic flood in 1819 that destroyed over fifty dwellings.

In the midst of these reverses, news of Mexico's independence from Spain arrived in Texas anticlimactically in the summer of 1821. Having suffered the consequences of local initiatives in favor of independence, Tejanos were not eager to anticipate any further change. In July 1821 the residents of Béxar and La Bahía took oaths to defend the Mexican nation *after* receiving word of Commandant General Joaquín Arredondo's acquiescence. Under such circumstances did Juan Seguín spend his childhood, learning the lessons of political action and war in the swirl of ambiguous and shifting allegiances.

Béxar in the 1820s was desperate to find a way out of its poverty-stricken existence. The soldiery went unpaid for months at a time, fields remained abandoned because of the Indian menace, the ranches were little more than temporary shelters during brief excursions into the countryside. Appeals for greater military resources to fight the Indians and to provide a market for local produce were not heeded by a national government more absorbed with political and military threats closer to home. It was not surprising, therefore, that Bexareños turned to Anglo-American immigration as the remedy for what ailed Texas.

Even as an adolescent Juan must have appreciated the importance his father and other prominent Bexareños attached to Stephen Austin and his colonists. The significance of his father's hosting James E. B. Austin, Stephen's brother, for over a year could not have been lost on Juan. The young Tejano also witnessed the growing frustration of Bexareños as they saw the Anglo-American colonies prosper while San Antonio remained stagnant, caught between the political power of Monclova and Saltillo and the economic power of San Felipe, Nacogdoches and the other Anglo-American settlements.

Juan matured quickly in this environment. During the time his father served as Texas deputy to the Constituent Congress, Juan handled the postmaster's duties, helped his mother tend to the fields, and to some degree acted as intermediary between Erasmo and Austin. The responsibilities thrust on Juan were not light, as is made clear in his plaintive letter to Erasmo of September 1824 in which he complained of the family's having run out of money and being assigned thirty cartloads of stone for the irrigation works.[49] Yet Juan remained "the boy,"[50] and he and his sister were admonished by their absent father to "read and write and not be out on the streets."[51]

There is some evidence that Juan heeded his father's advice. Although little is known of his education, which took place under very trying circumstances at best, there are hints of Juan's cultural aspirations and interests, particularly his interest in the political news. In a postscript to one of his mother's 1824 letters to his father, Juan asked for news and books, along with a saddle and "good hat"; in a subsequent letter of his own, he asked for a violin.[52] Writing to Austin of his father's return from Mexico, Juan included a copy of the new Mexican constitution and a number of newspapers, instructing Austin: "the former I send as a gift, but the latter you will do me the favor of returning at your first opportunity after acquainting yourself with them."[53] His interest in sharing news continued later in life; writing from New Orleans to President Lamar, Juan also forwarded "gazettes" from which the former could "be informed of the latest news of this republic and that of Mexico."[54] In December 1832, Juan helped organize and became president of a Society of Friends, the purpose of which was to sponsor a "tragedy, dance, and one-act farce."[55]

In 1826, twenty-year-old Juan took his first business trip. The journey to New Orleans, undertaken in late August in the company of Juan Martín Veramendi (another political ally of the Anglo

Americans and future governor of Coahuila y Texas), was made overland with a mule train and included a stop at San Felipe, Stephen F. Austin's capital on the Brazos River. The one thousand or so pesos of merchandise that he brought back most probably consisted of dry goods.[56] Erasmo, obviously anxious over his son, sent fresh mounts to San Felipe in mid-November, asking Austin to have his colonists keep an eye out for the young man. The venture launched Juan on a commercial career that saw him import goods at least twice more during the Mexican period, in 1831 and 1832.[57]

It was probably in the course of one of these commercial undertakings that Juan first became involved in land speculation. Various Mexican and Coahuiltexan laws made ownership of more than a league of land difficult for Anglo Americans. One increasingly popular method of getting around the problem consisted of Anglo Americans' posing as attorneys for bona fide claimants who sold their rights to them. Michel B. Menard was one of these American speculators. A business acquaintance of Samuel M. Williams and José Antonio Navarro, he probably met Juan during one of the latter's business trips to Louisiana. Menard succeeded in acquiring both Juan's and Erasmo's one league entitlements, which they petitioned for on January 18, 1833, for an unspecified amount of money. Both petitions having been approved by the governor, Menard located Juan's on the eastern end of Galveston Island in July 1834, and Erasmo's in the Nacogdoches region. Neither grant proved legal for reasons unrelated to the Seguíns, and in the case of Galveston Island Menard was forced to spend an additional fifty thousand dollars to obtain legal title.[58] Juan would follow up this brief flirtation with land speculation with a more concerted effort after Texas independence.

At the same time that he was establishing himself financially, Juan was starting what grew to be a very large family. His bride was María Gertrudis Flores de Abrego, a native of San Antonio and member of one of the town's most important ranching families. Little is known about Mrs. Seguín. The deeds to which she was a party demonstrate that she could not read or write. The only physical description we have of her comes from Mary A. Maverick, whose memoirs describe Mrs. Seguín during a dance held in President

Lamar's honor in June 1841: "Mrs. Seguin was so fat that the General [Lamar] had great difficulty in getting a firm hold on her waist."[59]

Gertrudis's father, José Antonio Flores de Abrego, was one of a group of Flores men who operated ranches east of present-day Graytown. Aside from holding a number of public offices in the 1810s and 1820s, her father at one time served as an officer in the Béxar militia. Four of Gertrudis's brothers saw action during the Texas War of Independence, including Salvador, who served in Juan's company during the fall 1835 campaign and later as a company commander in Juan's cavalry regiment. Salvador must have had a particularly close relationship with the Seguíns, for on his death in 1855 Juan became administrator of his estate and guardian of his family. Another of her brothers, José María Victoriano, who married Juan's sister María Leonides, owned a ranch on the site of present-day Floresville, for which land was donated for the townsite sometime before 1885 by Josefa Flores, their daughter.[60]

Juan's marriage to Gertrudis, in January 1826, was blessed the following year with the birth of Antonia, the first of ten children. The next two years saw the births of Teresa and their first son, José Erasmo. A daughter, María Josefa, born in October 1831, died at the end of April the following year. Juan Nepomuceno Jr., was born in 1833. The onset of rebellion in Texas interrupted the continued growth of Juan's family until 1838, when Josefa was born. Santiago followed in 1840 and María Gertrudis in 1841. During the family's Mexican exile only one child, Eugenio, was born on August 12, 1843, in the town of Zaragoza, Coahuila. Following their return to San Antonio their last child, María Guadalupe, was born in 1849.[61]

Juan's economic and social development brought about quick political maturity. Despite being just twenty-two years old at the time, Juan was elected as one of two San Antonio *regidores* for 1829, on occasion serving as *alcalde* during the absences of the incumbent, Gaspar Flores. Regarding the young office holder's political skills, the political chief, Ramón Músquiz, confided in Stephen Austin "Don Juan Nepomuceno Segin [Seguín] is very talented for his age, but he needs practice in order to be a good administrator of Justice."[62] During his tenure Juan was asked to perform what could only be considered thankless tasks. His efforts to collect the voluntary contribution for the local primary school proved a failure because of the lack of money in the town. Juan had to suggest to the political chief that the collection be suspended until such time as some hard cash came into town. Only a few days later he found out that he had to enforce a new state law requiring each citizen to contribute the proceeds from three days' labor to the local school. Only slightly less demanding was the compilation of the municipality's annual statistical report, for which he and the other *regidor* were responsible. On occasion he served as judge in minor civil and criminal cases.[63]

His success in handling his first elective office made Juan a prime candidate for future political activities. In the complicated world of post-independence Mexican politics, elections beyond the local level were indirect; the eligible citizens voted for electors who in turn voted for representatives to state and national offices. In 1833 he won twenty-six of thirty-three votes for secretary of the electoral assembly, and was subsequently elected as one of twenty-one electors. The following year he served as president of the electoral assembly.[64]

By 1833 some of the cracks in the Texas-Coahuila union had begun to appear. In December 1832, the *ayuntamiento* of San Antonio, independently of the Anglo Americans but in support of their grievances, lashed out at the state and national governments for their treatment of Texas. Not waiting to see what effect their convention of October 1832 and San Antonio's complaints might have on the authorities, the Anglo Texans held another meeting in April 1833 at which they decided to take their grievances to the national congress. Austin, one of the men chosen for the delegation, successfully delivered the grievance to the national government but was subsequently arrested while on his return to Texas for having written a letter to the *ayuntamiento* of Béxar in October in which he opined that if congress did not grant Texas separate statehood, Texas should declare it unilaterally.

Even as the Anglo Texans met in April 1833 and Austin made his way to Mexico City, the state government took some steps to meet Texan demands. The measures included: revamping the judicial

system and implementation of trial by jury; subdividing Texas into
two (and in 1834 into three) political departments, thus giving Texas
more representation in the legislature; and transferring the capital
to the more liberal confines of Monclova. The national government,
spurred on by Austin, annulled the anti-immigration provisions of
the law of April 6, 1830.

By the time the annual *ayuntamiento* elections were held in
December 1833 it seemed that the disturbances of the previous two
years were giving way to a more liberal and progressive period.
Although Juan won the race for *alcalde*, circumstances were to thrust
him onto an even bigger political stage, in a role that forced him to
define his political allegiances publicly. On January 1, 1834, the day
he was to take office, the interim political chief, José Miguel Arciniega, notified Juan that he was stepping down. Under the law,
Juan, not yet twenty-eight, assumed the top administrative office in
the department until the governor could appoint a permanent re-
placement.[65]

Just a few days after becoming political chief Juan found out that
Austin had been arrested. The news could not have come as a
surprise. After all, it had been the *ayuntamiento* of San Antonio
which had disclosed Austin's letter to them in October. Juan must
have been relieved, however, when he received a letter from Austin
indicating his acceptance of the government's action and attempting
to portray the October letter as nothing more than his effort to
contain popular discontent among the Anglo Texans in the face of
an indecisive national congress.[66]

Ramón Músquiz's return as political chief, at the beginning of
March, relieved Juan of the office but not of continued involvement
in the state government's affairs. Less than two weeks after Juan's
return to the office of *alcalde*, Músquiz sent him to meet with the
Comanche leader Casimiro to discuss mutual problems with the
Tonkawa. Juan must have enjoyed some success for the Indian
leader visited San Antonio in April to begin peace negotiations,
followed in May by almost two hundred Comanche men, women,
and children. After his return, Juan presided over the *alcaldía* less
than three months before once again being asked to assume the reins
of the department as political chief.[67]

Juan's resumption as political chief coincided with renewed political upheaval in Mexico and Coahuila, the result of President Antonio López de Santa Anna's switching political camps. In the political and military struggle—between the centralists supporting a strong national government and continued privileges for the military and the Church, and the federalists advocating strong state governments and the abolition of special privileges for the clergy and military—Santa Anna had previously supported the federalists. But in May 1834 Santa Anna proclaimed himself a centralist under the slogan *"Religión y Fueros"* (religion, and military and clerical privileges), in what has come to be known as the Plan of Cuernavaca. In June the small group of Coahuila y Texas legislators, who formed a permanent commission responsible for overseeing governmental matters between legislative sessions and the executive branch of the government, declared themselves against Santa Anna's plan. The following month the politicians in Saltillo, still smarting from, among other things, the loss of the capital to Monclova a year earlier, declared the government in Monclova unconstitutional and appointed their own governor. In response, the *ayuntamiento* of Monclova, the council, the permanent commission, a handful of legislators still in town, and the local garrison prepared for a fight, removing the sitting governor and installing a sympathetic army colonel, Juan José Elguezábal.

Faced with quickly changing circumstances, Juan at first sought to stay on the sidelines. In response to Commandant General Pedro Lemus's letter of August 31, 1834, asking that he use his office and influence to keep the peace in Texas, Juan replied on September 22 that it was his intention to do so. The situation continued to deteriorate in Coahuila, however, to the point that there were a number of skirmishes between the pro-Monclova and pro-Saltillo militia units. The news reaching Béxar in early October must have been enough to suggest to Juan that an effective state government no longer existed. Seconding the resolution reached at a public meeting in San Antonio which called for a convention of Texas municipalities to decide on a course of action, Juan instructed the *ayuntamientos* of his district and the other political chiefs to hold elections for delegates to meet at Béxar on November 15.[68]

In the memoirs, Juan claims that all the municipalities appointed their delegates, but there is evidence to the contrary. Henry Rueg, the political chief at Nacogdoches, apparently took no action. Most of the settlers of that area had yet to receive titles to their lands from the government, and there was little interest in disrupting the process. The political chief of the Brazos department, Henry Smith, long an advocate of Texas independence, saw an opportunity to advance the cause of Texas' separation from Coahuila and possibly from Mexico, but did not receive the support of the majority of residents within his jurisdiction. Some feared for Stephen Austin's safety; he was still under arrest in Mexico and might be held responsible for a disturbance in Texas. Others felt the reforms enacted by the legislature proved the good intentions of the government, and that Texas had yet to be adversely affected by the dispute between Monclova and Saltillo. The convention never met, the new commandant general, Martín Perfecto de Cos, although a centralist and sympathetic to Saltillo, acquiesced in Santa Anna's orders that Monclova be recognized as the capital and that all government officials there remain in place until new elections could be held. Juan, his position undermined by Santa Anna's acceptance of the Monclova government and chastised by Commandant General Cos for taking matters into his own hands, must have been happy to give up direction of the department to Ángel Navarro at the beginning of 1835.[69]

Peace proved illusory, however. When the newly elected Coahuila y Texas legislature met in Monclova on March 1, 1835, tensions developed between a majority of deputies and Governor Juan José Elguezábal on the one hand, and the deputies from Saltillo and the rest of the legislators on the other hand. The governor did not submit the annual report required of him on the state of the state and intimated his resignation. The legislature took advantage of Elguezábal's actions to replace him with yet another interim governor until the election results for the governorship were complete. The deputies from Saltillo declared the majority's actions unconstitutional and walked out of the legislature. Upon receiving a report that the state treasury was empty, the legislature quickly passed a law authorizing the governor to raise cash by disposing of four hundred leagues of land in Texas. General Cos declared the legislature's actions unconstitutional and sent a detachment to Monclova. The legislature responded by passing another law authorizing the governor to take the necessary measures to protect the government. When the duly elected governor, Agustín Viesca, took the oath of office in mid-April he faced insurrection in Saltillo, a thinly disguised threat of force from the commandant general, and a legislature intent on granting every desire of a handful of land speculators.

These events widened the schism between Anglo Americans and Tejanos that had developed the previous October when the departments of Brazos and Nacogdoches refused to send delegates to San Antonio. Governor Viesca's call for money and militiamen went unheeded in the Anglo-American controlled departments, where the government had lost credibility. Disgusted by the legislature's acquiescence in the speculators' designs on Texas public lands, the Anglo Americans turned their backs on Monclova without understanding that Cos intended to do away entirely with the pro-federalist government.

Only Béxar responded to the governor's call. Merchants José María Balmaceda and José Antonio and Eugenio Navarro offered to loan the amount necessary to meet the one thousand peso quota the governor set for the department. Juan volunteered for militia service and, with the rank of ensign, was placed at the head of the force of twenty-five that also included Ben Milam and John K. Allen. Unlike the Anglo Texans, the Tejanos recognized the political consequences of General Cos's moves against Monclova. For them, the struggle for the federalist cause was not just a pretext for launching a war of independence, as it was to become for the Anglo Americans later in the year.

When they arrived in Monclova, Juan and his fellow militiamen discovered that Governor Viesca was preparing to move the state government to San Antonio. The legislature, having recognized the possibility that General Cos might try to close down the government, had pre-authorized the governor to move it wherever he saw fit. On May 25, 1835, Viesca, 150 militiamen and approximately twenty Anglo Americans set out from Monclova on the road to San Antonio. Little more than thirty miles out of Monclova, and after a delay of two days, the governor had a change of heart, perhaps on hearing the news that an order for his arrest had been sent to the garrisons ahead. Returning to Monclova, Viesca dismissed the militia units who had assisted him and then made a new, though this time clandestine, effort to reach Texas. He and the few government officials with him were arrested less than a day's ride from the Rio Grande on June 5, 1835.

Juan's comment in the memoirs that, "we had agreed that the movement should begin in the center of Texas," makes it clear that the Tejanos were not about to expose themselves to Santa Anna's wrath on their own. They were aware of Zacatecas's fate for resisting the new centralist government: a large force composed of local militias had been routed by Santa Anna's army, which sacked the city before withdrawing. Juan and other Tejano leaders also knew that, despite the existence of a "War Party," the commonly held sentiment among the Anglo Americans was against an uprising so long as their own rights were not violated.

The violation, whether orchestrated by war party members or not, came by way of General Cos, who asked that William B. Travis, the leader of a group of settlers who had ousted the customs officer at Anahuac, be delivered to him. Cos also issued arrest orders for a large group of federalists including Samuel Williams, Mosley Baker, Lorenzo de Zavala, and José María Carbajal. At the same time he issued a proclamation advising the settlers that they had nothing to fear from the new government, but made it clear they must accept the changes without recourse. Not only did the Texans refuse to comply with Cos's orders, they violently resisted the army's effort to collect a cannon that had been lent to the town of Gonzales for Indian defense.

This action at Gonzales, which took place on October 2, mobilized the Anglo Texans and the Tejanos. Juan, commissioned "captain of the Federal Army of Texas,"[70] raised a company of thirty-seven men. His brother-in-law, Salvador Flores, and Manuel Leal organized another company from the San Antonio ranches. The Mexican settlers from the Victoria area organized themselves into a company of twenty-eight under Placido Benavides's command.

Desertions from the San Antonio and Goliad garrisons brought additional Tejanos into the ranks of the Texas Army.[71]

The roles assigned to the Tejanos—foraging, spying, harassments, and raids—clearly aimed at taking advantage of their knowledge of the countryside and their horsemanship. This is not to say that the Tejanos did not take part in the major engagement of the early struggle. There is considerable evidence that at least part of Juan's company, probably including himself, took part in the storming of San Antonio, which began on December 5. Immediately after General Cos's withdrawal from San Antonio, Seguín's company joined Travis's in raiding the Mexican army's horse herd.[72]

By January 1836 the Mexican army had been driven from Texas and Juan's company of mounted volunteers had disbanded. Juan himself had been chosen judge of San Antonio, a position he held until returning to military service in February, when Santa Anna advanced on Texas. Also in January, the government commissioned Juan a captain in the cavalry corps, although there apparently was some confusion regarding the appointment. In any case, Juan was busy acting as intermediary between the Tejanos, the Anglo Texans, and the revolutionary government, as well as attending to town business. Among these activities was a run-in with James Bowie over the latter's unauthorized release of a prisoner. As judge, Juan also was responsible for conducting the election that sent Francisco Ruiz and José Antonio Navarro as the only native-born Texans to the convention that declared Texas independence.[73]

Once Santa Anna arrived in Béxar, Juan withdrew into the Alamo along with an unspecified number of Tejanos. There are a number of reports which suggest that between Santa Anna's arrival on February 23 and March 3, some individuals had an opportunity to withdraw; more probably however, they withdrew between the time Santa Anna was spotted and the time he entered Béxar. Among those who chose not to remain were a number of Tejanos who probably felt it was useless to remain in the fort when Houston was organizing an army in the interior.[74]

Juan left the Alamo as a messenger, probably on the night of February 28. Apparently his knowledge of the area and his Spanish made him the logical choice in an attempt to get through the Mexican

lines. He never made it to Goliad, his original destination, for on
the road he met one of Colonel James Fannin's officers, who informed him that the Goliad garrison was on its way. Soon, however,
Seguín was informed by another of Fannin's men that the colonel
had decided to return to Goliad. Juan now headed for Gonzales
where, upon his arrival, he found many of the Tejanos who had been
in San Antonio until Santa Anna's approach. There he reorganized
his company, part of which was ordered by Sam Houston to help
protect the evacuation of the San Antonio River valley ranches.
Juan specifically sent three men from his unit to help his family leave
the area while he and the rest of the company made up the rear-guard
of the main body of Houston's army. Before taking up the march,
Juan took the time to inform the Bexareño delegates at Washington-
on-the-Brazos, Francisco Ruiz and José Antonio Navarro, about
the fall of the Alamo.[75]

According to the muster roll of Colonel Sidney Sherman's second
regiment of which it was a part, Seguín's small company at San
Jacinto consisted of nineteen men.[76] There was another individual
to whom Juan extended the honor of joining the fray. Juan López,
a sixteen-year-old orphan who had joined a body of Texan troops
as a cart driver, "became acquainted with some of the men belonging
to the Company of J. N. Seguin." Accompanying the army to San
Jacinto, he "joined the men of Seguin's Company whom he considered as being more his countrymen than the other troops, in
reason of their language." Seguín, one of the later affiants for
López's pension application, remembered having seen "the young
man in Mexican garb," during the time the army was crossing
Buffalo Bayou "looking more like an Indian than anything else."
He only saw the boy again at the start of the battle, "entering boldly
the fight, brandishing on one hand an old rusty sword, holding on
the other a gun stick at the top of which was fastened a red kind of
rag." Knowing that López was not a member of his company, but
not sure whether he was a soldier, Seguín

> ordered him to through [sic] away his pole, and to take the
> rifle of the private Manuel Tarín who declared himself
> sick and unable to fight. The lad abided by the order of

Affiant, fought as bravely as any man in the Army and recd. a slight flesh wound in the left knee.[77]

Juan and his men earned Sam Houston's respect at San Jacinto. Writing a letter of introduction for Juan to the governor of Louisiana, Houston stated: "The Colonel commanded the only Mexican company who fought in the cause of Texas at the Battle of San Jacinto. His chivalrous and estimable conduct in the battle won for him my warmest regard and esteem."[78] Writing to Juan's father some years later, Houston extended his compliments to the company in general, citing Juan's conduct and that of "his brave company in the army of 1836, and his brave and gallant bearing in the battle of San Jacinto, with that of his men."[79]

Houston was not the only military man impressed by the Tejanos. Edward Burleson wrote Colonel Thomas Rusk in early May regarding his concerns that four hundred Mexican troops with two pieces of artillery remained at Bexar. He noted that many Tejanos had fought hard for independence and, in his own inimitable style, asked Rusk to tell the cabinet

> that there is soldiers with us that has fought Brave and has bin faithful and I should be pleased to see them Enjoy Liberty to the full Extent I mean Capt Seguins company and himself and all others that has bin honestly Engaged in the noble cause of freedom.

His fear centered on the fact that, until Santa Anna's army was completely across the Rio Grande, the population on the frontier would not be safe: "Capt Seguins home is in the vicinity of Sanantonio and he cannot settle there with out suffering the insults of Santanas soldiers. I am clean for leaving none on this side of Riogrande."[80]

The *Telegraph and Texas Register* on September 21, 1836, introducing correspondence between Juan and Mexican commanders Vicente Filisola and Pedro de Ampudia,[81] commented:

> We judge that the following authentic articles will be perused with satisfaction, as they afford proofs of the services and patriotism of Lieut. Col. John N. Seguin, who

has persevered in his attachment to the cause of liberal
principles, and whose gallantry at San Jacinto, was conspicuous.[82]

But Juan earned another kind of notoriety during the war; he was
one of the few Tejanos to be singled out by the Mexicans for his
participation in the war. For instance, José Enrique de la Peña, a
participant in Santa Anna's expedition, published a diary of the
campaign in 1836. In it he attacked the ingratitude of the Anglo-
American settlers and the credulousness of many Tejanos. But for
Juan and two others he reserved the harshest judgment:

> The cry of independence darkened the magic of liberty
> that had misled some of the less careful thinkers . . .
> there remaining with the colonists only Don Lorenzo de
> Zavala and Béjar natives, Don Antonio Navarro and Don
> Juan N. Seguín, the only intelligent men who incurred the
> name of traitor, a label both ugly and deserved.[83]

Houston's and the other Texan commanders' trust in Juan was
evident in the assignments given his company following San Jacinto.
The first consisted of observing the Mexican army's withdrawal from
Texas. The Tejanos' responsibilities included making sure that the
departing Mexicans did not take Texan property with them, including slaves. Soon, however, Juan found himself with the additional
burden of having to care for a number of sick and wounded
Mexicans left behind during the retreat.[84]

By the end of May, Juan received orders to take possession of San
Antonio and raise a battalion of men for the purpose of defending
the frontier. General Thomas J. Rusk, who had taken command of
the Texas Army, asked Juan to be particularly watchful of Mexican
movements along the various roads leading from the Rio Grande.
Juan entered San Antonio on June 4, 1836, at the head of a company
consisting of twenty-two men; the few Mexican soldiers on station
there departed on the sixth.[85] In one of the war's minor ironies, Juan
accepted San Antonio's surrender from Lieutenant Francisco
Castañeda, the same officer who had been involved in the opening
skirmish of the war at Gonzales the previous October.

Juan's command proved to be both short and troubled. He was unable to raise the authorized ninety men for a battalion because "the majority of citizens do not want to take up arms against Mexican soldiers, they wish to remain neutral," and the twenty-two men at his disposal were not enough to make his decisions respected.[86] General Rusk responded by sending a detachment of 180 men through San Antonio to help Juan maintain control, but their temporary stay was not enough to make Juan comfortable in the city. On June 21, Juan informed his fellow Bexareños that he was evacuating the town, and requested their help in driving the cattle into the interior so that they would not fall into Mexican hands.[87]

In the flush of his recent successes, Juan appears to have decided to act as mediator between Anglos and Tejanos. Having previously noted their neutrality in the independence struggle to Rusk, he now appealed to his fellow Bexareños to prove their "attachment to the just cause, and the beloved liberty we are contending for." He then admonished them "If you maintain your post as mere lookers-on; if you do not abandon the city and retire [to] the interior of Texas, that its army may protect you, you will, without fail, be treated as real enemies, and will suffer accordingly."[88] The townspeople did not abandon San Antonio, however, and suffered the consequences. In October 1836, a company of Mexican cavalry entered an unprotected San Antonio in search of cattle. The *Telegraph and Texas Register* soon chided the townspeople, "they will perhaps in the future better appreciate the advice and orders of our friend, Col. Seguin, who cautioned them of the danger of remaining in Bexar."[89]

Matters soon reversed themselves, however, as the government called on Juan to garrison the city. Upon his return to the army following a furlough during which he had helped his family return to Béxar, Juan discovered that he had been promoted and instructed to return to San Antonio. On September 17, 1836, President David G. Burnet commissioned Juan a lieutenant colonel and ordered him to raise a battalion and take command of Béxar. That very day Juan enlisted forty-two men and an announcement in the *Telegraph and Texas Register* resulted in further enlistments, so that by the time he entered San Antonio in November, he had eighty men under his

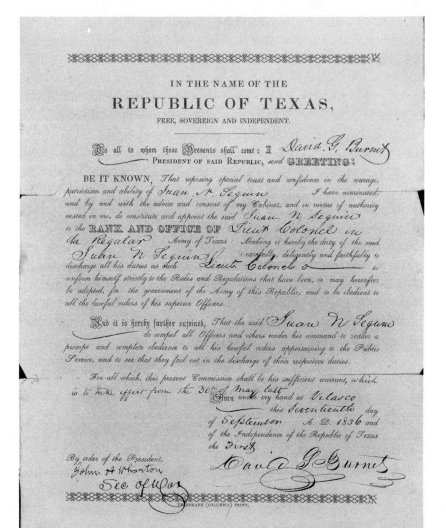

Certificate of Juan N. Seguín's commission as a Lieutenant Colonel in
the Texas Army. Courtesy Texas State Library, Austin, Texas.

command.[90] His obvious pride in the government's restated faith in his military service is evident in a letter of introduction he wrote for a fellow officer on October 22, 1836: "I believe it has come to your attention that I embraced the cause of Texas from the beginning. In that army I am now employed with the rank of Lieutenant Colonel, in which position I offer myself at your disposal and that of your kind family."[91]

Juan's command turned out to be full of controversy and turmoil. Felix Huston, who became commander of the army in October, after Sam Houston's election to the presidency and Thomas Rusk's appointment as secretary of war, was opposed to Seguín's holding the command. One of the "American straggling adventurers" of whom Juan complains in his memoirs, Huston had arrived in Texas well after San Jacinto with ambitious plans for invading Mexico. The general obviously had little respect for Juan, complaining in letters to Houston in November 1836 that Seguín was unfit for command because "he cannot speak our language" and was calling for the abandonment of Béxar.[92]

When General Huston tried to carry out the evacuation and destruction of San Antonio at the beginning of 1837, Juan successfully appealed the order to President Houston. Although Juan's appeal has not surfaced, the tenor of Houston's reply suggests the Tejano was deeply insulted by the order. After discussing the steps taken to undo Huston's orders, the president concluded: "You will, I confidently hope, be satisfied that no intention has been entertained to wound your feelings, or to compromise your honor! You will therefore retain your command, and command of the post of Bexar."[93] Juan was satisfied, but he apparently made an enemy of Huston and his associates, who may have been involved in a scheme to buy up land in San Antonio cheaply as a result of the abandonment.[94]

Despite winning this battle of wills, Juan was soon forced to retire from Béxar. Although his force consisted of 118 men in three companies at the end of 1836, neither the number nor the condition of his command inspired confidence. Short of money and supplies, Juan confiscated city funds for the relief of his regiment, which received no support from the army. As early as December Juan asked for but never received a reinforcement of two hundred cavalry or infantry, and his letters complain of his inability to get supplies from the quartermaster. In an effort to mount his men, Juan ordered, pursuant to an order from headquarters, the confiscation of all horses and mules in Béxar, a move which alienated him from his fellow Bexareños as it imperiled the livelihood of many. By the beginning of March 1837 he had withdrawn from San Antonio and was on his way to Gonzales, where he felt he could husband his scanty resources more efficiently.[95] For, as he explained to General Johnston, his men were "chiefly on foot, naked and barefoot."[96]

His stay in San Antonio, while difficult, was not without its accomplishments. Juan's regiment made its contributions to the country's defense by remaining in contact with Mexico, and thus providing intelligence to the Texas government on Mexican military movements. Houston trusted Juan as a contact with the Mexicans, and requested that he contact General Juan Valentín Amador to warn of the consequences of a new invasion by Mexico.[97] Juan, of course, took the request as another signal of the government's approbation: "I feel myself highly flattered by the discretionary power which you confide to me and being on the spot shall continue to exert my judgement and act as circumstances and necessities may require for the good of our cause and our country."[98] And, despite finding it difficult to obtain supplies from the army, Juan collected beef cattle for the main body of the army, at a time when he could ill afford to spare horses to herd the animals.[99]

Juan also had the singular honor of burying the remains of the defenders of the Alamo. Following the storming of the old mission on the morning of March 6, 1836, General Santa Anna ordered the bodies of the defenders burned. On February 25, 1837, before withdrawing from San Antonio, Juan ordered the ashes collected and military honors extended. He addressed the audience in Spanish; Major Thomas Western, Seguín's second-in-command, delivered a speech in English. Although a controversy exists regarding the burial site's location (to which Juan himself added fuel in a letter he wrote not long before his death), his letter to General Johnston of March 1837 describing the ceremony indicates the burial took place at the site of the largest mound of ashes.[100]

The withdrawal from San Antonio proved propitious, however, for in April Juan claimed to be in a position both to mount those yet on foot and to return to the vicinity of Béxar. It would seem, however, that Juan was growing increasingly eager to take care of personal interests. Confident that the Mexicans would not soon attack and that his command was on a stable footing, he asked for a month-long furlough. By the fall of 1837 he was again away from his command, on his way to New Orleans where he remained until early 1838. When he returned to Béxar in March he discovered that he had been elected Béxar's senator to the Texas Congress. Traveling to Houston, then the capital of the young republic, he resigned his commission on May 14, 1838, and four days later obtained his pay in bounty land—1,280 acres. He also acquired a donation grant of 640 acres of land for his service at San Jacinto.[101] Having made significant military contributions to the young republic, Juan now turned his talents to the political field, where his efforts were directed at making the coexistence of Tejano and Texan a reality.

Juan again found himself breaking ground, this time as the only Tejano senator to serve during the republic. He could not have had much time to formulate an agenda for himself, however, given the suddenness of the news of his election and the fact that the Second Congress was nearing the end. But even during the remaining nine days Juan proved to be a man of action. He introduced a bill for the relief of the widows and orphans of those who died at the Alamo, and even joined in the debate, though he did so in Spanish. Despite his need for a translator, Juan served during the Third and Fourth Congresses as chair of the Committee on Military Affairs, and had a seat on the Committee of Claims and Accounts.[102]

As the only Tejano in the senate it was clearly up to Juan to represent the interests not only of Bexareños but of all Tejanos. Juan clearly was concerned both that Tejanos understood the new system of government by which they were quickly being overwhelmed and that their interests were properly represented in congress.[103] His only surviving speech, made during the Fourth Congress, came as result of a Treasury report stating that $15,000 had been appropriated for the translation and publication of laws into Spanish. Perhaps Juan noted a growing disregard for the interests of Tejanos, a sense of their increasing isolation within a now overwhelmingly Anglo-American Texas. If so, his comments ring eloquently for the rights of his minority:

> Mr. President, the dearest rights of my constituents as Mexico-Texians are guaranteed by the Constitution and the Laws of the Republic of Texas; and at the formation of the social compact between the Mexicans and the Texians, they had rights guaranteed to them; they also contracted certain legal obligations—of all of which they are ignorant . . . . The Mexico-Texians were among the first who sacrificed their all in our glorious Revolution, and the disasters of war weighed heavy upon them, to achieve those blessings which, it appears, [they] are destined to be the last to enjoy.[104]

Juan's interest in instruction extended beyond expanding his constituency's understanding of the law. Given his own educational concerns, it is not surprising that he and José Antonio Navarro (the only Tejano serving in the house of representatives during the Third Congress) attempted to use their offices to obtain academic institutions for San Antonio. As Catholics, they found in Father John Timon, appointed by the bishop of New Orleans in 1838 to assess the Church's state of affairs in Texas, an opportunity to provide Béxar with a preparatory school and college of liberal arts and sciences while at the same time bringing needed reform to the spiritual life of Tejanos. Although Seguín and Navarro offered to endow a Catholic college with four leagues (17,714 acres) of land from the Republic,[105] conditions were not yet right and the plan fell through. Juan was able to influence the religious situation in San Antonio, however. After discussing the improprieties of the San Antonio and Goliad clergy with Father Timon, he provided an affidavit on the subject in January 1839 which contributed to their removal the following year.[106]

Despite Juan's apparent pursuit of his own programs, it was impossible for him not to become embroiled in both local and national political factionalism. Moreover, the emerging schism between Texans and Tejanos was bound, sooner or later, to have an impact on Juan's relationships with San Antonio's growing Anglo population. In the summer of 1838 Launcelot Smithers, an English doctor who settled in San Antonio shortly after independence, declared erroneously: "there is not any 'danger' of Seguin being elected another term to Congress. His conduct has ruined him with the Mexicans: they supported him before thro' fear of his strength and of his resentment."[107] Adjutant General Hugh McLeod was even more blunt about Juan: "Seguine [*sic*] is my enemy, independent of his Houston allegiance, at least so I think, and yet the fellow *smiles and smiles,* but the Navarro family can neutralize him, & I may count upon the Beramendi's."[108] Speaking of a failed 1839 campaign by companies of Anglos and Tejanos against the Comanche, in which Seguín led the Tejanos,[109] Mary Maverick suggested a less than courageous character on Juan's part: "They had been away from San Antonio ten days, when Captain Seguin returned reporting the woods full of Indians and predicting that our men would surely be killed."[110]

To understand the growing complexity of Juan's political situation it is necessary to trace his business interests in the post-independence period. Juan's most controversial business activity was his participation in land speculation. Juan had early experience with land speculation, having sold his right to land from the Mexican government to Michel B. Menard in 1833. Immediately after occupying San Antonio in June 1836, he purchased a league and one mile of land from Justo Travieso, the latter's inheritance from Vicente Travieso's four league ranch. On his arrival at Velasco on his return from New Orleans in February 1838, Juan wrote to Thomas J. Green regarding the possibility of claiming salt lakes below the Nueces River. This contact came to naught, but it may have something to do with the rancor with which Green speaks of Juan and Erasmo in his memoirs of the Somervell and Mier Expeditions.[111]

The real money in speculation lay in the headright system adopted by congress to promote settlement. The government, seeking to promote settlement and fearful of losing many of those colonists who came to Texas before independence but had not obtained land from the Mexican government, decided to grant such individuals the same amount of land to which they would have been entitled from the state of Coahuila y Texas. To distribute the land, boards of land commissioners in each county were to accept petitions and take testimony, upon the acceptance of which they would issue certificates. Considering the decentralized nature of the procedures and the great confusion regarding entry dates for individuals, the system soon became subject to abuse. False claimants, false testimony, and illegal locations became common.[112] Dr. Smithers provides a colorful rendition of the practices common in San Antonio:

> the citizens of Laredo are (as good Texians) to be brought to Calvios Ranch and other hiding places in this neighborhood and make oath before a judge of their citizenship & other qualifications & to transfer their headright which the assignee is to shove thro' the board.

> A great many claims already obtained are notoriously false. I have seen a mexican receive money for having sworn before the Board & proving out a head right; and any man can see the like if he will open his eyes. A silversmith of this town, who was acting political chief under Santa Ana, and everybody knows it—has recd. his lg & labor. I know many mexicans (3 in one hour) who ran away as enemies, who have lately come back (leaving their families beyond the Rio Grande) and who have recd. certificates for the Lg & [labor.] I believe all of Santa Ana's soldiers have had certificates, those who had wives 1 Lg & 1 labor & in some instances the women have again proved that they were widows & got another Lg.[113]

These were practices in which some speculators indulged throughout 1837 and 1838. They had willing victims among the poor and frightened Tejanos who inhabited the frontier between Mexico, Anglo-American Texas, and the Comanche. Abused by Anglo-American adventurers, under chronic attack by unchecked Comanche war parties, and ignorant of the potential of their headrights, most of them willingly sold out for what seemed to them fabulous amounts of money.

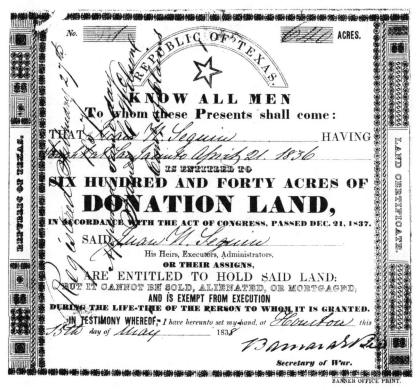

Certificate for land awarded to Juan N. Seguín for his service at San Jacinto. Despite the admonishment prohibiting transfer of the land during the lifetime of the recipient, donation and bounty certificates were commonly sold to speculators. Courtesy Texas General Land Office, Austin, Texas.

Prominent Tejanos, Juan among them, were secondary players, and the degree to which they participated in fraudulent practices cannot be determined from the information available. Rafael de la Garza, the most involved of them, acquired thirteen certificates. Juan was second in certificates acquired with ten. His first transaction dates from July 1837 and six others from September, the month before he left for New Orleans; all but one of the headrights were acquired while he was in uniform. Among the Anglo Americans, the partnership of Ludovic Colquhoun and William H. Steele acquired rights to seventy-three certificates, while John W. Smith, soon to become Seguín's opponent, acquired thirty-eight on his own and an additional nine in partnership with Enoch Jones.[114]

Whether or not he acquired his certificates in a legitimate fashion—the acquisition of certificates was not illegal if done in a lawful way—is of small consequence. Juan, in addition to purchasing certificates, associated himself with Juan Zambrano, president of the Bexar County Board of Land Commissioners in June 1838 and one of the Tejanos most disliked by the Anglo Americans, by serving as one of the individuals who signed his $20,000 surety bond.[115] To some degree, therefore, he was guilty by association. On the one hand, as William Pitts writes regarding Juan's involvement: "At the time when land speculation occupied the attention of the opportunistic and financially able of the city, he and his friends joined in buying the headrights of their impoverished countrymen."[116] On the other hand, the buying and selling of certificates was a widespread practice and Juan was on both ends of the operation. In May 1838, only days after receiving his bounty certificate for military service, he sold the entitlement to 1,280 acres for $250.[117]

Even while serving in the Army of the Republic, Seguín pursued a number of other economic enterprises, some of which left him open to political and ultimately to personal attacks. As commander at San Antonio Juan sold supplies to his command, a practice which, while not illegal, must certainly have been looked on unfavorably by local merchants. Juan also created opposition by refusing to refund the money he confiscated from the city during his tenure. He was finally taken to court over the matter and, having lost the verdict, was appealing the case at the time he fled to Mexico in 1842.[118]

Another type of opportunity presented itself to Juan in the spring of 1840. A renewal of hostilities between federalists and centralists in Mexico not only served to distract the Mexicans but actually strengthened the Texans' position in negotiations toward a permanent peace. Despite their mutual enmity, neither centralists nor federalists had been willing to accept the Treaty of Velasco, signed by Santa Anna while in captivity, as granting independence to Texas. Mexican public opinion continued to insist that Texas was an integral part of Mexico and no politician felt secure in contradicting that consensus. There was, however, some room for maneuver and General Antonio Canales, one of the founders of the short-lived Republic of the Rio Grande, hoped to draw Texan support for the country newly created from the states of Tamaulipas, Nuevo León, and Coahuila. The rebellious federalist, whose army had been defeated near the Rio Grande by centralist forces, thus appeared in San Antonio at the beginning of April 1840 seeking help from Seguín for the federalist cause.[119] Juan could now again cast himself in roles with which he was most familiar: defender of Mexican federalism; intermediary between Mexican and Texan; military man.

Advising Canales to present his plan to President Lamar, Juan, along with Cornelius Van Ness, provided the Mexican federalist with a letter of introduction. In meetings at the end of April, Canales would not promise to recognize Texan independence while Lamar would not promise his government's open support of the federalist cause. For the Mexican, premature recognition of Texas independence might jeopardize support among his fellow countrymen. For the Texan, open support of the federalists and the Republic of the Rio Grande might jeopardize British-sponsored negotiations with the centralist government in Mexico City over the recognition of Texas. In any case, Lamar did not impede Canales's efforts to raise troops in Texas for an expedition into Mexico.[120]

Juan quite possibly saw Canales and the Republic of the Rio Grande as a justification for his controversial actions in 1835-1836. After all, these Mexicans were federalists as he was, they too were declaring their independence in the face of hostilities from a centralist government in Mexico City, and they too were depending on Anglo-American assistance in carrying out their struggle. By October 1840 Juan was ready to join them. He resigned his seat in the Texas Senate as he raised approximately one hundred volunteers for the cause. Convinced he had Lamar's blessing and accompanied by S. W. Jordan and his 110 men, Juan marched south toward the Rio Grande.[121]

He was in for a sore disappointment. On November 5, 1840, Canales signed an armistice with the centralist general Isidro Reyes. The war over, the Republic of the Rio Grande was no more. Federalists and centralists now united to protect Mexico from Comanches and Texans. Seguín's and Jordan's volunteers, according to the agreement, were to disband and return home or face the consequences.

For Juan, Canales's defection was more than a political setback. He had invested over $3,000 in equipping his troops, a financial loss he could ill afford to sustain. Moreover, none of the Texan troops had been paid. Yet his efforts to have Canales meet his obligations proved fruitless. When he met in Monterrey with the general's superior, Mariano Arista, all Juan got was an earful of plans for the invasion of Texas and inducements to switch allegiances. Juan returned to Texas in mid-December 1840 with no money but much intelligence regarding the strength and distribution of Mexican forces along the Texas border.[122]

The return to San Antonio proved disappointing in another respect, for in January 1841 the first skirmish in Mexico's renewed campaign against Texas took place and Juan was one of its first victims. During a raid on the San Antonio River ranches by a company belonging to the Mexican general Rafael Vázquez's command, Juan lost a number of head of cattle. It was a loss he could not afford at the time, not only because his investment in the Canales Expedition was in jeopardy but because the size of his herd was still small. Juan now set out with Major George T. Howard on a fruitless pursuit of the Mexicans.[123]

Before he left, Juan received a small token of the aldermen's continuing appreciation for him as the mayor of San Antonio, a position which proved a heavy burden, particularly as it brought him into increasingly hostile contact with a growing body of Anglo-

American vagrants and adventurers. As early as May of that year the town council found it necessary to formally voice their support for Juan:

> RESOLVED BY THIS BOARD OF ALDERMEN, that the Mayor of this City in their opinion is fully authorised [*sic*] and empowered by the Act of incorporating said city to execute and carry into effect all laws passed by this body and they hereby vest him with full Executive Powers to that effect.[124]

Juan's efforts to contain the vagrant problem was seconded by none other than Launcelot Smithers, now a member of the board of aldermen, and a strong critic of Seguín three years before. At the September 9, 1841, meeting of the city council he proposed that all individuals in the city who were not residents of the Republic should register with the mayor, and that anyone harboring a suspicious individual should be fined by the mayor.[125] Considering his previously stated attitude, it is quite possible that Smithers meant "Mexicans" when he referred to suspicious individuals and not the Anglo Americans against whom Seguín directed his efforts.

Juan also faced financial difficulties at this time. Having borrowed over $3,000 to equip the companies he took to Mexico in answer to General Canales's call and having failed to collect on either his investment or his men's salaries, Juan was in need of raising the money by some means. He found an opportunity in the summer of 1841 when Rafael Uribe came to Texas on behalf of General Mariano Arista to discuss cooperating on measures against the Indians who were making assaults on both sides of the border. On his return to Mexico, Juan decided, as he says in the memoirs, to enter "with him into a smuggling operation." Juan mortgaged a sizeable amount of property to Duncan C. Ogden and George T. Howard in order to obtain the goods he took to Mexico: his residence, a house and lot fronting on Flores Street in San Antonio; a house and lot fronting on Main Street on the main plaza; and a league of land adjoining his father's ranch, Casa Blanca.[126]

This trip, though of a strictly private nature for Juan, proved no more successful than his military project of the previous year. Mistaken by General Arista for one of the delegates from the Texas government, Seguín was ordered to leave the country. Juan was now the victim of his previous efforts in support of federalism. In the face of reports that he was recruiting volunteers for a possible revolt by the general against the centralist government in Mexico City, Arista could not afford to have Seguín around. Hoping to make the best of the situation, Juan left his goods behind, only to discover later that his money and remaining goods had been confiscated.

On his return to San Antonio Juan resumed his duties as mayor under a cloud of suspicion, for a rumor arose that he had betrayed the Santa Fe Expedition to the Mexicans. Since President Lamar's ill-advised effort to conquer New Mexico had left only a day before Uribe arrived in Austin, it is clear that Uribe had ample opportunity to learn about the expedition and report to his government. Uribe hurried back to Mexico, and soon after his return "Governor Francisco G. Conde of the Department of Chihuahua published the news of the Texan expedition toward Nuevo México and warned his people against being led astray by the flattering talk of the Texans."[127]

The rumor of Juan's betrayal, in its most eloquent form, is found in the memoirs of Mary Maverick:

> It was strongly believed by many that Juan Nepomicino [sic] Seguin, who had held the honorable position of Mayor of San Antonio, and Representative to Congress, from Bexar, and being a man of great pride and ambition, had found himself surpassed by Americans, and somewhat overlooked in official places, had become dissatisfied with the Americans, and had opened communications with the officials of Mexico, exposing the entire plan from its inception as "invading Mexican soil." . . . From this time Seguin was suspected and Padre Garza, a rich and influential priest, was known to carry on traitorous correspondence with the Mexican authorities. Positive proof, however, was not obtained until Padre Garza escaped. Seguin indignantly denied the charge and many suspended judgement.[128]

Judgment was indeed suspended, for Juan not only resumed his duties as mayor, he was reelected at the end of the year.

After reelection Juan had to face the continuing problem of squatters on city property. As early as 1838, Mayor pro-tem Antonio Menchaca wrote to the commissioner of the General Land Office that a number of individuals, including Cornelius Van Ness, John W. Smith, and William Daingerfield among others, were attempting to take possession of land within the corporate boundaries of San Antonio. James Goodman, the single most visible offender at the time Seguín was mayor, was ousted from the property he claimed by Seguín, acting at the direction of the Board of Aldermen. Dr. Cupples, who settled in San Antonio in 1844, remembered Goodman in an interview he gave William Corner in 1890:

> I knew the man Goodman, you speak of; I remember him well, and the years of trouble he gave the city before he was finally ousted from the property on the Plaza, just opposite where Kalteyer's drug store is now was the location of the property he claimed. I remember he once came near to killing Ed Dwyer over that and other matters.[129]

Despite Juan's best efforts, the squatters problem escaped a solution. All Seguín managed was to make an enemy of Goodman.

The Goodman episode turned out to be one of Seguín's last actions as mayor of San Antonio. In the memoirs, Juan maintains that his efforts to repay the loan of $3,000 for which he had mortgaged his property led him to ask General Rafael Vázquez for a pass so that he might conduct some business. Juan, suspecting an invasion, shared Vázquez's letter of reply with the city council and the citizenry, and wrote President Houston for help on January 30, 1842. The response, which came from Secretary of War George Hockley, proved a disappointment: "I regret exceedingly that [the] impoverished condition of our country renders it almo[st] helpless, and that we must depend upon the patrio[tism] of those who are willing to defend it."[130]

Understanding that he and San Antonio could expect no help from the government, Seguín counseled a withdrawal from San

Antonio. Many of the Mexican families began leaving and Juan retired to his ranch. The Anglo Americans, in the meantime, decided to stay and organize a defense. The effort proved useless, however, and when Vázquez arrived in March, the defenders quickly withdrew to the town of Seguin. Although the Mexican forces remained in San Antonio for only two days, from March 5 to 7, they sowed enough suspicion and animosity against Seguín that it became impossible for him to recover.

Despite his joining Captain Jack Hays' company in pursuit of Vázquez, Juan returned to find that he had been branded a traitor. Even enjoying General Edward Burleson's favor—the general refused to hear any charges against Juan but instead ordered him to forage for the army among the ranches of the San Antonio River— Seguín could find no peace. Judging it impossible to remain in the city, Seguín went to the ranches but was constantly harassed. On April 18, 1842, citing "the turbulent state in which this unfortunate county finds itself," he resigned as mayor of San Antonio.[131] By May Juan was on his way to Mexico, "a victim to the wickedness of a few men whose imposture was favored by their origin and recent domination over the country," as he states in the preface to his memoirs. In far-away Nacogdoches Adolphus Sterne wrote in his diary for May 27: "Col. Seguin has joined them, and as is usually the case, when our warm Friends turn against us, they become the most inveterate foes, I am satisfied, that it will be so in this case."[132]

Even aside from the pain of being labeled a traitor, being hounded by the men against whom he had acted as mayor, and being forced to abandon his native land, Juan must have been extremely confused. With the advantage of hindsight, we can sort things out. Vázquez, perhaps hoping to force a break that would bring the Tejanos over to the Mexican side, probably did attempt to discredit Juan and thus further confuse Texans about the loyalty of the Tejano population. Goodman, and the other Anglo-American latecomers with whom Juan had dealt harshly, thus had an opportunity to take their revenge and gain the upper hand over the Bexareños.

But from their perspective—to Seguín, his family, and friends— the situation was too tangled to properly sort out. A. A. Alsbury explained to President Houston in June:

I regret very much to be compelled to say to you that Col.
Seguin has been led and has dragged by his influence a
large portion of his fellow citizens to Ruin; It appears from
what I can learn from *his* friends & family that he has been
in correspondence for some time past with our enemy &
that his pledges had brought the invasion of General
Vasquez[.] many of them tell me that Vasquez called on
them to know whether they would sustain him in keeping
possession of Bejar and told them that Seguin had
deceived him, they even now expect him with a considerable force to take & fortify & keep this place until more
forces arrive; Capt Menchaca who bears this will communicate to you many facts, of which I know nothing.[133]

There had been correspondence: Juan's efforts to reclaim his goods
and money, and other contacts made with the knowledge, and
possibly at the request, of the government. Moreover, it is hard to
imagine General Vázquez' giving Seguín command of a large force
to occupy San Antonio if he felt Juan had betrayed him.[134]

No records regarding Seguín's encounter with Mexican
authorities remain. He was well-enough known to Vázquez, Arista,
and other north Mexican leaders that it might have seemed to them
that Juan could be of some use. The large numbers of Tejanos on
the border, who had fled the Anglo Americans, were in need of
leadership, and among Bexareños there might be a strong sense of
loyalty to Juan which might be tapped. It is not surprising, therefore,
that Juan claims to have been given a choice in Mexico—military
service or jail. With a large family to feed and no livelihood at hand,
his choice was rather obvious.

It would be wrong to believe, however, that the Mexicans completely accepted Seguín. Although Woll gave him command of a
unit called the *Defensores de Béjar* (Bexar Defenders), he apparently received no official military title. General Woll's communications with the government routinely refer to Juan as "Don," "Señor"
or as commander of the unit, but never by a military rank. As for
the *Defensores,* it was a unit composed of Tejanos who fled Texas
following the Anglo-Texan victory at San Jacinto. They were used

by the Mexican army in much the same way Tejanos had been used
by the Army of the Republic, as the vanguard, as scouts, as foragers.

Juan's presence in the Woll Expedition, which captured San Antonio on September 11, 1842, served to condemn him. Although he
was responsible for obtaining Bryan Callaghan's release by Woll, it
became fashionable to blame him for all the perceived excess of the
invasion.[135]   One incident occurred at what was then known as
Sulphur Springs (now Sutherland Springs, Wilson County).   A
detachment from Seguín's command encountered three Texans at
the springs who reportedly offered resistance and were killed. By
September, despite the absence of eyewitnesses, there were reports
that "Col. Seguin has killed three sick men at the Sulphur Spring."[136]
Mary Maverick, reflecting the talk in San Antonio, blamed Seguín
for the incident in her diary. Thomas J. Green reduced Juan to
murderer and horse thief. Explaining that Woll had ordered Seguín
and part of his command to reconnoiter as far as the Guadalupe
River, he writes:

> It is *believed* that Seguin never went farther than the
> Cibelo Mineral Springs, where he knew that Dr. Smithers
> and two others were staying for their health. These three
> sick men he barbarously murdered, and thereby made
> himself the master of Dr. Smithers's fine American horse,
> which his family drove in a buggy to the Rio Grande.[137]

Soon newspapers in the United States were carrying the story.
Piecing together rumors, half-truths and misconceptions, a reporter
for the New Orleans *Crescent City* told the following story:

> It seems that the late expedition of the Mexicans against
> San Antonio is not of the general character supposed, but
> the work of Juan N. Seguin, the traitor, who it appears
> had mortgaged his landed property to Colonel D.C.
> Ogden, formerly a merchant of Bexar, for security, for
> about $10,000 worth of merchandise purchased of him.
> Seguin, it will be remembered, on his expedition to the Rio
> Grande, was robbed by Mexicans; returning to San An-
> tonio, raised a party and in retaliation robbed a party of

Mexican traders on the Texas side of the Rio Grande. The authorities of Texas not sanctioning this robbery by Seguin, he deserted the country with his followers from San Antonio and joined Vasquiz and his party. Now the court, which was in session at Bexar when the last (Woll) expedition of the Mexicans surprised them, would have decided a suit which Colonel Ogden had instituted against Seguin and Seguin knowing this was instrumental in raising off the Archives of Bexar County, in which he succeeded, and had also taken Colonel Ogden among the prisoners captured. There is little hope for the life of Colonel Ogden in the hands of this traitor. Dr. Smithers and others whom he had shot are supposed to have been witnesses to the mortgage.[138]

A review of the article reveals the following discrepancies: Juan's debt to D. C. Ogden and George T. Howard was $3,000, not $10,000; Juan was not robbed by Mexican bandits but had his goods confiscated after leaving them behind in the hopes of selling them; there is no evidence that Seguín robbed any traders; he did not join Vázquez but went in his pursuit; the archives of Bexar County were not carried off by Seguín and the Mexicans; and the suit proceeded in 1844, at which time Ogden and Howard won an award against Seguín's property; Ogden not only lived but returned to Texas in 1844, was elected to the Texas Congress, later to the legislature, and ultimately served as adjutant general of Texas; Howard met Seguín in Saltillo in 1848 and described him as a "worthy friend"; whether or not Launcelot Smithers and the others shot at Sutherland Springs were witnesses to the mortgage, it is clear from Juan's own report to General Woll at the time of the incident that he was not present.[139]

Some also held Seguín responsible for the so-called "Dawson Massacre." Nicholas Mosby Dawson had taken a group of fifty-three men to reinforce Mathew Caldwell's force which had marched against Woll from Gonzales. When they were discovered before reaching the main Texas force which was engaged in a battle against the Mexicans on the Salado River, Dawson's men took cover in a grove from which they put up resistance. By the time they tried to surrender it was too late. Thirty-five Texans died, fifteen were captured, and three escaped. Yet, again, Woll's reports on the battle do not mention Seguín's being involved in the "massacre."[140] To this is added the weight of the comments by one of the men captured. Norman Woods, writing from Mexico in July 1843, explained that "at the time that captain Dawson ran out with a white flag[,] it was Corascoes [Carrasco's] order for his soldiers to disarm us and put us to death[.]"[141]

Texans continued to find fault with Juan even as he withdrew with Woll on September 20. Accompanying the retiring Mexicans were approximately two hundred families, the charge for whom Woll gave to Seguín. According to the *Telegraph and Texas Register* many of these Tejanos later returned to Texas, justifying their flight by saying that Juan Seguín had warned that they would all be massacred by the Texans. The departing families were accused of plundering the town of anything not nailed down, including the archives, although the accusations proved largely false and Woll told a quite different story regarding their plight in his report from the Medina on the first day of the withdrawal:

> Having arrived at this place at four in the afternoon and having camped my division, I was surprised to discover that more than 150 carts belonging to the Mexican families residing in Béxar, loaded with furniture and the few belongings which Texan rapacity left those unfortunates, were retiring to the towns situated on the other side of the Rio Grande, fearing that the [Anglo-American] volunteers on their return to the city after its evacuation by our troops might want to avenge their ignominious defeats on those defenseless families.[142]

Juan spent his six-year exile under arms. At least part of the *Defensores de Béjar* enlisted into a unit under his command, the *Escuadrón Auxiliar de Béjar* (Béxar Auxiliary Squadron). The unit ranged between Laredo and Presidio Río Grande (now Guerrero, Coahuila), and in 1845 its orders required Juan to protect the crossings on the Rio Grande in the vicinity of Presidio Río Grande. The Bexareños also saw action against Indians during this period and made incursions across the Rio Grande.[143]

It cannot be said that Juan Seguín began his six-year exile totally alienated from Texas, for he had at least one well placed supporter. Sam Houston appears to have kept an open mind about Juan's actions. Soon after hearing of Juan's flight, Houston wrote Erasmo to console the old man. "I pray, Sir, that you will not suppose for one moment, that I will denounce Colonel John N. Seguin, without a most perfect understanding of the circumstances of his absence. I rely upon his honor, his worth, and his chivalry."[144] There is also some indication that Houston corresponded with Seguín for a time. In his published journal of the 1842 Texan expedition against Mexico, Thomas J. Green wrote that, despite Seguín's treachery, "his friend, President Houston, pronounces him as pure a patriot as any in the land."[145] The Clarksville *Northern Standard,* in a defense of Sam Houston against political attacks, concluded: "the alledged [*sic*] correspondence with Seguin and others, even if true, proves nothing of itself."[146]

There is other evidence that all of Juan's bridges had not burned behind him. In the summer of 1845, with the annexation of Texas to the United States looming, he once again stepped into the role of intermediary, advising President Anson Jones on Mexico's attitude toward the status of Texas. Under what authority Juan spoke is not known, but he assured the Texan that Mexico would recognize Texas independence if the Republic remained independent. Jones's comments to Juan's letter express sentiments that paralleled those of Sam Houston: "Col. Seguin fought as well at San Jacinto as any man there; but has been forced by bad usage to quit the country, and, as is said, has turned traitor; but I am unwilling to believe it. I think this letter expresses his *true* sentiments, but it is unnecessary for me to reply."[147] A reply was not necessary because a special convention called by Jones at the beginning of July had already voted in favor of annexation.

Most Texans shared quite a different view of Seguín, however, and the war that followed the American annexation of Texas brought Juan into confrontation with some of these Texans. Seguín and his company of approximately forty men were operating in the area north of Monterrey in the summer of 1846, when Ben McCulloch and his company of Texas Rangers crossed the Rio Grande. McCulloch's opinion of Seguín, like that of many others, was based on hearsay regarding Juan's role during the Woll expedition, and McCulloch's brother had once compared the Tejano to "Benedict Arnold and Judas Iscariot." Anxious to go after Seguín and his "forty thieves and murderers," the ranger declared that to kill them "would be doing God a service. It would be ridding the world of those that are not fit to live in it."[148] The rangers never did catch Juan who went on to fight at the Battle of Buena Vista and subsequent campaigns.

The war took its toll on Juan. At forty-three he had little to show for an adult life spent mostly fighting in the saddle. Near the end of the war, he showed up at Presidio Río Grande and made contact with the Texans there. In February 1848 John A. Veatch, captain in the regiment of Texas Mounted Volunteers, informed Mirabeau B. Lamar that "our *Texian-Mexican* Seguin, presented himself a few days since desiring permission to bring his family—which he thinks is in Saltillo—to this place. He says he will return to Texas and risk consiquences [*sic*]. He looks careworn & *thread-bare.*"[149] Finding his family in Saltillo, Juan determined to return to Texas and wrote in April to Sam Houston, asking for the Texan's "weighty and important recommendation to my former fellow citizens, as also a protection from the President of your Republic." Seguín did not enter into explanations: "You are I think acquainted with the causes which obliged me to leave my country, and as the explanation of them would be long, I defer it till I have the gratification of seeing you."[150] By the end of the year he was back in San Antonio, where he and his family settled down with Erasmo at Casa Blanca.[151]

As public a man as Juan had been throughout his adult life, it proved impossible for him to remain quietly on the ranch for long. In his April 1848 letter to Houston he already hinted at his interest in returning to local politics in San Antonio. In 1852 his interest became reality and Juan won election as Bexar County justice of the peace; he was reelected two years later. He also served as president of his election precinct, which included the ranches along the San Antonio River near his home.[152]

The last important event in Juan's public career was his participation in the establishment of the Democratic Party in Bexar County. The move to found a local Democratic Party stemmed from efforts to offset the growing popularity of the anti-Catholic, anti-masonic, anti-immigration, and anti-naturalization Know-Nothing Party. Although some Tejanos favored the Know-Nothings, many, including Seguín, saw in it the seeds of even worse discrimination against Tejanos. It is a testament to Juan's talents that, despite the presence of other prominent Tejanos in the community who had never been accused of disloyalty, particularly José Antonio Navarro, it was Seguín who became the featured Tejano in the Democratic Party, and Samuel Maverick, the local party president, named Juan to the platform writing committee. Juan also became a member of the Democratic committee of the "Mexican Texan citizens of Bexar County."[153]

His acceptance by Tejanos and Anglo Texans gave Seguín a new sense of responsibility. It did not come without a price, however. His political activities brought renewed personal attacks from which he had to defend himself. Juan looked upon the memoirs, which he wrote in 1858, not only as a defense against "the barbarous and unworthy deeds" of which he was accused but as a means of keeping alive the possibility of future public service.

His belief that he could once again act as intermediary between Texas and Mexico surfaced that same year when, perhaps fearing designs floating about Texas and Washington, D.C., regarding an American annexation of Mexico, Juan offered his services to Governor Santiago Vidaurri of Nuevo León. Sam Houston, then a member of the United States Senate, offered a bill calling for the United States to establish a protectorate over Mexico and Central America.[154] Juan, who traveled to Monterrey with his wife in the fall of 1858, returned to Texas with a special commission from Governor Vidaurri; he wrote Texas governor Hardin R. Runnels in January 1859 that Vidaurri wished to enter into a treaty with Texas "for the extradition of fugitive slaves, peons, robbers, murderers and incendiaries."[155] Governor Vidaurri thus thought to defuse the Texans' hostility by offering to eliminate their more important grievances against Mexico.

At this point, it becomes necessary to discuss what for historians has been the most confusing aspect of Juan's life. According to some students of Seguín, he participated in the 1850s and 1860s wars of the Reform and French Intervention and later on in Porfirio Díaz's 1871 revolt against Benito Juárez.[156] There is evidence, however, indicating that the Seguín who participated in these wars was not Juan but Juan Jr. For instance, at the very time Seguín and his wife made their trip to Monterrey in 1858, Santiago Vidaurri received word that a Juan N. Seguín and his cousin Miguel Zaragoza (General Ignacio Zaragoza's brother) were on their way to San Antonio with a mule train.[157] A biography of General Zaragoza makes the following claim in a genealogical note regarding the Seguín-Zaragoza family: "Juan N. Seguín, born in 1833, who was the one who accompanied Zaragoza during the War of the Reform with the rank of colonel and who was his third cousin."[158] Moreover, Seguín would have been sixty-five years old in 1871, the year Díaz rebelled against Juárez.

Beginning in the late 1850s Juan began attempts to take advantage, for himself and his men, of various government military pension programs. In 1854 he applied for and received a bounty certificate of 320 acres for having "participated in the Storming of Bexar as Captain Dec. 1835." However when the certificate was presented to the Commissioner of Claims, a special office established to verify the validity of all Texas land claims, the commissioner rejected Juan's claim on the grounds that Juan had previously been compensated for that service. At the time he presented his certificate to the commissioner, Juan also presented an affidavit listing the members of his company during the Siege of Bexar in December 1835. In 1860 and 1861 Seguín also made efforts to obtain compensation for the Indian campaign of 1839 in which he had led a company of Tejanos. Lastly, in 1874, Juan applied for and received a pension for his service to the Republic; his widow continued receiving the pension after his death.[159]

Little is known of Juan's private life during these later years. During the mid-1850s Juan built a house for his family about three-quarters mile north of Erasmo's Casa Blanca, and there followed a gradual selling of their other property. After Erasmo died in 1857 Juan and his sister Leonides sold Casa Blanca to Teresa

Photograph of Juan N. Seguín's home near Floresville, Texas, circa
1930s shortly before its demoliton. Courtesy Library of Congress,
Washington, D.C.

Seguín de Soto, Juan's daughter. By 1860 all that remained in real
property was in his wife Gertrudis's name, a house fronting the
military plaza in San Antonio which she had inherited from her
parents and one thousand acres of land near Casa Blanca which she
had received as a gift from Erasmo. The house in town was sold in
May 1866, and Santiago Seguín, Juan's youngest son, sold the ranch
property in 1875 using a power of attorney from the family.[160]

Despite his participation in local politics following his return from
exile, Juan must have felt an increasing sense of alienation in Texas.
He never acquired command of English at a time when Anglo-
American domination was extending into the Tejano countryside.
His reaction to growing discrimination and such incidents as the
Cart War, a series of attacks against Mexican freight haulers in 1857,
is nowhere recorded. Neither is there any evidence of his attitude
toward Secession and the Civil War. This silence may itself be a
comment on his growing alienation from Texas society. Selected to
serve as Wilson County judge in 1869, during Reconstruction, he
served only through the remainder of the year. By this time the
decision for the family to move to Mexico had probably been made,
for Santiago Seguín, one of Juan's sons, wrote sixty years later that
the family moved back to Mexico at about this time. It was with

Left: Tomb of Juan N. Seguín at Nuevo Laredo, Mexico, as restored circa 1970. Courtesy of the DRT Library, San Antonio, Texas

Below: The remains of Juan N. Seguín were moved from Nuevo Laredo to this pastoral site on the outskirts of Seguin, Texas, as part of the U.S. Bicentennial celebrations. The new tomb, inscription on facing page, was dedicated on July 4, 1976.

JUAN NEPOMUCENO SEGUIN
OCT. 27, 1806 – AUG. 27, 1890
"TEXAS PATRIOT, STATESMAN
FOR WHOM THE CITY OF SEGUIN WAS NAMED"

* ———————— *

SON OF ERASMO AND MARIA SEGUIN, SPANISH DESCENDANTS FROM THE CANARY ISLANDS WHO HELPED SETTLE TEXAS[1] • YOUNG JUAN ASSEMBLED MEXICAN-TEXAN TROOPS AND FOUGHT IN THE 1835 'SIEGE OF BEXAR' • PROVIDED HORSES AND AID FOR TROOPS OF COL. WILLIAM B. TRAVIS, FURTHER AIDING AS COURIER DURING SIEGE OF THE ALAMO • DEFENDED FLEEING SETTLERS IN 'RUNAWAY SCRAPE' AFTER THE FALL OF THE ALAMO • DIRECTED BURIAL OF THE REMAINS OF ALL COMBATANTS OF THE ALAMO, MAY, 1836[2] • COMMANDED COMPANY "A" (CAVALRY), 2ND REGIMENT DURING SAN JACINTO VICTORY • COMMANDED PURSUIT OF MEXICAN ARMY REMNANTS FOLLOWING SAN JACINTO BATTLE • WALNUT SPRINGS CITIZENS VOTED TO RENAME THIS COMMUNITY "SEGUIN" IN HIS HONOR ON FEB. 25, 1838[3] • SERVED AS MAYOR OF SAN ANTONIO, 1841-48[4] • 3-TERM SENATOR, REPUBLIC OF TEXAS, 1837-40, SUPPORTED BI-LINGUAL PUBLISHING OF TEXTBOOKS;[5] HELPED SELECT SITE FOR STATE CAPITOL [sic] • DIED 1890, NUEVO LAREDO, MEXICO • REMAINS RETURNED TO SEGUIN, SEPTEMBER, 1974 •

REINTERRED WITH SPECIAL HONORS ON JULY 4, 1976 BY THE CITY OF SEGUIN AND SEGUIN BICENTENNIAL COMMISSION

---

[1] Juan did not have any Canary Islander ancestors, though his wife did.

[2] Juan directed the funeral services for the remains of the Alamo defenders on February 25, 1837.

[3] The author could find no evidence supporting this date. According to the most plausible of the stories for the renaming of Walnut Springs, the residents changed the name to Seguin in gratitude for Juan's efforts, while in the senate, to obtain a post office for the town on the Austin-San Antonio route. If this story is true, it could not have happened before the end of May 1838, when Juan joined the session. A.J. Sowell, in his *Early Settlers and Indian Fighters of Southwest Texas*, first published in 1900, says the change of name was made at a town meeting on February 25, 1839.

[4] Juan served as mayor in 1841-1842 only.

[5] Although Juan supported Spanish language publication of the state's laws, there is no evidence regarding his support for "bilingual" textbooks.

Santiago, himself prominent in Nuevo Laredo and border politics during the 1870s and 1880s, that Juan and Gertrudis lived out the last years of their lives in Mexico.[161]

Texas did not entirely forget Juan, nor did Texans view him in an unfavorable light during the last years of his life. During his return to Texas in 1874 to apply for his pension, Edward Miles, secretary of the Texas Veterans Association, asked Juan to write some reminiscences for a "Log Cabin History of Texas," a work that was never published. In 1882 the San Antonio *Light* reported that the Seguin family, "one of the oldest and most respected of San Antonio" was visiting from Mexico. Five years later the Clarksville *Northern Standard* published a premature and quite odd obituary of him: "Capt. JUAN N. SEGUIN, of Laredo, the last surviving captain of the battle of San Jacinto, died in London, England, a few days since. The flag over the capitol building in Austin was run down to half mast on the 9th in his honor." In the last eighteen months of his life Juan also answered requests for information from Texans regarding his activities during the War of Independence.[162]

What is remarkable about these late communications is that there is no sense of hostility, bitterness or regret in Juan's words. His 1887 interview with a reporter from the Laredo *Times*, which was reprinted in other Texas newspapers, evidences a man at peace with himself and with the world around him. Even allowing for some literary license, Juan's questions regarding his former compatriots and their descendants, naming John J. and Edward Linn, John S. Menefee, Thomas O'Connor, and others, suggests that he had many fond memories. This was especially true of Houston: "The old veteran recalled with evidences of pride and pleasure the fact of Houston's friendship, and even partiality, for him, saying that 'Old Sam' was wont to call him his son."[163]

Death came for Juan on August 27, 1890, at age eighty-three. This time there were no obituaries, no ceremonies, no notice of his passing. His memoirs have long remained his only epitaph, yet his achievements and travails have not permitted Texas to forget him. As Tejanos rediscover their contributions to Texas history, as they overcome the barriers that separate Texan and Tejano, Juan Seguín has again returned to serve as intermediary between the two.

Endnotes To
"The Making Of A Tejano"

1. For Santiago Seguín's baptism see San Fernando Church Baptismals, 1731-1760, June 8, 1754, SF; for Erasmo, ibid., 1761-1793, June 2, 1782; for Juan Nepomuceno, ibid., 1793-1812, November 3, 1806.

2. For the marriage see Marriages of Mission San Antonio de Valero, 1709-1797, June 19, 1728, SF. For details of Pedro Ocón y Trillo's career see: Proceedings concerning charges against Captain Urrutia, 1735, Archivo General de la Nación de México, ramo Provincias Internas, vol. 163; Notary Protocol, March 22, 1738, BA; Notary Protocol, September 15, 1747, ibid.; Petition of the cabildo and citizens to the Governor, [August 12, 1749], ibid.; Proceedings of Martín Lorenzo de Armas, 1st alcalde, June 13, 1760, ibid.; Petition of Fr. Pedro Ramírez, June 6, 1762, ibid.; Inspection of Villa by Gov. Navarrete, June 20, 1762, ibid.; Election book, January 1, 1763, ibid.; Autos formados contra Juan José Flores de Abrego y otros Rancheros por varios robos de ganado orejano en los agostaderos de la Misión de Espíritu Santo, con un Informe del Ayuntamiento de la Villa de Sn. Fernando, September 23, 1778, ibid.; Donación de un solar a favor de Pedro de Ocón y Trillo, September 6, 1762, Land Grants, Spanish Archives, BC.

3. "Spanish Volume, Records," Spanish Archives, BC, book 3, 317-48; Causa mortual del difunto D. Juan José Flores de Abrego, June 9, 1779, BA; Diligencias practicadas sobre la presentación de Juan José Flores, April 26, 1780, ibid.; diligencias practicadas sobre la muerte que dieron los indios Comanches a Felipe de Luna, November 5, 1780, ibid.; Diligencias seguidas sobre la causa criminal formada contra Tomás Travieso, February 14, 1782, ibid.; Causa mortual de D. Fernando Veramendi, April 28, 1783, ibid.; Expediente formado sobre el pago de los trabajos expendidos por los vecinos de la villa de Sn. Fernando y Presidio de Sn. Antonio, April 11, 1793, ibid.

4. Donación de tierra a favor de Bartolo Seguín, April 23, 1772, Land Grants, Spanish Archives, BC; Venta de tierra por Juan Antonio Navarro a favor de Bartolo Seguín, ibid.; Cabildo elections, January 5, 1777, BA;

Poseciones de oficios de alcaldes y regidores de esta villa de San Fernando, December 20, 1779, ibid.; Military roster, March 2, 1784, ibid.; Diligencias practicadas para poner en depósito consecuente a lo mandado por el Señor Comandante General, September 7, 1786, ibid.; Papers relative to religious feasts, February 12, 1772, Nacogdoches Archives Transcripts, BHC; Bartolo's burial record reads "widower for the third time of Bernarda Guerrero," San Fernando Church Burials, 1761-1801, January 11, 1791, SF. Although this record states his age as 79, the census of 1779 listed his age as 47, making him 59 or 60 in 1791.

5. Revista de Inspección del Presidio de San Antonio de Béxar, [1779], Archivo General de Indias, Audiencia de Guadalajara, legajo 283, microfilm in the author's possession; Autos formados contra Juan José Flores de Abrego y otros rancheros por varios robos de ganado orejano, September 23, 1778, BA; Información recivida . . . sobre junta hecha de 8 a 9 de la noche del día 15 de Noviembre, November 15, 1790, ibid.; Petition of Alguacil D. Amador Delgado, January 4, 1793, ibid.; Expediente formado sobre el pago de los trabajos expendidos por los vecinos de la villa de Sn. Fernando y Presidio de San Antonio, April 11, 1793, ibid; Causa criminal contra D. Santiago Seguín, por haber alevosamente ultrajado al regidor D. Manuel Berbán, August 12, 1796, ibid.

6. Jack Jackson, *Los Mesteños: Spanish Ranching in Texas, 1721-1821* (College Station: Texas A&M University Press, 1986), 312; Diligencias practicadas para que en los herraderos que deben hacer los dueños de ganados de los ranchos del arroyo del Cibolo y río de San Antonio cumplan, guarden y observen el no correr ni coger ganado orejano, November 7, 1779, BA; Diligencias practicadas sobre haber vendido de cuenta de SM cientosetenta y siete reses vacunas orejanas a D. Santiago Seguín vecino de este presidio, July 6, 1784, ibid.

7. Marriages 1775-1780, no. 133, July 28, 1778, SF; Poseciones de oficios de alcaldes y regidores de esta villa de San Fernando, December 20, 1779, BA; Diligencias practicadas para poner en depósito, September 7, 1786, ibid.

8. Representación, apología, o escudo, que la República de la Villa de San Fernando, Real Presidio de San Antonio de Béxar, [1787], BA; Información recivida de los testigos que adentro se expresan a vista del parte dado por el alcalde de segundo voto de esta villa D. Angel Navarro, November 15, 1790, ibid.; Lista de los individuos del Ayuntamiento de esta Villa de San Fernando de [Béxar y] vecindario de ella que voluntariamente han de contribuir con lo que [pueden a la] fatiga de la fábrica del nuevo

cuartel, October 14, 1793, ibid.; Muñoz to Cabildo, December 29, 1794, ibid.; Causa criminal contra D. Santiago Seguín, por haber alevosamente ultrajado al Regidor D. Manuel Berbán, August 12, 1796, ibid.

9. Nemecio Salcedo to Juan Bautista Elguezábal, August 2, 1803, BA; Elguezábal to Salcedo, August 31, 1803, in copy book of his letters to the commandant general, July 6, 1803, ibid.

10. Surety bond of José Erasmo Seguín, July 19, 1806, BA (this item is incorrectly identified in the calendar as an affidavit of good character); José Erasmo Seguín's statement of government services performed, October 15, 1826, ibid.

11. Frederick C. Chabot, *With the Makers of San Antonio* (San Antonio: Artes Gráficas, 1937), 122; Adán Benavides, ed., *The Béxar Archives (1717-1836): A Name Guide* (Austin, University of Texas Press, 1989), 100. For samples of María Josefa's writing, as well as her discussion of family business matters with Erasmo, see their letters during his stay in Mexico City as delegate to the Constituent Congress in 1823 and 1824, in BA.

12. Padrón de los ranchos comprehendidos en la jurisdicción del síndico D. Manuel Salinas, January 2, 1811, Nacogdoches Archives Transcripts, BHC; Petitions for return of property, November 15, 1818, BA; [Martínez] to commander of Bahía, April 22, 1820, BA. Erasmo formalized his title to the property in 1834, see: Title to Erasmo Seguín, Bexar Land Papers, Spanish Collection, GLO, box 120 folder 3.

13. Election of October 12, 1810, in: Expediente formado para la elección de diputado en Cortes de la Provincia de Texas, June 27, 1810, BA.

14. Junta gubernativa to Commandant General Salcedo, June 19, 1811, ibid; José Erasmo Seguín's statement of government service, October 15, 1826, ibid; Frederick C. Chabot, ed., *Texas in 1811: The Las Casas and Sambrano Revolutions* (San Antonio: Yanaguana Press, 1941), 111.

15. [?] to [?], May 31, 1814, BA; [Commandant General] to Governor of Texas, November 2, 1814, ibid; Petitions for return of property, November 15, 1818, ibid; Gaspar Flores to Governor Martínez, June 24, 1819, ibid; [Governor Martínez] to commander at La Bahía, April 22, 1820, ibid; Joaquín de Arredondo to the governor of Texas, November 2, 1814, Nacogdoches Archives Transcripts, BHC.

16. María Josefa Becerra to Erasmo, February 20, 1824, BA; Juan N. Seguín to Erasmo, September 6, 1824, ibid.; Erasmo to Becerra, September 21, 1824, ibid.; [José Ignacio] Esteva to Military Commander of Texas, July 2, 1825, ibid.; Francisco Rojo's invoice, March 24, 1826, ibid.; Erasmo to

Antonio Pereyda, January 20, 1828, ibid.; Erasmo to Francisco Ugartechea, September 15, 1835, ibid; Oficio sobre el traslado de la administración de correos a José Erasmo Seguín, 1822, Oficios, Spanish Archives, BC.

17. Erasmo acquired the land from some of the heirs of Simón de Arocha: From Ignacio Arocha he acquired an unspecified amount of land for $200 (Transcribed Record, Spanish Archives, BC, vol. C-1, p. 261); from Ignacia, Juana, and Consolacíon Leal, heirs of Ana María Arocha, he obtained another unspecified amount of land for $125 (Land Grants, Spanish Collection, BC). The original 36,000 acre tract had been partitioned eight ways for the Arocha heirs, thus Erasmo acquired approximately 4,500 acres in each of these transactions.

18. William Kennedy, *Texas The Rise, Progress and Prospects of the Republic of Texas* (reprint, Clifton, N.J: Augustus M. Kelley, 1974), 404.

19. Proceedings of Béxar ayuntamiento, July 25, 1820, BA; Oficio sobre el traslado de la administración de correos a José Erasmo Seguín, December 31, 1822, Oficios, Spanish Archives, BC; Governor Martínez to Félix Trudeau, February 26, 1821, AP, I: 383.

20. In his biography of Austin, *Moses Austin: His Life* (San Antonio: Trinity University Press, 1987), page 207, David Gracy maintains that Erasmo must have caught up with Austin one or two days before the latter reached Herculaneum, Missouri. There is, however, no indication of a meeting between the two. In fact, Stephen Austin's letter to his father, written from Natchitoches on July 4, 1821 (AP, I: 400), includes a rough translation of the order authorizing the colonization project, thus suggesting that the older Austin had only received word of his success.

21. Stephen F. Austin to Maria Austin, July 13, 1821, AP, I: 401.

22. José Erasmo Seguín to Austin, August 30, 1821, AP, I: 411; Voluntary Subscription for Congressman's Expenses, November 22, 1823, ibid., I: 709; Austin to Seguín, [January 1, 1824], ibid., I: 718-19; Seguín to Austin and Bastrop, January 14, 1824, ibid., I: 723-24; Eugene C. Barker, *Life of Stephen F. Austin* (Austin: University of Texas Press, 1969), 113-14.

23. Austin to Gaspar Flores, [December 1824], AP, I: 986. In his recent book, *Rise of the Lone Star: The Making of Texas* (College Station: Texas A&M University Press, 1989), page 71, Andreas V. Reichstein implies that Austin's espousal of Seguín was a snub of the Baron of Bastrop, who had acted as go-between for Moses, and later Stephen Austin, in their dealings with the authorities.

24. Austin to James E. B. Austin, May 22, 1822, AP, I: 517; James E. B. Austin to Austin, May 4, 1823, ibid. I: 636; Seguín to Austin, July 24, 1825, ibid. I: 1156-58.

25. James E. B. Austin to Austin, August 22, 1826, AP, II: 1433.

26. Austin to Samuel M. Williams, May 9, 1833, AP, I: 966.

27. No evidence survives of Austin's attempt to give Erasmo a league of land. Erasmo subsequently sold his entitlement to Michel B. Menard. See: Erasmo Seguín, Spanish Collection, GLO, box 116 folder 12.

28. Erasmo Seguín to Austin, October 30, 1828, AP, II: 136-37; Erasmo Seguín to Austin, January 24, 1828, January 22, 1829, and April 2, 1829, Austin Papers, Series IV, BHC; Erasmo Seguín to Samuel M. Williams, August 5, 1830, and February 17, 1831, Samuel May Williams Papers, Rosenberg Library, Galveston, Texas.

29. Voluntary Subscription for Congressman's Expenses, November 22, 1823, AP, I: 709.

30. Erasmo to Austin and Baron of Bastrop, January 14, 1824, AP, I: 724.

31. Erasmo to Josefa Becerra, January 7, 1824, BA. Adán Benavides, in his paper "Spanish and Mexican Letters on the Texas Frontier, 1795-1835" (presented at the 1991 meeting of the Texas State Historical Association), points out that the two dozen letters between Erasmo and his family "form the largest block of family correspondence in Spanish . . . for the history of Texas prior to 1836" (p. 6).

32. Erasmo to the Provincial Deputation, December 23, 1823, in Provincial Deputation of Bexar to Ayuntamiento, February 12, 1824, AP, I: 741.

33. Erasmo to Bastrop, April 21, 1824, AP, I: 775-77.

34. Erasmo to Austin and Bastrop, January 14, 1824, AP, I: 723; Barker, *Life of Stephen F. Austin*, 119-20.

35. Erasmo to Austin and Bastrop, January 14, 1824, AP, I: 723.

36. Erasmo to Austin, July 24, 1825, AP, I: 1157.

37. Erasmo to Bastrop, March 24, 1824, AP, I: 758; Erasmo to Austin, July 24, 1825, ibid. I: 1157; Barker, *Life of Stephen F. Austin*, 201-25; 1820 census of San Antonio, BA, lists María Feliciana Cureste, as a single mulatto slave in Erasmo's household; he is also reported as having a slave in 1840, see Gifford White, *The 1840 Census of the Republic of Texas* (Austin: Pemberton, 1966), 17.

38. Erasmo to Bastrop, March 24, 1824, AP, I: 758, Erasmo to Austin, August 11, 1824, ibid. I: 873.

39. Austin to Luke Lesassier, May 6, 1833, AP, II: 961; Balmaceda to José Francisco Madero, April [sic] 6, 1833, quoted in *Gaceta del gobierno supremo del estado de Coahuila y Tejas,* May 27, 1833, reproduced in Celia Gutiérrez Ibarra, *Cómo México perdió Texas* (Mexico: Instituto Nacional de Antropología, 1987), appendix, 45.

40. John W. Smith to Thomas Jefferson Chambers, September 2, 1835, in Macolm D. McLean, comp. and ed., *Papers Concerning Robertson's Colony in Texas* (Arlington: University of Texas at Arlington Press, 1984), 11: 384-85.

41. Bowie and Fannin to Austin, October 22, 1835, in: John J. Jenkins III, comp., *The Papers of the Texas Revolution* (Austin: Jenkins Publishing Company, 1973), II: 191.

42. Bexar County Boundary Line File #2, GLO.

43. Gifford White, ed., *The 1840 Census,* 17; 1850 Census of the United States, Bexar County Texas, #146 (typescript copy, Texas State Library).

44. *Telegraph and Texas Register,* June 15, 1842.

45. Thomas J. Green, *Journal of the Texian Expedition Against Mier; Subsequent Imprisonment of the Author, His Sufferings, and Final Escape from the Castle of Perote* (New York, Harper & Brothers, 1845), 35.

46. Green, Rena Maverick, ed., *Memoirs of Mary A. Maverick,* arranged by Mary A. Maverick and George Madison Maverick (San Antonio: Alamo Printing Company, 1921), 59.

47. William Corner, comp. and ed., *San Antonio de Bexar: A Guide and History* (San Antonio, 1890), 113.

48. Joseph Nance, *Attack and Counterattack: The Texas-Mexican Frontier, 1842* (Austin: University of Texas Press, 1964), 383.

49. Erasmo to Josefa Becerra, January 7, 1824, BA; Josefa Becerra to Erasmo, February 20, 1824, ibid.; Erasmo to Josefa Becerra, August 11, 1824, ibid.; Juan to Erasmo, September 6, 1824, ibid.

50. Erasmo to Josefa Becerra, September 8, 1824, ibid.

51. Erasmo to Josefa Becerra, August 11, 1824, ibid.

52. Josefa Becerra to Erasmo, February 20, 1824, ibid.; Juan to Erasmo, September 22, 1824, ibid.

53. Juan to Austin, April 22, 1825, AP, I: 1079.

54. See appendix 50.

55. Juan to Alcalde of Béxar, January 11, 1833, BA.

56. For an example of the types of goods commonly included in such shipments see appendix 2.

57. James E. B. Austin to Stephen F. Austin, August 22, 1826, AP, I: 1433; Erasmo to Austin, November 18, 1826, ibid.: 1506; Duty on goods imported by Juan N. Seguín, et al., July 21, 1831, and June 7, 1832, BA.

58. Erasmo Seguín, Spanish Collection, GLO, box 116 folder 12; Juan N. Seguín, ibid., box 130 folder 9; author's correspondence with Margaret Swett Henson regarding Menard and the Galveston City Company. The company's papers are found at the Rosenberg Library, Galveston, Texas.

59. *Memoirs of Mary A. Maverick*, 55.

60. Marriages, 1798-1856, SF, #297; Padrón de los ranchos comprehendidos en la jurisdicción del síndico D. Joaquín Leal, December 10, 1810, Nacogdoches Archives Transcripts, BHC; Order of the ayuntamiento, October 10, 1811, ibid.; Jackson, *Los Mesteños,* 69-70, 490, 576; Chabot, *With the Makers of San Antonio,* 57; "Floresville," *Handbook of Texas* (3 vols., Austin: TSHA, 1952, 1976), I:612. For Manuel and Salvador Flores's military service see appendices 35, 52, 66, 67, and 68; Juan's administration of Salvador's family and estate are noted in *El Bejareño*, February 7, 1855, and February 9, 1856.

61. Chabot, *With the Makers of San Antonio*, 128; note "Children of Juan Nepomuceno Seguin and Maria Gertrudes Flores," in folder "The Seguin Family," Family Genealogy Files, BC; 1850 and 1860 U.S. censuses, TSL.

62. Músquiz to Austin, January 22, 1828 [should be 1829], AP, II: 9.

63. Election returns, December 21, 1828, BA; Cuaderno borrador of Gaspar Flores and Juan N. Seguín, June 5, 1829, ibid.; Juan to Jefe Político, June 7 and 20, 1829, ibid.; Resumen general, August 10, 1829, ibid.

64. Election of electoral assembly officers, February 13, 1832, BA; Minutes of the electoral assembly, March 1, 1833, ibid.; Minutes of the electoral assembly, February 9, 1834, ibid.

65. See appendices 3 and 4.

66. See appendices 5 and 6.

67. See appendices 7-9; Juan to Músquiz (fragment), April 6, 1834, BA;

Músquiz to Secretary of the State Government, April 7 and 12, June 1, and July 7, 1834, ibid.

68. See appendices 10-14.

69. Titles issued in East Texas under the empresario contracts made with Lorenzo de Zavala, David G. Burnet, and Joseph Vehlein, date from November 1834; titles issued by special commissioners George H. Smyth and Charles Taylor date from 1835 (Spanish Collection, GLO). See also appendices 15 and 16.

70. See appendix 17.

71. Paul Lack, "Los Tejanos: Texas Mexicans in the Revolution," MSS chapter in forthcoming book on Texas War of Independence, 451-52.

72. Lack, "Los Tejanos", 453-54; Antonio Cruz, Audited Military Claims, TSL; Juan Rodríguez, Republic Pension Applications, ibid.; appendices 18 and 66.

73. Nicolás Flores to Juan, January 23, 1836, BA; [San Antonio Meeting], January 26, 1836, Jenkins, *Papers of the Revolution,* 4: 153-55; J. J. Baugh to Henry Smith, February 13, 1836, ibid.; Harbert Davenport, "Captain Jesus Cuellar, Texas Cavalry, Otherwise Comanche," SWHQ 30 (July 1926): 58; Antonio Menchaca, *Memoirs* (San Antonio: Yanaguana Press, 1937), 23. For Juan's notification to Ruiz of his election see appendix 19.

74. "Alamo's Only Survivor," San Antonio *Express,* May 12, 1907; Menchaca, *Memoirs,* 23; José María Rodríguez, *Rodriguez Memoirs of Early Texas* (reprint, San Antonio: Standard Printing Company, 1961); Lack, "Los Tejanos," 478.

75. Juan Rodríguez, Republic Pension Applications, TSL; Lack, "Los Tejanos," 479-80; William F. Gray, *From Virginia to Texas* (Houston: Gray, Dillaye & Company, 1909), 131, appendices 68 and 70.

76. Appendix 20.

77. Juan López, Republic Pension Applications, Comptroller's Records, TSL.

78. Houston to E.D. White, October 31, 1837, James Grizzard Collection, TSL.

79. Houston to Erasmo, July 6, 1842, *The Writings of Sam Houston, 1813-1863,* ed. by Amelia W. Williams and Eugene C. Barker (10 vols., Austin: University of Texas Press, 1938-1943), 4: 125.

80. Burleson to Rusk, May 5, 1836, Army Papers, Adjutant General Records, TSL.

81. Appendices 21, 24, and 25.

82. *Telegraph and Texas Register,* September 21, 1836.

83. José Enrique de la Peña, *With Santa Anna in Texas: A Personal Narrative of the Revolution* (College Station: Texas A&M University Press, 1975), 4.

84. Appendices 21-25.

85. Appendices 26 and 27.

86. Appendix 27.

87. Appendices 28 and 29.

88. Appendix 29.

89. *Telegraph and Texas Register,* November 9, 1836.

90. Juan N. Seguín, Service Records, Adjutant General Records, TSL; Juan N. Seguín, Audited Military Claims, Comptroller of Public Accounts Records, ibid.; Felix Huston to Sam Houston, November 10, 1836, Houston Collection, Texas Catholic Archives, Austin; appendices 30 and 31.

91. Appendix 32.

92. Felix Huston to Sam Houston, November 14, 1836, Houston Collection, Catholic Archives of Texas.

93. Appendix 36.

94. Jack C. Butterfield, "Juan N. Seguín: A Vindication" (MSS, DRT, n.d.), 12-14.

95. Appendices 33, 35, 40-45; folder entitled "Case of City of San Antonio vs Juan N. Seguin for debt, Bexar County, Nov. 16, 1836 [*sic*]," Juan N. Seguín Collection, DRT.

96. Appendix 42.

97. Appendices 34, 36, 37, 38, 40, 41, 46.

98. Appendix 40.

99. Appendices 41 and 42.

100. Appendix 39. Conflicting descriptions of the burial are found in appendices 42 and 72. In the letter to General Johnston, no mention is made of an urn into which were placed "the few fragments" mentioned in the letter to Hamilton P. Bee. On the other hand, the Johnston letter does

mention the coffin containing ashes from two of the pyres having been taken to the parish church, from whence the procession began. The discovery of human remains inside the parish church in 1937, near the spot described by Juan in his letter to Bee, occasioned Archbishop Arthur J. Drossaerts of San Antonio to publish a pamphlet on the matter: *The Truth About the Burial of the Remains of the Alamo Heroes* (San Antonio: private printing, 1938). In his section on Juan Seguín, Rubén Rendón Lozano in *Viva Tejas: The Story of the Mexican-born Patriots of the Republic of Texas* (San Antonio: Southern Literary Institute, 1936), 37-38, quoting "old documents," states that ashes from two locations were placed in a coffin, which was subsequently placed on the third, largest heap of ashes, which became the burial site.

101. Appendices 46 and 47; Refugio B-5 and Fannin B-440, Original Land Grant Collection, GLO; Juan N. Seguin, Audited Civil Service Claims, Comptroller's Records, TSL.

102. *Telegraph and Texas Register*, May 19, 1838; Ida Vernon, "Activities of the Seguins in Early Texas History" (West Texas Historical Association Year Book 25, 1949), 28; Joseph M. Nance, *After San Jacinto: The Texas Mexican Frontier, 1836-1841* (Austin: University of Texas Press, 1963), 281.

103. Appendices 54, 55, 58.

104. Appendix 56.

105. Unable to afford the expenses of public colleges, Congress promoted the establishment of private institutions through grants of public land.

106. Charles E. Castañeda, *Our Catholic Heritage in Texas, 1519-1936* (New York: Arno, 1976), 7:25-27; appendix 53.

107. Smithers to John P. Borden, July 13, 1838, Early Letters Received, GLO (microfilm).

108. McLeod to Lamar, August 24, 1840, Lamar Papers, TSL.

109. Appendix 67.

110. *Memoirs of Mary A. Maverick*, 29.

111. Appendix 51; folder: "Feb. 17, 1870-Nov. 27, 1879," George Thomas and Mary F. Howard Papers, BHC; Green, *Journal of the Texian Expedition*, 34-35. The Somervell and Mier expeditions were launched in the fall of 1842 in an effort to punish the Mexicans for General Woll's invasion of San Antonio. When Alexander Somervell decided to return to

Texas after capturing Laredo and Guerrero only part of his command obeyed. The majority of the force, under command of William S. Fisher continued to Mier, where it was defeated and the majority of members captured.

112. For a report on the problem throughout the republic see: John P. Borden to Lamar, October 23, 1839, Letters, 1837-1841, vol. 2: 258-64, GLO.

113. Smithers to Borden, July 13, 1838, Early Letters Received, GLO.

114. John Bost Pitts III, "Speculation in Headright Land Grants in San Antonio From 1837 to 1842," (M.A. thesis, Trinity University, San Antonio, 1966), appendix.

115. Folder 82, Casiano-Pérez Collection, DRT.

116. Ibid., folder 51.

117. Refugio B-5, Original Land Grant Collection, GLO.

118. Juan N. Seguin, Audited Military Claims, Comptroller's Records, TSL; folder: "Case of the City of San Antonio vs. Juan N. Seguin for debt," Juan N. Seguin Collection, DRT; folder: Summons to appear in district Court, San Antonio, 1840, ibid.

119. The events of this period are extremely complex and are here summarized only briefly. For a detailed account of the Republic of the Rio Grande, see Nance, *After San Jacinto*, 252-377.

120. Nance, *After San Jacinto*, 281-82; appendix 57.

121. Appendix 59; "Information derived from J.M. Monchaca, San Fernando, related to the Manchacas in Bexar [1857?]," doc. 2567, Lamar Papers, TSL; Nance, *After San Jacinto*, 328-29.

122. Appendix 60.

123. Benjamin Gillam to Hugh McLeod, January 10, 1841, Army Papers, Adjutant General's Records, TSL; White, *The 1840 Census of the Republic of Texas*, 16; Nance, *After San Jacinto,* 409.

124. Journal A, Records of the City of San Antonio from 1837 to 1849, Material from Various Sources, BHC, vol. 815: 79.

125. Journal A, Records of the City of San Antonio, vol. 815: 87, 89, BHC; Vernon, "Activities of the Seguins," 31-32.

126. Journal A, Records of the City of San Antonio, BHC, vol. 815: 82; Juan and Gertrudis Seguín to Howard and Ogden, July 2, 1841, Deed

Records of Bexar County, vol. A-2: 447-48; Nance, *After San Jacinto*, 431-34.

127. Nance, *After San Jacinto*, 434.

128. *Memoirs of Mary A. Maverick*, 59.

129. Corner, *San Antonio*, 113.

130. Appendix 61.

131. Appendix 62.

132. Harriet Smither, ed., "Diary of Adolphus Sterne," Part XV, SWHQ 33 (April 1930): 318.

133. A. A. Alsbury to Houston, June 16, 1842, A. J. Houston Collection, TSL, #2504.

134. *Telegraph and Texas Register*, June 15, 1842; Samuel Maverick to Mary Maverick, October 6, 1842, Maverick Family Papers, General Correspondence, BHC.

135. List of persons captured in San Antonio, Texas, on the 11th of Sep 1842, in folder: "Battle—Mier, San Jacinto," Texas Veterans Association Collection, BHC; Vernon, "Activities of the Seguins," 34; Nance, *Attack and Counterattack,* 353.

136. *Telegraph and Texas Register*, October 5, 1842.

137. Green, *Journal of the Texian Expedition,* 34.

138. Quoted in Sam Houston Dixon and Louis Wiltz Kemp, *The Heroes of San Jacinto* (Houston: Anson Jones Press, 1932), 438.

139. Vernon, "Activities of the Seguins," 34-35; Execution of judgement of District court against Juan and wife in favor of Howard and Ogden, for $3,000 debt owed since October 2, 1841, Deed Records, BC vol. B-2: 265-66; Melchor Travieso to Juan N. Seguin, ibid., vol. C-2: 142; "Ogden, Duncan Campbell," *Handbook of Texas* 2: 303; Nance, *Attack and Counterattack*, 353; appendices 63 and 65.

140. Thomas Cutrer, Biography of Ben McCulloch (MS), states: "McCulloch, in common with most Anglo-Texans, held [Seguín and his men] responsible for murdering Captain Nicholas M. Dawson and his men after they had surrendered near Salado Creek in September, 1842;" *Expedición hecha en Tejas par una parte de la División del Cuerpo de Egército del Norte* (Monterrey, 1842), 36, 40-43.

141. Norman Woods to H. G. Woods, July 5, 1843, in L. U. Spellmann,

comp., "Letters of the 'Dawson Men' from Perote Prison, Mexico, 1842-1843," SWHQ 38 (April 1935): 258.

142. *Expedición hecha en Tejas*, 48.

143. Complaint against the Escuadrón Auxiliar de Béjar, Saltillo Archives, vol. 42, leg. 38, 1845, exp. 1472, BHC; Juan to [Dolores García, alcalde of Laredo], May 19, 1846, Laredo Archives (microfilm), reel 14, TSL; *Telegraph and Texas Register*, October 26, 1842 and January 15, 1845; Richard Santos, "Juan Nepomuceno Seguín," *Humanitas: Anuario del Centro de Estudios Humanísticos de la Universidad Autónoma de Nuevo León* (Nuevo Leon: Universidad, 1976), 562.

144. Houston to Erasmo, July 6, 1842, *The Writings of Sam Houston, 1813-1863*, 4: 125.

145. Green, *Journal of the Texian Expedition*, 35.

146. Clarksville *Northern Standard*, February 23, 1843.

147. Appendix 64.

148. Ben McCulloch to William W. S. Bliss, June 23, 1846, McCulloch Papers, BHC, cited in Cutrer, biography of Ben McCulloch manuscript.

149. Veatch to Lamar, February 23, 1848, Lamar Papers, doc. 2377, TSL.

150. Appendix 65.

151. Vernon, "Activities of the Seguins," 36; 1850 Census of the United States, Bexar County (microfilm), #146, TSL.

152. *El Bejareño,* July 7, 1855; Santos, "Juan Nepomuceno Seguín," 563.

153. *El Bejareño*, July 21, 1855.

154. Santos, "Juan Nepomuceno Seguín," 564-65; Llerena Friend, *Sam Houston: The Great Designer* (reprint, Austin: University of Texas Press, 1969), 298-300.

155. Juan to Hardin R. Runnels, January 8, 1859, Hardin Richard Runnels Correspondence, Governors Papers, TSL.

156. Jack Jackson, *Los Tejanos* (Stamford: Fantagraphics Press, 1982), 121; Santos, in "Juan Nepomuceno Seguín," 565 (fn. 44), 566, cites the Archivo de la Defensa Nacional, where he examined a folder on "Juan N. Seguín." The author could not consult this folder as it is now unavailable.

157. *La Voz de Zaragoza*, 1 (December 1961): 27; Guillermo Colin Sánchez, *Ignacio Zaragoza: Evocación de un héroe* (Mexico: Editorial

Porrúa, 1963), 41.

158. Federico Berrueto Ramón, *Ignacio Zaragoza* (Mexico: Secretaría de Gobernación, 1962), 329, n. 2.

159. Bexar B-1347, Original Land Grant Collection, GLO; Juan N. Seguín, Audited Military Claims, Comptroller's Records, TSL; appendices 66-70.

160. Juan and Gertrudis to Jacob Waelder, April 19, 1856, Deed Records, BC, vol. N-2: 620; Juan to Teresa Seguin de Soto, February 15, 1858, ibid., vol. R-2: 199; Schedule of the separate property of Gertrudis Flores de Seguin wife of Juan N. Seguin, August 14, 1860, ibid.; vol. S-1: 223; Juan and Gertrudis to A. B. Frank, May 4, 1866, ibid., vol. T-2: 736; 1860 Census of the United States, Bexar County (microfilm, TSL), #1848; Santiago Seguín to R. A. Wiseman, June 12, 1927, copy of letter in possession of Jack Jackson, Austin.

161. G. Treviño to Porfirio Díaz, April 7, 1875, *Archivo del General Porfirio Díaz: Memorias y Documentos* (Mexico: Editorial Elade, 1951), 11: 259; Porfirio Díaz to Francisco Naranjo, April 22, 1876, ibid., 13: 236; Santiago Seguín to R. A. Wiseman, June 12, 1927, copy of letter in possession of Jack Jackson, Austin; Dallas *Weekly Herald*, July 3, 1884; Santos, "Juan Nepomuceno Seguín," 566; Vernon, "Activities of the Seguins," 38; appendix 71.

162. San Antonio *Light*, November 13, 1882; Clarksville *Northern Standard*, August 18, 1887; appendices 69, 72, and 73.

163. Appendix 71.

PERSONAL MEMOIRS

OF

JOHN N. SEGUIN,

FROM THE YEAR 1834

TO THE

RETREAT OF GENERAL WOLL

FROM

THE CITY OF SAN ANTONIO

1842.

SAN ANTONIO:

PRINTED AT THE LEDGER BOOK AND JOB OFFICE.

1858.

Preface

A native of the city of San Antonio de Béxar, I embraced the cause of Texas at the sound of the first cannon which foretold her liberty, filled an honorable role within the ranks of the conquerors of San Jacinto, and was a member of the legislative body of the Republic. In the very land which in other times bestowed on me such bright and repeated evidences of trust and esteem, I now find myself exposed to the attacks of scribblers and personal enemies who, to serve *political purposes* and engender strife, falsify historical fact with which they are but imperfectly acquainted. I owe it to myself, my children and friends to answer them with a short but true exposition of my acts, from the beginning of my public career up to the time of the return of General Woll from the Rio Grande with the Mexican forces, among which I was then serving.

I address myself to the American people, to that people impetuous as the whirlwind when aroused by the hypocritical clamors of designing men but just, impartial, and composed whenever men and facts are submitted to their judgment.

I have been the object of the hatred and passionate attacks of a few troublemakers who, for a time, ruled as masters over the poor and oppressed population of San Antonio. Harpy-like, ready to pounce on everything that attracted the notice of their rapacious avarice, I was an obstacle to the execution of their vile designs. They therefore leagued together to exasperate and ruin me, spread malignant calumnies against me, and made use of odious machinations to sully my honor and tarnish my well earned reputation.

A victim to the wickedness of a few men whose false pretenses were favored because of their origin and recent domination over the country, a foreigner in my native land, could I stoically be expected to endure their outrages and insults? Crushed by sorrow, convinced that only my death would satisfy my enemies, I sought shelter among those against whom I had fought. I separated from my country, parents, family, relatives and friends and, what was more, from the institutions on behalf of which I had drawn my sword with an earnest wish to see Texas free and happy. In that involuntary exile my only ambition was to devote my time, far from the tumult of war, to the support of my family who shared in my sad condition.

Fate, however, had not exhausted its cup of bitterness. Thrown into a prison in a foreign country, I had no alternatives left but to linger in a loathsome confinement or to accept military service.

On one hand, my wife and children, reduced to beggary and separated from me; on the other hand, to turn my arms against my own country. The alternatives were sad, the struggle of feelings violent. At last the father triumphed over the citizen; I seized a sword that pained my hand. (Who among my readers will not understand my situation?) I served Mexico; I served her loyally and faithfully. I was compelled to fight my own countrymen, but I was never guilty of the barbarous and unworthy deeds of which I am accused by my enemies.

Ere the tomb closes over me and my contemporaries, I wish to publicize this stormy period of my life. I do it for my friends as well as for my enemies. I challenge the latter to contest with facts the statements I am about to make, and I confidently leave the decision to those who witnessed the events.

Memoirs, &c.

In October 1834 I was political chief of the department of Béxar.[1] Dissatisfied with the reactionary designs of General Antonio López de Santa Anna, who was at that time president of the Republic of Mexico and endeavoring to overthrow the federal system, I issued a circular in which I urged every municipality in Texas to appoint delegates to a convention that was to meet at San Antonio to consider the impending dangers and to devise means to avert them.[2]

All the municipalities appointed their delegates but the convention never met, the general government having ordered Colonel José María Mendoza to march with his forces from Matamoros to San Antonio and prevent the meeting of the delegates. Proof of the above facts exists in the archives of the county of Béxar.[3]

In April 1835 the governor of Coahuila and Texas, Don Agustín Viesca, called for assistance from the various departments to resist the aggressions of Santa Anna against that state. I volunteered my services and received from the political chief, Don Angel Navarro, the command of a party of national guards sent from San Antonio

---

[1] Seguín, elected alcalde of San Antonio for 1834, served as interim political chief upon José Miguel Arciniega's resignation from the same post at the beginning of January. Seguín gave up the office to the incumbent Ramón Músquiz, but resumed the office in July upon the latter's resignation for poor health. He surrendered the post to Angel Navarro in December 1834. See appendices 3, 4, 7, 8, 9 and 16.

[2] Two previous conventions (October 1 to 6, 1832, and April 1 to 13, 1833) organized by Anglo-American settlers at San Felipe suffered from lack of support from the Tejano population. Both gatherings had stressed the need for separate statehood for Texas, repeal or relaxation of the anti-immigration clause of the Law April 6, 1830, and tariff reductions.

[3] Now the Bexar Archives, University of Texas at Austin, Barker Texas History Center. Reproduced in this volume as appendices 10 through 15.

to Monclova.[4] In our encounters with the troops of Santa Anna, I
was efficiently assisted by Colonel Benjamin R. Milam and Major
John K. Allen. On our withdrawal from Monclova, disgusted with
the weakness of the governor who had given up the struggle, we
pledged ourselves to use all our influence to rouse Texas against the
tyrannical government of Santa Anna.

We returned to San Antonio in the beginning of June. The
military commander, Colonel Domingo Ugartechea, considering me
opposed to the existing government, ordered two officers to watch
my movements in secret. This, however, did not prevent my working
diligently to prepare for the intended campaign.

We had agreed that the campaign should begin in the center of
Texas[5] but, not hearing from that quarter, I determined to send an
agent, Juan A. Zambrano, to Brazoria with directions to sound out
the temperament of the people. On the return of the agent, we were
apprised that there was a great deal of talk about a revolution in
public meetings but that the moment for an armed movement was
still remote. Our agent was sent to Victoria where he called a meeting
of the citizens,[6] but the military commander of Goliad, Manuel
Sabariego, sent down a detachment of troops to prevent the assembly and arrest the promoters.

We despaired of a successful issue until the military commander
of Texas, Ugartechea, after being informed of the revolutionary
feelings which were spreading through the American colonies,
decided to remove from the town of Gonzales a piece of artillery lent
to that municipality by the former political chief, Antonio Saucedo.[7]

---

[4] The militiamen were sent to Monclova in response to a request from
the governor for protection from General Cos, who was moving to occupy
the city for the centralist cause. Of the three Texas districts, Nacogdoches,
Brazos, and Béxar, only the latter sent twenty-five men, led by Seguín, far
short of the one hundred men requested.

[5] That is, Austin's Colony on the Brazos and Colorado rivers.

[6] Victoria was the center of Martín de León's colony. The area had the
heaviest concentration of Tejanos after San Antonio.

[7] The cannon had been loaned in 1831 at the request of empresario Green
DeWitt for the purpose of establishing defenses against hostile Indians.

At the time this was a delicate undertaking. A lieutenant, Francisco Castañeda, was detailed to carry it into execution, with orders to use force if necessary. On the same day that the military detachment started for Gonzales, I went to the lower ranchos on the San Antonio River.[8] At Salvador Flores' I held a meeting of the neighbors and induced several to take up arms, well satisfied that the beginning of the revolution was close at hand. The officer sent to Gonzales met some resistance at the "Perra"[9] and thought it prudent to beat a hasty retreat. Colonel Ugartechea was making preparations to proceed in person towards Gonzales, with a substantial force, when he received orders from General Martín Perfecto de Cos to await his arrival.

A few days after the entry of General Cos into San Antonio Major George Collinsworth, surprising the garrison of Goliad, took possession of that place.[10] As soon as I was informed of that circumstance, I marched with my company to reinforce the major. But, at the "Conquista" crossing[11] on the San Antonio River, I was overtaken by a dispatch from General Stephen F. Austin, who informed me that he was marching on San Antonio and requested me to join him in order to attack General Cos. I retraced my steps after having requested Captain Manuel Flores to go and meet General Austin and inform him of my readiness to comply with his wishes, and that I would take with me all the men I could possibly enlist en route.

On the 13th of October I met Austin on the Salado, at the crossing of the Gonzales road, and joined my forces with his small army. Upon this occasion I had the honor to become acquainted with General Sam Houston, who accompanied Austin. On the same day

---

[8] Most of the established Tejano families of San Antonio had their ranches in the San Antonio River valley between Béxar and Goliad.

[9] This episode later came to be known as the Battle of Gonzales. It took place on October 2, 1835, on the west bank of the Guadalupe River about four miles from Gonzales on the road to San Antonio.

[10] Colonel Francisco Sandoval had taken command of Goliad just eight days before its capture on the evening of October 10, 1835.

[11] About half-way between Béxar and Goliad at Conquista Creek.

we had a slight engagement with the forces under Cos, who retired into San Antonio. Austin, as commander-in-chief of the army, gave me the appointment of captain.[12]

I was commanded to accompany Colonel James Bowie, with my company, to the Mission of San José with orders to approach the city as close as possible, following the banks of the river. We arrived at the Mission of Concepción on the evening of the 21st of November and, noticing that we had been observed by the scouts of General Cos, passed the night in making preparations to resist an attack which we considered imminent. We were not deceived; on the morning of the 22d a force was seen moving along the road from San Antonio to the Mission. A few men, sent by Bowie to reconnoitre, made such a rash charge that they were cut off from their line of retreat and had to barricade themselves in the steeple of the church, where they remained during the action. The day was soon ours, the enemy retreating with the loss of one piece of artillery.

I was detailed to forage for the army and was successful in doing so, returning to the camp with a liberal supply of provisions.[13] Our camp was soon moved to within one mile of the Alamo, whence we proceeded to the "Molino Blanco" and established headquarters. On the 11th of December we entered the city and, after having taken possession of the houses of the curate, Refugio de la Garza, and the Veramendi, Garza, Flores and other families, we forced the enemy to capitulate and withdraw towards Laredo.[14]

After the capture of San Antonio Captain William B. Travis' company and mine were detailed to pursue the Mexican forces and capture from them a caballado [horse herd] which they had in the Parrita, on the Laredo road. We succeeded, taking nearly one

---

[12] See appendices 17 and 18.

[13] As the people best acquainted with the country, Tejanos were often detailed to foraging, escorting, and scouting activities. This is possibly why relatively few Tejanos took part in the major engagements. See appendices 26 and 30.

[14] For a list of those Tejanos Seguín claims served under him during this campaign see appendix 66.

hundred head of horses which were sent to San Felipe de Austin for the benefit of the public service. I was afterwards detailed to the ranchos on the San Antonio River, to see if I could find more horses belonging to the Mexican troops.

On the 2d of January, 1836, I received from the Provisional Government[15] the commission of captain of regular cavalry, with orders to report to Lieutenant Colonel Travis in San Antonio.[16]

On the 22d of February, at 2:00 P.M., General Santa Anna with over four thousand men took possession of the city. In the meantime, we fell back into the Alamo.

On the 28th the enemy commenced the bombardment while we met in a council of war. Taking into consideration our perilous situation, a majority of the council resolved that I should leave the fort and proceed with a communication to Colonel James W. Fannin, requesting him to come to our assistance. I left the Alamo on the night of the council. On the following day at the San Bartolo Ranch on the Cibolo, I met Captain Francis L. Desauque who, by orders of Fannin, had foraged on my ranch, carrying off a great number of cattle, corn, and other provisions. Desauque informed me that Fannin's arrival at the Cibolo, on his way to render assistance

---

[15] The Consultation, a meeting of delegates from Texas municipalities, met in November 1835 to resolve a course of action. On November 7 the Consultation proclaimed Texas an independent state within the Mexican Republic under the Constitution of 1824 and established a temporary government. The Provisional Government, composed of a governor, lieutenant governor, and legislative body known as the General Council, was inactive for much of the period preceding its dissolution when the Texas Declaration of Independence was signed.

[16] Available documentation seems to contradict Seguín's account of his appointment. According to the record of the proceedings of the Convention at Washington, February 9, 1836, Seguín did not take up the commission: "From information recently received that Juan N. Seguín, who was appointed Captain in the Cavalry corps has not accepted his appointment, the Advisory Committee would recommend to your excellency that [Jesús Cuellar], who so gallantly Piloted the brave army into Bexar the morning of the 5th December last should be appointed to fill his place." Hans P.N. Gammel, ed., The Laws of Texas, 1822-1897 (10 vols., Austin, 1898), I: 878.

to the defenders of the Alamo, could not be more than two days away. I therefore determined to wait for him. By dispatch I sent Fannin the communication from Travis, informing him at the same time of the critical position of the defenders of the Alamo. Fannin answered me, through Lieutenant Charles Finley, that he had advanced as far as "Rancho Nuevo"[17] but, being informed of the movements of General José Urrea, had countermarched to Goliad to defend that place. Fannin added that he was unable to respond to Travis' call, their respective commands being separate, and assistance depended upon General Houston, then at Gonzales, with whom he advised me to communicate. I lost no time in repairing to Gonzales and reported myself to the general, informing him of the purport of my mission. He commanded me to wait at Gonzales for further orders. General Houston ordered Captain Salvador Flores, with twenty-five men of my company, to the lower ranchos on the San Antonio River, to protect the inhabitants from the depredations of the Indians.[18]

Afterwards, I was ordered with the balance of my company to take possession of the "Perra," about four miles away on the road to San Antonio, with instructions to report every evening at headquarters. Thus my company formed the vanguard of the Texan army on the San Antonio road.

On the 6th of March I received orders to go to San Antonio with my company and a party of American citizens, carrying provisions for the defenders of the Alamo on the horses.

Arriving at the Cibolo and not hearing the signal gun which was to be discharged every fifteen minutes as long as the place held out, we retraced our steps to convey to the general-in-chief the sad tidings. Another party was sent out which soon came back, having met with Anselmo Vergara and Andres Barcena, both soldiers of my company whom I had left in the vicinity of San Antonio for purposes of observation. They brought the intelligence of the fall of the Alamo,

---

[17] About two miles west of Goliad on the San Antonio River.

[18] Two more detailed, though slightly differing accounts by Seguín of his activities during the Alamo campaign may be seen in appendices 71 and 73.

and their report was so detailed as to preclude any doubts about that disastrous event.

The Texan army began its retreat towards the center of the country. I was put in command of the rear guard, with orders not to leave behind any families. I continued covering the rear guard until we had crossed the Arenoso Creek near the Brazos River where, by orders of the general, I was detached with Captain Mosley Baker to the town of San Felipe de Austin to cut off the enemy from the river crossing. We remained in that position and within sight of the brigade of General Joaquín Ramírez y Sesma, who occupied San Felipe. I was subsequently ordered with my company to occupy the house of Leonard W. Groce, farther up the river. Our main army was then encamped in the bottom of the Paloma or Molino Creek, on the western bank of the Brazos River, where it remained until information was received that the enemy had crossed the river at Fort Bend and was marching towards Harrisburg. Our army began at once to cross the river on board the steamer *Yellow Stone* and, when the whole force had crossed, took up the march with the intention of harassing the enemy's rear guard.

The army was taking its noon rest near Buffalo Bayou when two soldiers of my company, who had gone out to water horses, reported that they had seen three Mexicans riding at full speed over the prairie. Without delay I advised the general, who immediately sent Captains Henry Karnes and Deaf Smith in pursuit. These officers returned shortly, bringing as prisoners a captain, a citizen, and an express bearer of dispatches from Mexico to the enemy.

We were apprised by the prisoners that Santa Anna was at Harrisburg with eight hundred men, and a perusal of their papers acquainted us with the fact that Cos was to bring him reinforcements. To prevent the concentration of forces, General Sam Houston gave the order to resume the march. The army, artillery and train crossed over Buffalo Bayou on rafts, during which operation General Thomas Rusk, then secretary of war, did not spare his personal labor. It was dark when the crossing was effected. In the course of the night we passed through Harrisburg, the ruins of which were still smoking, having been set on fire by the enemy. We continued our march all night. At daybreak a man was taken prisoner who, on discovering us, had attempted to escape. He was a printer belonging to San Felipe, who informed us that the enemy was about eight miles away on the way back to Harrisburg. Our scouts soon came in with the information that the enemy was countermarching towards Buffalo Bayou.

Conscious of the starving condition of the troops, who had not eaten for twenty-four hours, General Houston resolved on camping on a small rise contiguous to the San Jacinto River.

We were beginning to cook our meal when the enemy showed themselves nearby. We rushed to arms and formed in line of battle. As they approached we were ordered to lie down on the ground, thus concealing ourselves in the grass. A piece of high ground adjacent to our position was soon occupied by the enemy, upon which the general ordered the band to strike up "Will you come to the bower?" The enemy answered with its artillery, and we joined the chorus with a brisk musketry. We were soon charged by a skirmishing party on foot, detached from the right wing of the enemy. They were quickly driven back by a party of our cavalry, supported by the artillery. The enemy kept up their fire until they had selected a camping ground about four hundred steps away from ours and protected by two hillocks. Both armies ceased firing. We resumed the cooking of our meal of only meat, but had the good fortune to capture a boat loaded with provisions which afforded some seasoning to a repast that otherwise would have been rather scanty.

On the same evening General Mirabeau B. Lamar went out with a party of cavalry to draw the enemy into a fight. The result was a slight skirmish ending in the wounding of two or three on each side.

On the morning of the 21st of April General Houston, for the purpose of cutting off the communication of General Cos' forces with those of Santa Anna, ordered Deaf Smith to burn the bridge over the river,[19] but on reaching it he saw that he had come too late. The enemy's reinforcements had already crossed. However, the

---

[19] The bridge referred to spanned Vince's Bayou, less than ten miles east of the battlefield.

bridge was destroyed and Smith returned to our camp at the very moment when Cos joined forces with Santa Anna.

At noon, General Rusk came to partake of dinner in my tent. When he had done eating he asked me if the Mexicans were not in the habit of taking a siesta at that hour. I answered in the affirmative adding, moreover, that in such cases they kept their main and advanced guards under arms with a line of sentinels. General Rusk observed that he thought so too, however the moment seemed to him favorable to attack the enemy. He added: "Do you feel like fighting?" I answered that I was always ready and willing to fight, upon which the general rose, saying: "Well, let us go!" I made my dispositions at once. The general proceeded along the line speaking to the captains, and our force was soon under arms. Generals Houston and Rusk delivered short addresses, and we formed in line of battle in front of the enemy. My company was in the left wing, under Colonel Sidney Sherman.[20] We marched out onto the prairie and were met by a column of infantry, which we drove back briskly. Before engaging that column, we had dispersed an ambuscade that had opened fire against us within pistol shot. The entire enemy line, panic struck, took to flight. We were already on the bank of the river in pursuit of the fugitives when my attention was called to a Mexican officer who, emerging from the river where he had kept himself concealed, gave himself up and requested me to spare his life. Protected by weeds and grass, he seemed afraid to leave his shelter because of the fire which was being maintained against the fugitives. I ordered those who were close to me to cease firing, an order which was extended along the line to a considerable distance. Then the officer who had addressed me came out, followed by Colonels Juan María Bringas, Juan N. Almonte, Dias, and quite a number of other officers.

On my way to the camp with the prisoners, an officer named Sánchez conducted me to a place where $25,000 had been concealed. I reached the camp at dark and presented my prisoners to the general, who congratulated me, and I reported to him the discovery of the

---

[20] For the muster roll of Seguín's company at San Jacinto, see appendix 20.

money. Colonel John Forbes was at once detailed to go and bring it in.[21]

On this great and glorious day my company was conspicuous for efficiency and gallantry yet we did not lose one single man, to the surprise of those who had witnessed our honorable and perilous situation.

Two days after the capture of Santa Anna, and four days after the battle, Captain Karnes and I were detailed with our companies to observe the retreat of the remains of the Mexican army. We overtook their rear guard at the "Contrabando" Marsh, where some of their wagons had broken down. As soon as the escort saw us they took to flight, leaving the whole property in our possession. General Pedro de Ampudia sent me a communication requesting me to attend to the sick and wounded whom he had left behind.[22]

We crossed the Colorado River at the heels of the enemy and, after proceeding a short distance, met General Adrián Woll, who was bearer of a safe conduct. We camped every night on the ground abandoned each morning by the enemy until we reached Victoria, which had already been evacuated by them. Shortly afterwards Colonel Sherman arrived, in command of the vanguard of our army, and subsequently General Rusk, then commander-in-chief, who established his headquarters in that town.

On the 30th of May, I received from the general-in-chief my promotion to the rank of lieutenant colonel of the Texan army, and

---

[21] No record corroborating Seguín's claim about this money has been discovered; however, estimates of the specie taken from the Mexicans range from $12,000 to $45,000. Most of these estimates came as a result of claims made by Nicholas Labadie in the *Texas Almanac* (1859) that John Forbes, commissary general of the Texas army during the battle and responsible for the distribution of spoils, had pilfered a large part of the captured money. Labadie's assertions led to a law suit for libel by Forbes, during which much testimony was taken on the amount of specie captured from the Mexicans (John Forbes vs. Nicholas D. Labadie, Robert Bruce Blake Research Collection, XXXI, BHC).

[22] For the extent of Seguín's contacts with the retreating Mexican forces see appendices 21 through 25.

was ordered to take possession of San Antonio.[23] I left Victoria on the 1st of June and, on the Cabeza Creek, met General Juan José Andrade who was retreating towards Matamoros.

In conformance with my instructions, I sent to that general a communication informing him that my orders were to take possession of San Antonio. His answer was that the place was occupied by Captain Francisco Castañeda, who was instructed to surrender it to the first Texas officer who should come to demand it.

I took possession of San Antonio on the 4th of June.[24] On the 10th Colonel Smith came to occupy it with the regiment of Mississippi Mounted Volunteers. On the 24th I received orders to fall back with my command to headquarters at Victoria, information having been received that the Mexican army was marching from Matamoros to Texas.[25]

When we were convinced of the falseness of that report, I applied to the general for leave to go to Nacogdoches on a visit to my family, then in that town on their return from the Sabine where they had sought refuge from the Mexican army. My application was favorably received and leave of absence for twenty-two days granted to me.

I found all the members of my family sick with fever. The disease did not spare me either and I was compelled to exceed the term of my leave. General Houston, who was then at Nacogdoches recuperating from the wounds he received at San Jacinto, gave me a certificate stating the causes of my delay in returning to my post. I left Nacogdoches on the 20th of August, and on my passage through Columbus I received orders from the secretary of war to report myself to the president, David G. Burnet, for instructions.

I arrived at Velasco on the 10th of September. On the next day, the president handed to me my commission of lieutenant colonel and

---

[23] For a copy of the order see appendix 26.

[24] For Seguín's letter advising Rusk of his occupation of San Antonio see appendix 27.

[25] Two documents regarding Seguín's brief stay in San Antonio during June 1836 are found in appendices 28 and 29.

appointed me to the command of the city of San Antonio with orders to proceed to my destination without delay.[26]

I arrived at headquarters at Lavaca on the 15th of the same month and reported to General Rusk, who ordered me to begin recruiting my regiment in that town.[27]

On the 11th of October I left headquarters with my regiment dismounted and with instructions to procure horses in San Antonio, where I arrived on the 17th.[28]

In March of 1837, in command of San Antonio, I received orders from General Felix Huston to destroy that city and relocate its inhabitants to the east bank of the Brazos. At the same time, Lieutenant Colonel Alonzo B. Sweitzer of the volunteers arrived with instructions to assist me in carrying out the order. Considering the measure premature and unjust, I took upon myself the responsibility of disobeying the order until I had referred the matter to President Sam Houston, with whom I made use of all my influence to have the order rescinded. The president prevailed upon General Huston to desist. I thus averted the impending destruction of San Antonio but, in consequence, made General Felix Huston my bitter enemy.[29]

---

[26] For a copy of the commission see illustration on page 30. Seguín's instructions for the reoccupation of San Antonio and the raising of a battalion are found in appendix 30.

[27] Apparently Seguín was forced to cast a wide net for volunteers. He even posted a recruitment notice in the *Telegraph and Texas Register*, see appendix 31. For the muster roll of Seguín's regiment, see appendix 35.

[28] What means Seguín employed for detailing the dates of his movements is not known, but on more than one occasion his sources failed him. On October 22, 1836, Seguín had yet to arrive in San Antonio for he wrote a letter of recommendation for a fellow officer dated at Lavaca. On December 6, 1836, Seguín wrote Sam Houston stating that he had left headquarters for San Antonio on November 4. See appendices 32 and 34.

[29] Huston had already made his position regarding Seguín known to President Houston in November 1836: "I do not believe that Col. Seguin or that Major Western can command the men and they have no American officer but a smart litle [Lt.?] named Miller." (Huston to Houston, November 10, 1836, Houston Collection, Catholic Archives of Texas, Austin.)

As I had received neither funds nor stores for the subsistence of my command, I was compelled to make requisitions upon the citizens for corn and cattle. At this time Don José Antonio Navarro delivered to me, for the subsistence of my command, goods to the amount of over $3,000.[30]

In April I received orders to requisition the horses of the citizens of San Antonio to mount my command. I was instructed to act with "discernment" in the discharge of this duty but, however prudent I might be, I could not avoid creating a good deal of dissatisfaction, and several complaints were transmitted to the government.[31]

In March of 1838, on obtaining a leave of absence for three months to go to New Orleans, I turned over the command of San Antonio to Colonel Karnes.[32] On my return I was apprised that my fellow citizens had done me the honor to elect me as senator to congress. During my term, I was appointed as chairman of the Committee on Military Affairs.[33] At the expiration of my term as senator I was

---

For Houston's letter to Seguín countermanding General Huston's order see appendix 36.

[30] It was also during this time that Seguín conducted a military funeral for the remains of the Alamo defenders; see appendices 39 and 42. For Seguín's description of his command's condition, see appendices 40, 41 and 42.

[31] Seguín received this order on March 24 according to his reply dated April 10, 1837. For the orders, as well as the protests raised by Bexareños, see appendices 43 through 46.

[32] The 1858 translator of the memoirs apparently had some problem with this passage, for Seguín made his trip at the end of 1837, and was back in San Antonio by March 1838. Sam Houston wrote a letter of recommendation on Seguín's behalf to the governor of Louisiana in October 1837; Seguín wrote Mirabeau B. Lamar from New Orleans in January 1838, and Hamilton Stuart, a newspaper editor, was on board the same ship from New Orleans to Galveston in January 1838 (Ben C. Stuart, "Hamilton Stuart: Pioneer Editor," SWHQ 21:4 April 1918, 382). There must have been a stop at Velasco, for Seguín wrote Thomas Jefferson Green from there on February 4, 1838. For the letter to Lamar see appendix 50, for the letter to Green, which was misdated 1834, see appendix 51.

[33] For Seguín's activities as senator, see appendices 54, 56, 58 and 71.

elected mayor of the city of San Antonio.[34]

Here I must digress from my narrative to call attention to the situation of my family, in those times that daunted the stoutest hearts.

No sooner was General Cos informed that I had taken an active part in the revolution than he removed my father, Erasmo Seguín, from the office of postmaster which he had filled for several years. He forced him to leave San Antonio at once, and my father consequently had to walk the thirty-three miles which separated him from his rancho, where my family was living. Such was the hurry with which he was compelled to depart that he was obliged to leave his family, which remained exposed to our fire during the whole siege.

When we received intelligence from our spies on the Rio Grande that Santa Anna was preparing to invade Texas, my father with his, my own, and several other families, removed toward the center of the country.

My family took with them over three thousand head of sheep. They had reached Gonzales when Santa Anna took possession of San Antonio and, as soon as some other families joined them, they proceeded towards the Colorado via Columbus. On their arrival at San Felipe de Austin, the citizens of that place, terror struck at the sight of the hurried flight of such a number of families, endeavored to flee in front of them. The confusion and delay caused on the road by that immense, straggling column of fugitives were such that when my family was beginning to cross the Colorado with their livestock, the enemy was at their heels. General Ramírez y Sesma did not fail to take hold of that rich booty, and the shepherds escaped only by swimming over the river. The loss to three of the families was very severe, nay, irretrievable. They did not stop on their flight until they reached the town of San Augustine, east of Nacogdoches.

When the families received the welcome tidings of the victory of San Jacinto, they went to Nacogdoches. There all the members of

---

[34] Actually, Seguín resigned his senatorial seat on October 14, 1840, in order to take part in an expedition in support of General Antonio Canales' expedition.

my family, not excepting a single person, were attacked by fever. Thus, prostrated on their couches, deprived of all resources, they had to struggle in the midst of their sufferings to assist one another. Want of money compelled them to part, little by little, with their valuables and articles of clothing. A son, an uncle, and several more remote relatives of mine fell victims to the disease. Seeing that the fever did not abate, the families determined upon moving towards the interior.

The train presented a spectacle which beggars description. Old men and children were laid in the wagons, and for several days Captain Antonio Menchaca, who was the only person able to stand up, had to drive the whole train as well as attend to the sick.

The families reached San Antonio at last. There was not one of them who did not lament the loss of a relative and, to crown their misfortunes, they found their houses in ruins, their fields laid waste, and their cattle destroyed or dispersed. I myself found my ranch despoiled; what little was spared by the retreating enemy had been wasted by our own army. Ruin and misery met me on my return to my unpretentious home.

But let me draw a veil over those past and sorrowful days and resume my narrative.

The tokens of esteem and evidences of trust and confidence repeatedly bestowed upon me by the supreme magistrate, General Rusk, and other dignitaries of the Republic, could not fail to arouse a great deal of invidious and malignant feeling against me. The jealousy evinced against me by several officers of the companies recently arrived at San Antonio from the United States soon spread among the straggling American adventurers, who were already beginning to work their dark intrigues against the native families, whose only crime was that they owned large tracts of land and desirable property.

John W. Smith, a bitter enemy of several of the richest Mexican families of San Antonio by whom he had been covered with favors, joined the conspiracy which was organized to ruin me.[35]

---

[35] Another self-pronounced enemy was Adjutant General Hugh McLeod. (McLeod to Lamar, August 24, 1840, Lamar Papers, TSA.)

I will also point out the origin of another enmity which, on several occasions, endangered my life. In those evil days, San Antonio swarmed with adventurers from every quarter of the globe. Many a noble heart grasped the sword in the defense of the liberty of Texas, cheerfully pouring out their blood for our cause, and to them ever-lasting public gratitude is due. But there were also many bad men, fugitives from their country who found in this land an opportunity for their criminal designs.

San Antonio claimed then, as it claims now, to be the first city of Texas. It was also the receptacle of the scum of society. My political and social situation brought me into continual contact with that class of people. At every hour of the day and night my countrymen ran to me for protection against the assaults or exactions of those adventurers. Sometimes, by persuasion, I prevailed on them to desist; sometimes, also, force had to be resorted to. How could I have done otherwise? Were not the victims my own countrymen, friends, and associates? Could I leave them defenseless, exposed to the assaults of foreigners who, on the pretext that they were Mexicans, treated them worse than brutes? Sound reason and the dictates of humanity precluded any different conduct on my part.

In 1840 General Antonio Canales, who was at the head of a movement in the states of Tamaulipas, Nuevo León and Coahuila in favor of the federation, sought refuge in San Antonio after having been routed by the Mexican forces. There he endeavored to raise companies of volunteers to renew the struggle, and requested me to join him in the enterprise. I promised him my cooperation provided I could procure the consent of General Lamar, then president of the Republic. Canales proceeded to the capital and Galveston, and succeeded in raising some companies with which he went to Mexico to carry out his designs. In the meantime I had an interview with the president, who not only authorized me to raise volunteers but or-dered that I should be supplied with arms from the armories of Texas. General Lamar yielded to my request with evident satisfac-tion, as he thought and declared that any movement against the tyrannical government then existing in Mexico would promote the independence of Texas.

I recruited my men and marched to Mexico but, on reaching the frontier, I heard that Canales was in treaty with Mariano Arista, thus putting an end to the revolutionary attempt. One of the articles of the treaty stated that Mexico should pay for the services rendered by the volunteers. At the request of the officers and men of my brigade, I went to Monterrey to receive the money due them. But, on my arrival at Monterrey, Arista refused to pay me, alleging that he had to seek advice in the city of Mexico.

Fully aware that his only object was to search for a pretext to reject our claims and withhold payment, I determined to return to Texas. Immediately after my return, I went to the capital to report the result of the expedition to the president.[36]

In the same year Don Rafael Uribe, of Guerrero, Tamaulipas, passed through San Antonio on his way to the capital as bearer of a secret communication from General Arista to the president of Texas. Señor Uribe requested me to accompany him. I was present at several interviews between that gentleman and the president, and found out that Arista's intention was to obtain an understanding with the executive of Texas regarding pursuit of the Indians who committed depredations on both frontiers.

In fitting out my expedition to assist the federalists, I contracted some monetary obligations which it was necessary to fulfill. Availing myself of offers made by Señor Uribe, I entered into a smuggling operation with him. For this operation Messrs. Duncan C. Ogden and George Thomas Howard gave me a credit of $3,000 against a mortgage on part of my property.[37]

---

[36] For the documents relating to Seguín's involvement with Canales' federalist scheme see appendices 57 and 60.

[37] Juan and his wife indentured their residence in San Antonio, along with another house and lot there and one league of land (half of the ranch that Erasmo Seguín had acquired from the Arochas) on October 2, 1841 (BC, Deed Book A-2, pp. 447-448). For the kinds of goods typically taken into Mexico see the manifest of an earlier Seguín commercial venture into Mexico, appendix 2.

The president having appointed Messrs. Cornelius Van Ness and John D. Morris to discuss the subject of Uribe's mission, I proceeded in their company and that of Messrs. George W. Blow, Davis, David Murphree, Ogden, and Michael Chevallie, on a trip to Mexico. When Arista was apprised of our arrival at Guerrero, he made a good deal of fuss to exculpate himself in the eyes of his government. He ordered his forces to march from Matamoros to San Fernando, Coahuila, and issued orders to the effect that all the Americans at Guerrero should proceed to Monterrey, but that I should remain at Guerrero. Chevallie, who was sick of the fever, had to remain with me until the return of our associates.

Arista having ordered us to leave the country without delay, I was compelled to leave my goods on consignment to be disposed of. When I heard that they had been sold, I sent Chevallie with some men of San Antonio to the place appointed by my agent to receive the proceeds of the sale. When the agent did not appear, Chevallie returned to San Antonio empty handed. Shortly afterwards, an American who came from Mexico informed me that a certain Francisco Calvillo, who was on the lookout for smugglers, had seized my money.

After the retreat of the Mexican army under Santa Anna, until Vásquez' invasion in 1842, the war between Texas and Mexico ceased to be carried on actively. Although open commercial intercourse did not exist, it was carried on by smuggling, at which the Mexican authorities used to wink provided it was not carried on so openly as to oblige them to notice it, or so extensively as to arouse their avarice.

In the beginning of this year [1842] I was elected mayor of San Antonio. Two years previously a gunsmith named James Goodman had taken possession of certain houses, situated on the Military Plaza, which were the property of the city. He used to shoe the horses of the volunteers who passed through San Antonio. Thus the Republic owed him a debt, for the payment of which he applied to the president to give him possession of the buildings referred to, which had always been known as city property.

The board of aldermen passed a resolution to the effect that Goodman should be compelled to leave the premises. Goodman resisted, alleging that the houses had been given to him by the president, in payment for public services. The board could not, of course, acknowledge any power of the president to dispose of the city property and, consequently, directed me to carry the resolution into effect. My compliance with the instructions of the board caused Goodman to become my most bitter and inveterate enemy in the city.[38]

The term for the mortgage, that Messrs. Ogden and Howard held on my property, had run out. In order to raise money and comply with my obligations, I determined to go to Mexico for a drove of sheep. But, fearful that this new trip would prove as fatal as the one already alluded to, I wrote to General Rafael Vásquez, who was then in command of the Mexican frontier, requesting him to give me a pass. The tenor of Vásquez' answer caused me to apprehend that an expedition against Texas was in preparation for the following month of March.

I called a session of the board of aldermen (of which the Hon. Samuel A. Maverick was a member) and laid before them the communication of General Vásquez, stating that according to my interpretation of the letter we might soon expect the approach of the Mexicans. A few days afterwards Don José María García, of Laredo, came to San Antonio. His report was so detailed as to preclude all possible doubts as to the imminent approach of Vásquez to San Antonio.

Notice of the impending danger was sent immediately to the government. In the various meetings held to devise means of defense, I expressed my candid opinion as to the impossibility of defending San Antonio. I observed that, for myself, I was going to

---

[38] Seguín's and the board's positions were ultimately validated by the Texas Supreme Court in Lewis v. San Antonio (7 Texas 288) which found that the city of San Antonio had complete control of land distribution within the city limits.

the town of Seguin and advised everyone to do the same.[39]

On leaving the city, I passed through a street where some men were making breastworks. I told them I was going to my rancho and thence to Seguin, in case the Mexican forces should take possession of San Antonio.

From the Nueces River, Vásquez forwarded a proclamation by Arista to the inhabitants of Texas. At my rancho I received a bundle of those proclamations, which I transmitted at once to the municipality of San Antonio.

As soon as Vásquez entered the city, those who had been determined to defend the place withdrew to Seguin. Among them were James Dunn and Chevallie, both of whom had succeeded in escaping from the Mexican hands into which they had fallen while on a reconnoitering expedition on the Medina River.

Chevallie told me that Vásquez and his officers stated that I was on the side of the Mexicans. Chevallie further added that one day as he was talking with Vásquez, a man named Sánchez came within sight, whereupon the General observed: "You see that man? Well, Colonel Seguín sent him to me when he was at Rio Grande. Seguín is with us." He then drew a letter from his pocket, stating that it was from me. Chevallie asked to be allowed to see it, as he knew my handwriting, but the general refused and cut short the interview.

On my return to San Antonio, several persons told me that the Mexican officers had declared that I was on their side. This rumor, and some threats uttered against me by Goodman, left me but little doubt that my enemies would try to ruin me.

Some of the citizens of San Antonio had taken up arms on the side of the enemy. Judge John Hemphill advised me to have them arrested and tried but, as I was starting out with the party that was to go in pursuit of the Mexicans, I could not follow his advice.

Having observed that Vásquez gained ground on us, we fell back

---

[39] In fact, Seguín did get a reply to his request for help from the central government. On February 3, 1842, George W. Hockley informed Seguín that no forces were available to help in San Antonio's defense. See appendix 61.

on the Nueces River. When we came back to San Antonio, reports about my implausible treason were spreading widely. Captain Manuel Flores, Lieutenant Ambrosio Rodríguez, Matías Curbier and five or six other Mexicans joined me to find out the origin of the false rumors. I went out with several friends, leaving Curbier in my house. I had reached the Main Plaza when several persons came running to inform me that some Americans were murdering Curbier. We ran back to the house where we found poor Curbier covered with blood. On being asked who assaulted him he answered that the gunsmith Goodman, in company with several Americans, had struck him with a rifle. A few minutes later Goodman returned to my house with about thirty volunteers but, observing that we were prepared to meet them, they did not attempt to attack us. We went out of the house and then to Mr. Francois Guilbeau's, who offered me his protection. He went out into the street, pistol in hand, and succeeded in dispersing the mob which had formed in front of my house. Mr. John Twohig offered me a shelter for that night. The next morning, I went under disguise to Mr. Van Ness' house. Twohig, who recognized me in the street, warned me to "keep my eyes open." I remained one day at Mr. Van Ness'.

The next day General Edward Burleson arrived at San Antonio, commanding a respectable force of volunteers. I presented myself to him, asking for a court of inquiry. He answered that there were no grounds for such proceedings. In the evening I went to the camp and, jointly with Colonel William H. Patton, received a commission to forage for provisions in the lower ranchos. I complied with this assignment.

I remained, hiding from rancho to rancho for over fifteen days. All the parties of volunteers en route to San Antonio declared "they wanted to kill Seguín." I could no longer go from rancho to rancho, and determined to go to my own rancho and fortify it. Several of my relatives and friends joined me. Hardly a day elapsed without receiving notice that a party was preparing to attack me; we were constantly kept under arms. Several parties came in sight but, probably seeing that we were prepared to receive them, refrained from attacking.

On the 30th of April, a friend from San Antonio sent me word that Captain James W. Scott and his company were coming down by the river, burning the ranchos on their way. The inhabitants of the lower ranchos called on us for aid against Scott. With those in my house, and others to the number of about one hundred, I started to lend them aid. I proceeded, observing Scott's movements from the junction of the Medina to Pajaritos. At that place we dispersed and I returned to my wretched life. In those days I could not go to San Antonio without peril for my life.

Matters being in this state, I saw that it was necessary to take some step which would place me in security and save my family from constant wretchedness. I had to leave Texas, abandon all for which I had fought and spent my fortune, to become a wanderer. The ingratitude of those who had assumed onto themselves the right of convicting me, their credulity in declaring me a traitor on the basis of mere rumors, the necessity to defend myself for the loyal patriotism with which I had always served Texas, wounded me deeply.[40]

But before leaving my country, perhaps forever, I determined to consult with all those interested in my welfare. I held a family council. All were in favor of my removing for some time to the interior of Texas. But to accomplish this there were some unavoidable obstacles. I could not take one step from my rancho towards the Brazos without being exposed to the rifle of the first person who might meet me for, throughout the whole country, credit had been given to the rumors against me. To emigrate with my family was impossible as I was a ruined man after the invasion of

---

[40] Of Seguín, John Holland Jenkins wrote in his memoirs: "Juan N. Seguín, who had hitherto been true and loyal to Texas in all her troubles, even commanding a company against the Mexicans at the Battle of San Jacinto, now turned and became our enemy, giving as a reason for the change the fact that we destroyed many of his hogs and property while lying at San Antonio. Whatever might have been his true reasons, he went entirely over to Mexico." (John H. Jenkins III, ed., *Recollections of Early Texas: The Memoirs of John Holland Jenkins*, Austin: University of Texas Press, 1987, p. 96).

Santa Anna and our flight to Nacogdoches. Furthermore the country of the Brazos was unhealthier than that of Nacogdoches. What might we not expect to suffer from disease in a new country, without friends or means?

Seeing that all these plans were impracticable, I resolved to seek a refuge among my enemies, braving all dangers. But before taking this step, I sent in my resignation as mayor of the city to the municipality of San Antonio, stating to them that, unable any longer to suffer the persecutions of some ungrateful Americans who strove to murder me, I had determined to free my family and friends from their continual misery on my account, and go and live peaceably in Mexico. That for these reasons I resigned my office, with all my privileges and honors as a Texan.[41]

I left Béxar with no obligation to Texas, my services repaid with persecutions. Exiled and deprived of my privileges as a Texan citizen, I was outside the pale of society in Texas. If Texas could not protect the rights of her citizens, they were privileged to seek protection elsewhere. I had been tried by a rabble, condemned without a hearing, and consequently was at liberty to provide for my own safety.

When I arrived at Laredo the military commander of that place put me in prison, stating that he could not do otherwise until he had consulted with General Arista, whom he advised of my arrest. Arista ordered that I be sent to Monterrey. When I arrived in that city, I earnestly prayed the general to allow me to retire to Saltillo, where I had several relatives who could aid me. General Arista answered that, as he had informed Santa Anna of my imprisonment, he could not comply with my request. Santa Anna directed that I be sent to the City of Mexico but Arista, sympathetic to my unfortunate position, interceded with him in my behalf to have the order revoked. The latter complied, but on condition that I should return to Texas with a company of explorers to attack its citizens and, by spilling my blood, vindicate myself.

---

[41] For Seguín's resignation letter, see appendix 62.

Under the orders of General Arista, I proceeded to the Rio Grande to join General Woll, who told me that Santa Anna, at his request, had allowed me to go to Texas with Woll's expedition, but that I should receive no command until my services proved that I was worthy.

I set out with the expedition of General Woll.[42] In the vicinity of San Antonio, on the 10th of September, I received an order to take a company of cavalry and block the exits from the city. By this order the city was blockaded and, consequently, it was difficult for any person to escape. When I returned from complying with this order, at dawn of day, the general determined to enter the city with the infantry and artillery. I was sent to the vanguard with orders to take possession of the Military Square despite all obstacles. I entered the square without opposition and, shortly afterwards, the firing commenced on the Main Square. John Hernández came out of Goodman's shop with a message from him to the effect that if I would pardon him for what he had done against me he would leave his place of concealment and deliver himself up. I sent him word that I had no rancor against him. He delivered himself up, and I placed him under the special charge of Captain Manuel Leal.[43] Those who had made some show of resistance in the Main Square surrendered, and the whole city was in General Woll's possession.

The next day I was ordered, with two hundred men, to take the Gonzales road and approach that town. On the Cibolo I divided my forces, sending one detachment up the creek, another down the

---

[42] Seguín's position in the expedition was a nebulous one. In General Adrián Woll's published record of the campaign, *Expedición hecha en Tejas, por una parte de la División del Cuerpo de Egército del Norte* (Monterrey, 1842), Seguín is never referred to by military rank, but only as the commander of the Bexar Defenders, a company of irregulars made up of Tejanos loyal to Mexico.

[43] Seguín intervened in at least one other case. According to a list of Woll's prisoners prepared for the Texas Veterans Association, Bryan Callahan was freed by Woll "at the intercession of Col. Jno. N. Seguin," (Folder: "Battles—Mier, San Jacinto," Texas Veterans Association Collection, BHC).

creek, and with the main body proceeded on the Gonzales road. The following day, these parties joined the main body. Lieutenant Manuel Carvajal, who commanded one of the parties, reported that he had killed three Texans who would not surrender in the Azufrosa [Sulphur Springs].[44]

I returned to San Antonio. A party of Texans appeared by the Garita road and the troops were taken under arms. The general took one hundred infantry, the cavalry under Cayetano Montero, and one piece of artillery and proceeded towards the Salado. The general ordered one hundred *presidiales* [former garrison soldiers from Texas] to attack. The commander of those forces sent word that the enemy was in an advantageous position and that he required reinforcements. The answer of the general was to send me with orders "to attack at all costs." I obeyed. On the first charge I lost three killed and eight wounded, on the second seven killed and fifteen wounded. I was preparing for a third charge when Colonel José María Carrasco came to relieve me from my command. I returned to the side of the general and made my report, whereupon he ordered the firing to cease.

A new attack was in preparation when the attention of the general was called to some troops on our rear guard. The aides reported them to be enemies and near at hand. Colonel Montero was ordered to attack them with his cavalry. He called on them to surrender to the Mexican Government; they answered with scoffing and bantering. Montero formed his dragoons; the Texans commenced firing, killing two soldiers. Montero dismounted his troops, also began firing, and sent for more ammunition. The general angrily sent him a message asking whether his dragoons had no sabres or lances. Before Montero received this answer he had charged, sabre in hand, ending the engagement in a few minutes. Only some ten or fifteen

---

[44] The names of the three were Launcelot Smithers, John McDonald and John McRhea. Some Texans came to believe that Seguín was directly responsible for the "murders," but Seguín's own report at the time makes it clear he was not with the detachment involved in the incident; see appendix 63.

Texans survived. During this time, I remained by the side of General Woll and was there when Montero made his report and brought in the prisoners. At dusk the troops received orders to return to San Antonio.[45]

In accordance with his orders not to remain over a month on this side of the Rio Grande, General Woll began his retreat by the road he came. The Mexican families who left San Antonio were put under my charge and, consequently, I was not in the affair of "Arroyo Hondo."[46]

REMARKS

After General Woll's expedition I did not return to Texas until the treaty of Guadalupe Hidalgo.[47] During my absence nothing occurred that could stamp me as a traitor. My enemies had accomplished their object; they had killed me politically in Texas, and the less they spoke of me, the less risk they incurred of exposing the infamous means they had used to accomplish my ruin.

As to my reputed treason with Vásquez, when we consider that Don Antonio Navarro and I were the only Mexicans of note in

---

[45] Seguín's description appears to be collaborated by Woll's report of the engagement. The general does not mention Seguín in the description of the action, only at the end of the commendations where he receives only perfunctory mention. (Woll, *Expedición,* 38-45.) In a letter to his wife from his detention at San Fernando, Coahuila, Samuel Maverick stated: "You have heard all—We surrendered from necessity being hemmed in on all sides by 30 times our numbers, headed by genl. Wall [*sic*] and not by Seguin & Perez as we believed" (S.A. Maverick to wife, October 6, 1842, General Correspondence, Maverick Family Papers, BHC).

[46] Hondo Creek, a tributary of the Frio River, rises in Bandera County and flows southeast through Medina and Frio counties, and must be crossed on the way to Rio Grande. According to General Woll, "the Bexar and Rio Grande Defenders had left to escort the carts bringing the families of the former" (Woll, *Expedición,* 49).

[47] Seguín did contact President Anson Jones in the summer of 1845 proposing Mexico's terms for accepting Texas independence; see appendix 64. For his letter to Sam Houston seeking to return to Texas, see appendix 65.

western Texas who had taken a prominent part in the war, the interest the Mexican general had in causing us to be distrusted will be seen. Mr. Navarro was then a prisoner.[48] I alone remained, and if they were able to make the Texans distrust me, they gained a point. This is proved by the fact that, after I withdrew from the service, no other regiment of Mexican-Texans was ever seen. The rumor that I was a traitor was seized avidly by my enemies in San Antonio. Some envied my military position, as held by a *Mexican*; others found in me an obstacle to the accomplishment of their villainous plans. The number of land suits which still encumbers the docket of Bexar County would indicate the nature of these plans, and anyone who has listened to the evidence elicited in cases such as this will readily discover the base means adopted to deprive rightful owners of their property.

But, returning again to the charge of treason. If I had sold myself to Mexico, the bargain would, of course, have been with the government. It would have been in the interest of Mexico to keep the bargain a secret, and not allow inferior officers to know it. So long as I enjoyed the confidence of the Texans, I might have been useful in imparting secrets, *etc.*, but as soon as my fellow citizens distrusted me, I was absolutely useless. And is it not strange that the Mexican officers should have been so anxious to inform the Texans of my treason? General Vásquez took out a paper from his pocket and claimed to Chevallie that it was from me, but when the latter desired to see the letter, Vásquez refused to show it to him.

But I take the expedition of Vásquez to be my best defense. What did Vásquez accomplish in that expedition? The coming into and going out of San Antonio without taking any further steps. Undoubtedly, if I had been allied with him, I would have tried to make his expedition something more than a mere military promenade. Far from doing this, however, I presented the letter that I received from Vásquez to the municipality of San Antonio; I predicted the expedition and counseled such steps as I thought should be taken.

And why, if my treason were so clear, did the patriotic and brave

---

[48] As a result of the Santa Fe Expedition.

Burleson refuse to subject me to a court of inquiry? Undoubtedly he knew it to be his duty to put me on trial if the slightest suspicion existed as to my character. He refused, and this proved that Burleson and the superior officers were convinced of the shallowness of the charges against me.

During the electoral campaign of August 1855,[49] I was frequently attacked in newspapers and was styled in some "the murderer of the Salado."[50] For some time I had proposed to publish my memoirs, so I thought it useless to enter into a newspaper war, more particularly as the attacks against me were anonymous and were directed with a venom which made me conclude that I owed them to the malevolence of a personal enemy.

I have related my participation in Woll's expedition and have only to say that neither I nor any of my posterity will ever have reason to blush for it.

During my military career, I can proudly assert that I never deviated from the line of duty, that I never shed, or caused to be shed, human blood unnecessarily, that I never insulted a prisoner by word or deed, and that, in the fulfillment of my duty, I always drew a distinction between my obligations as a soldier on the battlefield and as a civilized man after the battle.

I have finished my memoirs; I have neither the capacity nor the desire to adorn my acts with literary phrases. I have attempted a short and clear narrative of my public life in relation to Texas. I publish it without omitting or suppressing anything that I thought of the least interest, and confidently I submit to the public verdict.

Several of those who witnessed the facts I have related are still alive and among us. They can state whether I have falsified the record in any way.

---

[49] Seguín had served as a justice of the peace since 1852 and was involved in forming the Democratic Party in Bexar County. He was a member of the *Junta Democrática de los Ciudadanos Mejico-Tejanos,* that is, Democratic Council of Mexican-Texan Citizens. Seguín also served as president of an election precinct whose polling place was at his ranch.

[50] Now commonly called the "Dawson Massacre."

Appendices

{1}
Seguín's Unedited Memoirs

Preface

A native of the City of San Antonio de Bexar, I embraced the cause of Texas at the report of the first cannon which foretold her liberty; filled an honorable situation in the ranks of the conquerors of San Jacinto, and was a member of the legislative body of the Republic. I now find myself, in the very land, which in other times bestowed on me such bright and repeated evidences of trust and esteem, exposed to the attacks of scribblers and personal enemies, who, to serve *political purposes*, and engender strife, falsify historical facts, which they are but imperfectly acquainted. I owe it to myself, my children and friends, to answer them with a short, but true exposition of my acts, from the beginning of my public career, to the time of the return of General Woll from the Rio Grande, with the Mexican forces, amongst which I was then serving.

I address myself to the American people; to that people impetuous, as the whirlwind, when aroused by the hypocritical clamors of designing men, but just, impartial and composed, whenever men and facts are submitted to their judgment.

I have been the object of the hatred and passionate attacks of some few disorganisers, who, for a time, ruled, as masters, over the poor and oppressed population of San Antonio. Harpy-like, ready to pounce on every thing that attracted the notice of their rapacious avarice, I was an obstacle to the execution of their vile designs. They, therefore, leagued together to exasperate and ruin me; spread against me malignant calumnies, and made use of odious machinations to sully my honor, and tarnish my well earned reputation.

A victim to the wickedness of a few men, whose imposture was favored by their origin, and recent domination over the country; a foreigner in my native land; could I be expected stoically to endure their outrages and insults? Crushed by sorrow, convinced that my death alone would satisfy my enemies, I sought for a shelter amongst those against whom I had fought; I separated from my country, parents, family, relatives and friends, and what was more, from the institutions, on behalf of which I had drawn my sword, with an earnest wish to see Texas free and happy.

In that involuntary exile, my only ambition was to devote my time, far from the tumult of war, to the support of my family, who shared in my sad condition.

Fate, however, had not exhausted its cup of bitterness. Thrown into a prison, in a foreign country, I had no alternative left, but, to linger in a loathsome confinement, or to accept military service. On one hand, my wife and children, reduced to beggary, and separated from me; on the other hand, to turn my arms against my own country. The alternative was sad, the struggle of feelings violent; at last the father triumphed over the citizen; I seized a sword that galled my hand. (Who amongst my readers will not understand my situation?) I served Mexico; I served her loyally and faithfully; I was compelled to fight my own countrymen, but I was never guilty of the barbarous and unworthy deeds of which I am accused by my enemies.

Ere the tomb closes over me and my cotemporaries [*sic*], I wish to lay open to publicity this stormy period of my life; I do it for friends as well as for my enemies, I challenge the latter to contest, with facts, the statements I am about to make, and I leave the decision unhesitatingly to the witnesses of the events.

Memoirs, &c.

In October 1834, I was Political Chief of the Department of Bejar. Dissatisfied with the reactionary designs of General Santa Anna, who was at that time President of the Republic of Mexico, and endeavored to overthrow the Federal system, I issued a circular, in which I urged every Municipality in Texas to appoint delegates to a convention that was to meet at San Antonio, for the purpose of taking into consideration the impending dangers, and for devising the means to avert them.

All the Municipalities appointed their delegates, but the convention never met, the General Government having ordered Col. José Maria Mendoza to march with his forces from Matamoras to San Antonio, and prevent the meeting of the delegates. The proofs of the above facts exist in the archives of the County of Bejar.

In April 1835, the Governor of Coahuila and Texas called for assistance from the various Departments, to resist the aggressions of Santa Anna against that State. I volunteered my services, and received from the Political Chief, Don Angel Navarro, the command of a party of National Guards, sent from San Antonio to Monclova. In our encounters with the troops of Santa Anna, I was efficiently assisted by Col. B. R. Milam and Maj. John R. Allen. On our withdrawal from Monclova, disgusted with the weakness of the Executive, who had given up the struggle, we pledged ourselves to use all our influence to rouse Texas against the tyrannical government of Santa Anna.

We returned to San Antonio in the beginning of June. The Military Commander, Col. Domingo Ugartchea, considering me opposed to the existing government, ordered two officers to watch secretly my motions. This, however, did not prevent me from working diligently to prepare for the intended movement.

We had agreed that the movement should begin in the center of Texas, but, not hearing from that quarter, I determined to send an agent to Brazoria, Juan A. Zambrano, with directions to sound the disposition of the people. On the return of the agent, we were apprized that there was a great deal of talk about a revolution, in public meetings, but that the moment for an armed movement was still remote. Our agent was sent to Victoria, and he there called a meeting of the citizens, but the Military Commander of Goliad sent down a detachment of troops to prevent the assembly and arrest the promoters.

We were despairing of a successful issue, when the Military Commander of Texas, informed of the revolutionary feelings which were spreading over the colonies, determined upon removing from the town of Gonzales a piece of artillery, lent to that Corporation by the Political Chief Saucedo. This was at the time a delicate undertaking. A lieutenant was detailed to carry it into execution, with orders to use force if necessary. On the same day that the military detachment started for Gonzales, I went to the lower ranchos on the San Antonio River; at Salvador Flores I held a meeting of the neighbors, and induced several to take up arms, well satisfied that the beginning of the revolution was close at hand. The officer sent to Gonzales met some resistance at the "Perra," and thought it prudent to beat a hasty retreat. Col. Ugartchea was making preparations to proceed in person towards Gonzales, with a respectable force, when he received orders from Gen. Cos to await his arrival.

A few days after the entry of Gen. Cos into San Antonio, Major Collinsworth, surprising the garrison of Goliad, took possession of that place. So soon as I was informed of that circumstance, I marched with my company to reinforce the Major, but, at the "Conquista" crossing on the San Antonio River, I was overtaken by an express from General Stephen F. Austin, who informed me that he was marching on San Antonio, and requested me to join him, in order to attack General Cos. I retraced my steps, after having requested Captain Manuel Flores to go and meet General Austin and inform him of my readiness to comply with his wishes, and that I would take with me all the men I could possibly enlist on my route.

On the 13th of October, I met Austin on the Salado, at the crossing of the Gonzales road, and joined my forces with his small army. Upon this occasion I had the honor to become acquainted with General Sam Houston, who accompanied Austin. On the same day we had a slight encounter with the forces under Cos, who retired into San Antonio. Austin, as Commander-in-Chief of the army, gave me the appointment of Captain.

I was commanded to accompany Col. Bowie to the Mission of San José, with my company, with orders to approach the city as nearly as possible, following the banks of the river. We arrived, on the evening of the 21st of November, at the Mission of Concepcion, and noticing that we had been observed by the scouts of Gen. Cos, passed the night in making preparations to resist an attack which we considered imminent. We were not deceived; on the morning of the 22d a force was seen moving along the road from San Antonio to the Mission. A few men, sent by Bowie to reconnoitre, made such a rash charge, that they were cut off from their line of retreat, and had to shut themselves up in the steeple of the church, where they remained during the action. The day was soon ours; the enemy retreating, with the loss of one piece of artillery.

I was detailed to forage for the army, and was successful in doing so, returning to the camp with a liberal supply of provisions. Our camp was shortly moved to within one mile of the Alamo, whence we proceeded to the "Molino Blanco," and established head-quarters. On the 11th of December we entered the city, and after having taken possession of the houses of the Curate Garza, Veramendi, Garza, Flores, and others, we obliged the enemy to capitulale [*sic*] and withdraw towards Laredo.

After the capture of San Antonio, Captain Travis' company and mine were detailed to go in pursuit of the Mexican forces, and capture from them a cavallado which they had in the Parrita, Laredo road; we succeeded, taking nearly one hundred head of horses, which were sent to San Felipe de Austin, for the benefit of the public service. I was afterwards detailed to the ranchos on the San Antonio river, to see if I could find more horses belonging to the Mexican troops.

On the 2d of January, 1836, I received from the Provisional Government
the commission of Captain of Regular Cavalry, with orders to report to
Lieutenant-Colonel Travis in San Antonio.

On the 22d of February, at 2 o'clock p.m., General Santa Anna took
possession of the city, with over 4000 men, and in the mean time we fell
back on the Alamo.

On the 28th, the enemy commenced the bombardment, meanwhile we
met in a Council of War, and taking into consideration our perilous
situation, it was resolved by a majority of the council, that I should leave
the fort, and proceed with a communication to Colonel Fannin, requesting
him to come to our assistance. I left the Alamo on the night of the council;
on the following day I met, at the Ranch of San Bartolo, on the Cibolo,
Captain Desac, who, by orders of Fannin, had foraged on my ranch,
carrying off a great number of beeves, corn, &c. Desac informed me that
Fannin could not delay more than two days his arrival at the Cibolo, on
his way to render assistance to the defenders of the Alamo. I therefore
determined to wait for him. I sent Fannin, by express, the communication
from Travis, informing him at the same time of the critical position of the
defenders of the Alamo. Fannin answered me, through Lieutenant Finley,
that he had advanced as far as "Rancho Nuevo," but, being informed of
the movements of General Urrea, he had countermarched to Goliad, to
defend that place; adding, that he could not respond to Travis' call, their
respective commands being separate, and depending upon General Houston, then at Gonzales, with whom he advised me to communicate. I lost
no time in repairing to Gonzales, and reported myself to the General,
informing him of the purport of my mission. He commanded me to wait
at Gonzales for further orders. General Houston ordered Captain Salvador
Flores with 25 men of my company to the lower ranchos on the San Antonio
river, to protect the inhabitants from the depredations of the Indians.

Afterwards, I was ordered to take possession, with the balance of my
company, of the "Perra," distant about four miles on the road to San
Antonio, with instructions to report every evening at head-quarters. Thus
my company was forming the vanguard of the Texan army, on the road to
San Antonio.

On the 6th of March, I received orders to go to San Antonio with my
company and a party of American citizens, carrying, on the horses,
provisions for the defenders of the Alamo.

Arrived at the Cibolo, and not hearing the signal gun which was to be
discharged every fifteen minutes, as long as the place held out, we retraced
our steps to convey to the General-in-Chief the sad tidings. A new party

was sent out, which soon came back, having met with Anselmo Vergara and Andres Barcena, both soldiers of my company, whom I had left for purposes of observation in the vicinity of San Antonio; they brought the intelligence of the fall of the Alamo. Their report was so circumstantial as to preclude any doubts about that disastrous event.

The Texan army began its retreat towards the centre of the country. I was put in command of the rear-guard, with orders not to leave any families behind. I continued covering the rear-guard, until we had crossed the Arenoso creek, near the Brazos, where I was, by orders of the General, detached with Captain Mosley Baker, to the town of San Felipe de Austin, to cut off the enemy from the passage of the river. We remained in that position, and within sight of the Brigade of General Ramirez, who occupied San Felipe. I was subsequently ordered to occupy with my company Gross' house, farther up the river. Our main army was then encamped in the bottom of the Paloma or Molino Creek, on the Western bank of the Brazos River, where it remained until information was received that the enemy had crossed the river at Fort Bend, and was marching towards Harrisburg. Our army began at once to cross the river, on board the steamer Yellow Stone, and when the whole force had crossed, took up the march, with the intention of harassing the enemy's rear-guard.

The army was taking its noon rest, near Buffalo Bayou, when two soldiers of my company, who had gone out to water horses, reported that they had seen three Mexicans riding at full speed over the prairie. Without delay, I advised the General, who immediately sent Captains Karnes and ____ in pursuit. These officers returned shortly, bringing as prisoners a captain, a citizen, and an express bearer of despatches from Mexico to the enemy.

We were apprised by the prisoners that Santa Anna was at Harrisburg with 800 men; and a perusal of their papers made us acquainted with the fact that Cos was to bring him reinforcements. To prevent the concentration of forces, General Sam Houston gave the order to resume the march. The army, artillery, and train, crossed over Buffalo Bayou on rafts, during which operation, General Rusk, then Secretary of War, did not spare his personal labor. It was dark when the crossing was effected. In the course of the night we passed through Harrisburg, the ruins of which were still smoking, having been set on fire by the enemy. We continued our march all night. At daybreak a man was taken prisoner, who, on discovering us, had attempted to escape. He was a printer belonging to San Felipe, and informed us that the enemy were at a distance of about 8 miles, on the way back to Harrisburg. Our scouts came in soon with the information that the enemy were countermarching towards Buffalo Bayou.

Conscious of the starving condition of the troops, who had not eaten for twenty-four hours, General Houston resolved on camping, in a small mott, contiguous to the San Jacinto River.

We were beginning to cook our meal, when the enemy showed themselves close to us. We rushed to arms, and formed in line of battle. On their nearer approach we were ordered to lay down on the ground, thus concealing ourselves in the grass. A height, adjacent to our position, was soon occupied by the enemy, upon which, the General ordered the band to strike up "Will you come to the bower." The enemy answered with its artillery, and we joined the chorus with a brisk musketry. We were soon charged by a skirmishing party on foot, detached from the right wing of the enemy; they were quickly driven back by a party of our cavalry, supported by the artillery. The enemy kept up their fire until they had selected a camping ground, distant about 400 steps from ours, and protected by two motts. Both armies ceased firing; we resumed the cooking of our meal, composed of meat only, but had the good fortune to capture a boat loaded with provisions, which afforded some seasoning to a repast that otherwise would have been rather scanty.

On the same evening General Lamar went out with a party of Cavalry, to draw the enemy into a fight; the result was a slight skirmish, ending in the wounding of two or three on each side.

On the morning of the 21st of April, General Houston, for the purpose of cutting off the communication of General Cos' forces with those of Santa Anna, ordered deaf Smith to burn the bridge over the river, but, on reaching it, he saw that he had come too late, the enemy's reinforcements had already crossed. However, the bridge was destroyed, and Smith returned to our camp at the very moment when Cos united with Santa Anna.

At noon, General Rusk came to partake of dinner in my tent. When he had done eating, he asked me if the Mexicans were not in the habit of taking a siesta at that hour. I answered in the affirmative, adding, moreover, that in such cases they kept under arms their main and advanced guards, and a line of sentinels. General Rusk observed that he thought so; however, the moment seemed to him favorable to attack the enemy, and he further said: "Do you feel like fighting?" I answered that I was always ready and willing to fight, upon which the General rose, saying: "Well, let us go!" I made at once my dispositions; the General proceeded along the line, speaking to the Captains, and our force was soon under arms. Generals Houston and Rusk delivered short addresses, and we formed into line of battle in front of the enemy. My company was in the left wing, under Colonel Sherman. We marched onward on the prairie, and were met by a column of infantry, which we drove back briskly. Before falling in with that column, we had dispersed an ambuscade that had opened their fire against us within pistol shot. The whole enemy's line, panic struck, took to flight. We were already on the bank of the river, in pursuit of the fugitives, when my attention was called to a Mexican officer, who, emerging from the river where he had kept himself concealed, gave himself up and requested me to spare his life. Being sheltered by weeds and grass, he seemed afraid to leave his retreat, owing to the fire which was kept up against the fugitives. I ordered those who were close to me to cease firing, which order was extended along the line to a considerable distance. Then, the officer who had addressed me came out, followed by Colonels Bringas, Almonte, Dias, and quite a number of other officers.

On my way to the camp with the prisoners, an officer, named Sanchez, conducted me to a place where $25,000 had been concealed. I reached the camp at dark, presented my prisoners to the General, who congratulated me, and I reported to him the discovery of the money. Colonel Forbes was at once detailed to go and bring it in.

On this great and glorious day my company was conspicuous for efficiency and gallantry; however, we did not lose one single man, to the surprise of those who had witnessed our honorable and perilous situation.

Two days after the capture of Santa Anna, and four days after the battle, Captain Karnes and myself were detailed with our companies to observe the retreat of the remains of the Mexican army. We overtook their rear-guard at the "Contrabando" marsh, where some of their wagons had broken down. As soon as the escort saw us they took to flight, leaving the whole property in our possession.

Gen. Ampudia sent me a communication requesting me to attend to the sick and wounded whom he had left behind.

We crossed the Colorado at the heels of the enemy, and after proceeding a short distance, we met General Woll, who was bearer of a safe conduct. We camped every night on the ground abandoned each morning by the enemy, until we reached Victoria, which had been already evacuated by them. Shortly afterwards Colonel Sherman arrived, in command of the vanguard of our army, and subsequently General Rusk, then Commander-in-Chief, who established his headquarters in that town.

On the 30th of May, I received from the General-in-Chief my promotion to the rank of Lieutenant-Colonel of the Texan army, and was ordered to take possession of San Antonio. I left Victoria on the 1st of June, and, on the Cabeza creek, met General Andrade, who was retreating towards

Matamoras.

Agreeably to my instructions, I sent to that General a communication, informing him that my orders were to take possession of San Antonio. His answer was that the place was occupied by Captain Castañeda, who was instructed to surrender it to the first Texan officer who should come to demand it.

I took possession of San Antonio on the 4th of June; on the 10th, Colonel Smith came to occupy it with the regiment of Mississippi Mounted Volunteers; on the 24th I received orders to fall back with my command to head-quarters at Victoria, information having been received that the Mexican army was marching from Matamoras to Texas.

When we were convinced of the falseness of that report, I applied to the General for leave to go to Nacogdoches on a visit to my family, then in that town on their return from the Sabine, where they had sought a refuge from the Mexican army. My application was favorably received, and leave of absence for twenty-two days granted to me.

I found all the members of my family sick with fever, and the disease did not spare me, but compelled me to exceed the term of my leave. General Houston, who was then at Nacogdoches, getting cured of the wounds he received at San Jacinto, gave me a certificate stating the causes of my delay in returning to my post. I left Nacogdoches on the 20th of August, and on my passage through Columbus I received, from the Secretary of War, orders to report myself to the President for instructions.

I arrived at Velasco on the 10th of September; on the next day the President handed to me my commission of Lieutenant-Colonel, appointing me to the command of the City of San Antonio, with orders to proceed to my destination without delay.

I arrived at head-quarters, at Lavaca, on the 15th of the same month, and reported to General Rusk, who ordered me to begin recruiting my regiment in that town.

On the 11th of October I left head-quarters, with my regiment dismounted, and with instructions to procure horses in San Antonio, where I arrived on the 17th.

1837. In March, being in command of San Antonio, I received orders from General Felix Houston to destroy that city and transfer its inhabitants to the east bank of the Brazos. At the same time, Lieutenant-Colonel Switzer of the Volunteers came, with instructions to assist me in carrying out the order. Considering the measure premature and unjust, I took upon myself the responsibility of disobeying the order, until I had referred the matter to the President, with whom I made use of all my influence to have the order rescinded. The President prevailed upon General Houston to desist; I thus averted the impending destruction of San Antonio, but, in consequence, made Gen. F. Houston my bitter enemy.

As I had received neither funds nor stores for the subsistence of my command, I was compelled to make requisitions upon the citizens for corn and beeves. At this time, Don José Antonio Navarro delivered to me, for that object, goods to over the amount of $3000.

In April, I received orders to seize upon the horses of the citizens of San Antonio, to mount my command. I was instructed to act with "discernment" in the discharge of this duty, but, however prudent I might be, I could not avoid creating a good deal of dissatisfaction, and several complaints were transmitted to the Government.

1838. In March, on obtaining a leave of absence for three months, to go to New Orleans, I turned over the command of San Antonio to Colonel Karnes. On my return, I was apprized that my fellow-citizens had done me the honor to elect me as Senator to Congress. During my term, I was appointed as Chairman of the Committee on Military Affairs. At the expiration of my term as Senator, I was elected Mayor of the City of San Antonio.

Here I must digress from my narrative, to call attention to the situation of my family in those times that tried the stoutest hearts.

No sooner was General Cos informed that I had taken an active part in the revolution, than he removed my father from the office of Postmaster, which he had filled for several years. He forced him to leave San Antonio at once, and he had consequently to walk the thirty-three miles which separated him from his rancho, where my family was living. Such was the hurry with which he was compelled to depart, that he was obliged to leave his family, who remained exposed to our fire during the whole siege.

When we received intelligence from our spies on the Rio Grande, that Santa Anna was preparing to invade Texas, my father, with his, my own, and several other families, removed toward the centre of the country.

My family took with them above three thousand head of sheep. They had reached Gonzales when Santa Anna took possession of San Antonio, and as soon as some other families joined them, they proceeded towards the Colorado, via Columbus. On their arrival at San Felipe de Austin, the citizens of that place, terror struck at the sight of the hurried flight of such a number of families, endeavored to take the advance. The confusion and delay caused on the road by that immense straggling column of fugitives were such, that when my family were beginning to cross the Colorado with their cattle, the enemy was at their heels. General Ramirez y Lesma did not fail to take hold of that rich booty, and the shepherds only escaped by swimming over the river. The loss to three of the families was very severe, nay, irretrievable. They did not stop on their flight, until they reached the town of San Augustine, east of Nacogdoches. When the families received the welcome tidings of the victory of San Jacinto, they went to Nacogdoches. There, all the members of my family, without excepting a single person, were attacked by fever. Thus, prostrated on their couches, deprived of all resources, they had to struggle in the midst of their sufferings, to assist one another. Want of money compelled them to part, little by little, with their valuables and articles of clothing. A son, an uncle, and several more remote relatives of mine fell victims to the disease. Seeing that the fever did not abate, the families determined upon moving towards the interior.

The train presented a spectacle which beggars description. Old men and children were lying in the wagons, and for several days, Captain Menchaca, who was the only person able to stand up, had to drive the whole train, as well as attend to the sick.

The families reached San Antonio at last. There was not one of them who had not to lament the loss of a relative, and to crown their misfortunes, they found their houses in ruins, their fields laid waste, and their cattle destroyed or dispersed.

I, myself, found my ranch despoiled; what little was spared by the retreating enemy, had been wasted by our own army; ruin and misery met me on my return to my unpretending home.

But let me draw a veil over those past and sorrowful days, and resume my narrative.

The tokens of esteem, and evidences of trust and confidence, repeatedly bestowed upon me by the Supreme Magistrate, General Rusk, and other dignitaries of the Republic, could not fail to arouse against me much invidious and malignant feeling. The jealousy evinced against me by several officers of the companies recently arrived at San Antonio, from the United States, soon spread amongst the American straggling adventurers, who were already beginning to work their dark intrigues against the native families, whose only crime was, that they owned large tracts of land and desirable property.

John W. Smith, a bitter enemy of several of the richest families of San Antonio, by whom he had been covered with favors, joined the conspiracy which was organized to ruin me.

I will also point out the origin of another enmity which, on several occasions, endangered my life. In those evil days, San Antonio was swarming with adventurers from every quarter of the globe. Many a noble heart grasped the sword in the defence of the liberty of Texas, cheerfully pouring out their blood for our cause, and to them everlasting public gratitude is due; but there were also many bad men, fugitives from their country, who found in this land an open field for their criminal designs.

San Antonio claimed then, as it claims now, to be the first city of Texas; it was also the receptacle of the scum of society. My political and social situation brought me into continual contact with that class of people. At every hour of the day and night, my countrymen ran to me for protection against the assaults or exactions of those adventurers. Some times, by persuasion, I prevailed on them to desist; some times, also, force had to be resorted to. How could I have done otherwise? Were not the victims my own countrymen, friends and associates? Could I leave them defenceless, exposed to the assaults of foreigners, who, on the pretext that they were Mexicans, treated them worse than brutes. Sound reason and the dictates of humanity would have precluded a different conduct on my part.

In 1840, General Canales, who was at the head of a movement in favor of the federation, in the States of Tamaulipas, Nueva Leon and Coahuila, after having been routed by the Mexican forces, sought refuge in San Antonio. There he endeavored to raise companies of volunteers, to renew the struggle, and requested me to join him in the enterprise. I promised him my co-operation, provided I could procure the consent of General Lamar, then President of the Republic. Canales proceeded to the Capital and Galveston, and succeeded in raising some companies, with which he went to Mexico to carry out his designs. In the meantime, I had an interview with the President, who not only authorized me to raise volunteers, but, ordered that I should be supplied with arms from the armories of Texas. General Lamar yielded to my request with evident satisfaction, as he thought and declared that any movement against the tyrannical government then existing in Mexico would be promotive of the independence of Texas.

I recruited my men and marched to Mexico, but on reaching the frontier, I heard that Canales was in treaty with Arista, thus putting an end to the revolutionary attempt. One of the articles of the treaty, stated that Mexico should pay for the services rendered by the volunteers. At the request of the officers and men of my brigade, I went to Monterey to receive the money due them. But on my arrival at Monterey, Arista refused to pay me, alleging that he had to take advice in the city of Mexico.

Fully aware that his only object was to seek for a pretext to reject our claims, and withhold payment, I determined to return to Texas.

Immediately after my return, I went to the capital to report to the President the result of the expedition.

In the same year, Don Rafael Uribe, of Guerrero, passed through San Antonio, on his way to the capital, as bearer of a secret communication from General Arista to the President of Texas. Señor Uribe requested me to accompany him. I attended at several interviews between that gentleman and the President, and found out that Arista's intention was to have an understanding with the Executive of Texas, to the effect of pursuing the Indians, who committed depredations on both frontiers.

In fitting out my expedition to assist the Federalists, I contracted some money obligations which it was necessary to comply with. Availing myself of offers made by Señor Uribe, I entered with him into a smuggling operation. For this object, Messrs. Ogden and Howard gave me a credit of $3000, on a mortgage on part of my property.

The President having appointed Messrs. Van Ness and Morris to treat upon the subject of Uribe's mission, in their company, and that of Messrs. Blo, Davis, Murphy, Ogden, and Chevallie, I proceeded on a trip to Mexico. When Arista was apprised of our arrival at Guerrero, he made a good deal of fuss to exculpate himself in the eyes of his government. He ordered his forces to march from Matamoras to San Fernando, and issued orders to the effect that all the Americans at Guerrero should proceed to Monterey, but that I should remain at Guerrero. Chevallie, who was sick of the fever, had to remain with me until the return of our associates.

Arista having ordered us to leave the country without delay, I was compelled to leave my goods on consignment to be disposed of. When I heard that they had been sold, I sent Chevallie with some men of San Antonio to the place appointed by my agent, to receive the proceeds of the sale, but the agent not having shown himself, Chevallie returned to San Antonio empty handed. Shortly afterwards, an American, who came from Mexico, informed me that a certain Calvillo, who was on the look out for smugglers, had seized upon my money.

1842. After the retreat of the Mexican army under Santa Anna, until Vasquez' invasion in 1842, the war between Texas and Mexico ceased to be carried on actively. Although open commercial intercourse did not exist, it was carried on by smuggling, at which the Mexican authorities used to wink, provided it was not carried on too openly, so as to oblige them to notice it, or so extensively as to arouse their avarice.

In the beginning of this year, I was elected Mayor of San Antonio. Two years previously a gunsmith, named Goodman, had taken possession of certain houses situated on the Military Plaza, which were the property of the city. He used to shoe the horses of the volunteers who passed through San Antonio, and thus accumulated a debt against the Republic, for the payment of which he applied to the President to give him possession of the buildings referred to, which had always been known as city property.

The board of Aldermen passed a resolution to the effect, that Goodman should be compelled to leave the premises; Goodman resisted, alleging that the houses had been given to him by the President, in payment for public services. The Board could not, of course, acknowledge in the President any power to dispose of the city property, and consequently directed me to carry the resolution into effect. My compliance with the instructions of the Board caused Goodman to become my most bitter and inveterate enemy in the city.

The term for the mortgage that Messrs. Ogden and Howard held on my property, had run out. In order to raise money and comply with my engagements, I determined to go to Mexico for a drove of sheep. But fearful that this new trip would prove as fatal as the one already alluded to, I wrote to General Vasquez, who was then in command of the Mexican frontier, requesting him to give me a pass. The tenor of Vasquez' answer caused me to apprehend that an expedition was preparing against Texas, for the following month of March.

I called a session of the Board of Aldermen, (of which the Hon. S. A. Maverick was a member,) and laid before them the communication of General Vasquez, stating, that according to my construction of the letter we might soon expect the approach of the Mexicans.

A few days afterwards, Don José Maria Garcia, of Laredo, came to San Antonio; his report was so circumstantial, as to preclude all possible doubts as to the near approach of Vasquez to San Antonio.

Notice was immediately sent to the Government of the impending danger. In the various meetings held to devise means of defence, I expressed my candid opinion as to the impossibility of defending San Antonio. I observed, that for myself, I was going to the town of Seguin, and advised every one to do the same.

On leaving the city, I passed through a street where some men were making breast-works; I stated to them that I was going to my ranch, and thence to Seguin, in case the Mexican forces should take possession of San Antonio.

From the Nueces river, Vasquez forwarded a proclamation by Arista, to the inhabitants of Texas. I received at my ranch, a bundle of those proclamations, which I transmitted at once to the Corporation of San Antonio.

As soon as Vasquez entered the city, those who had determined upon defending the place, withdrew to Seguin. Amongst them were Dunn and

Chevallie, who had succeeded in escaping from the hands of the Mexicans, into which they had fallen while on a reconnoitering expedition on the Medina.

The latter told me that Vasquez and his officers stated that I was in favor of the Mexicans; and Chevallie further added, that, one day as he was talking with Vasquez, a man, named Sanchez, came within sight, whereupon the General observed: "You see that man! Well, Colonel Seguin sent him to me, when he was at Rio Grande, Seguin is with us." He then drew a letter from his pocket, stating that it was from me. Chevallie asked to be allowed to see it, as he knew my handwriting, but the General refused and cut short the interview.

On my return to San Antonio, several persons told me that the Mexican officers had declared that I was in their favor. This rumor, and some threats uttered against me by Goodman, left me but little doubt that my enemies would try to ruin me.

Some of the citizens of San Antonio had taken up arms in favor of the enemy. Judge Hemphill advised me to have them arrested and tried, but as I started out with the party who went in pursuit of the Mexicans I could not follow his advice.

Having observed that Vasquez gained ground on us, we fell back on the Nueces river. When we came back to San Antonio, reports were widely spreading about my pretended treason. Captain Manuel Flores, Lieutenant Ambrosio Rodriguez, Matias Curbier, and five or six other Mexicans, dismounted with me to find out the origin of the imposture. I went out with several friends, leaving Curbier in my house. I had reached the Main Plaza, when several persons came running to inform me, that some Americans were murdering Curbier. We ran back to the house, where we found poor Curbier covered with blood. On being asked who assaulted him, he answered, that the gunsmith Goodman, in company with several Americans, had struck him with a rifle. A few minutes afterwards, Goodman returned to my house, with about thirty volunteers, but, observing that we were prepared to meet him, they did not attempt to attack us. We went out of the house and then to Mr. Guilbeau's, who offered me his protection. He went out into the street, pistol in hand, and succeeded in dispersing the mob, which had formed in front of my house. Mr. John Twohig offered me a shelter for that night; on the next morning, I went under disguise to Mr. Van Ness' house; Twohig, who recognised me in the street, warned me to "open my eyes." I remained one day at Mr. Van Ness'; next day General Burleson arrived at San Antonio, commanding a respectable force of volunteers. I presented myself to him, asking for a Court of Inquiry; he answered, that there were no grounds for such proceedings. In the evening I went to the camp, and, jointly with Colonel Patton, received a commission to forage for provisions in the lower ranchos. I complied with this trust.

I remained, hiding from rancho to rancho, for over fifteen days. Every party of volunteers en route to San Antonio, declared, "they want to kill Seguin." I could no longer go from farm to farm, and determined to go to my own farm and raise fortification, &c.

Several of my relatives and friends joined me. Hardly a day elapsed without receiving notice that a party was preparing to attack me; we were constantly kept under arms. Several parties came in sight, but, probably seeing that we were prepared to receive them, refrained from attacking. On the 30th of April, a friend from San Antonio sent me word that Captain Scott, and his company, were coming down by the river, burning the ranchos on their way. The inhabitants of the lower ranchos called on us for aid against Scott. With those in my house, and others to the number of about 100, I started to lend them aid. I proceeded, observing the movements of Scott, from the junction of the Medina to Pajaritos. At that place we dispersed and I returned to my wretched life. In those days I could not go to San Antonio without peril of my life.

Matters being in this state, I saw that it was necessary to take some step which would place me in security, and save my family from constant wretchedness. I had to leave Texas, abandon all, for which I had fought and spent my fortune, to become a wanderer. The ingratitude of those, who had assumed to themselves the right of convicting me; their credulity in declaring me a traitor, on mere rumors, when I had to plead in my favor the loyal patriotism with which I had always served Texas, wounded me deeply.

But, before leaving my country, perhaps for ever, I determined to consult with all those interested in my welfare. I held a family council. All were in favor of my removing for some time to the interior of Texas. But, to accomplish this, there were some unavoidable obstacles. I could not take one step, from my ranch towards the Brazos, without being exposed to the rifle of the first person who might meet me, for, through the whole country, credit had been given to the rumors against me. To emigrate with my family was impossible, as I was a ruined man, from the time of the invasion of Santa Anna and our flight to Nacogdoches; furthermore, the country of the Brazos was unhealthier than that of Nacogdoches, and what might we not expect to suffer from disease in a new country, and without friends or means.

Seeing that all these plans were impracticable, I resolved to seek a refuge amongst my enemies, braving all dangers. But before taking this step, I sent in my resignation to the Corporation of San Antonio, as Mayor of the city, stating to them, that, unable any longer to suffer the persecutions of some ungrateful Americans, who strove to murder me, I had determined to free my family and friends from their continual misery on my account, and go and live peaceably in Mexico. That for these reasons I resigned my office, with all the privileges and honors as a Texan.

I left Bexar without any engagements towards Texas; my services paid by persecutions, exiled and deprived of my privileges as a Texan citizen, I was in this country a being out of the pale of society, and when she could not protect the rights of her citizens, they were privileged to seek protection elsewhere. I had been tried by a rabble, condemned without a hearing, and consequently was at liberty to provide for my own safety.

I arrived at Laredo, and the Military Commander of that place put me in prison, stating, that he could not do otherwise, until he had consulted with General Arista, whom he advised of my arrest. Arista ordered that I should be sent to Monterey. I arrived in that city, and earnestly prayed the General to allow me to retire to Saltillo, where I had several relatives who could aid me. General Arista answered, that, as he had informed Santa Anna of my imprisonment, he could not comply with my request. Santa Anna directed, that I should be sent to the City of Mexico, but Arista, feeling for my unfortunate position, interceded with him in my behalf, to have the order revoked. The latter complied, but on condition, that I should return to Texas, with a company of explorers, to attack its citizens, and, by spilling my blood, vindicate myself.

By orders of General Arista, I proceeded to Rio Grande, to join General Woll, who told me, that Santa Anna, by his request, had allowed me to go with him, in his expedition to Texas, but, I should receive no command until my services proved if I were worthy.

I started with the expedition of General Woll. In the vicinity of San Antonio, on the 10th of September, I received an order to take a company of Cavalry, and keep the outlets of the city. By this order the city was blockaded, and consequently it was difficult for any person to escape. When I returned from complying with this order, at dawn of day, the General determined to enter the city with the Infantry and Artillery. I was sent to the vanguard, with orders to take possession of the Military Square at all hazards. I entered the Square without opposition, and shortly afterwards the firing commenced on the Main Square. John Hernandez came out of Goodman's shop, with a message from him to the effect, that, if I would pardon him for what he had done against me, he would leave his place of concealment and deliver himself up. I sent him word, that I had no rancor against him. He delivered himself up, and I placed him under the special charge of Captain Leal. Those who had made some show of resistance in the Main Square surrendered, and the whole city was in the possession of General Woll.

Next day, I was ordered, with 200 men, to take the Gonzales road, and go near that town. On the Cibolo I divided my forces, sending a portion up the creek, another down the creek, and with the main body proceeded on the Gonzales road. Next day, these parties joined the main body. Lieutenant Carvajal, who commanded one of the parties, reported, that he had killed, in the Azufrosa, three Texans, who would not surrender.

I returned to San Antonio. A party of Texans appeared by the Garita road, and the troops were put under arms. The General took one hundred Infantry, the Cavalry under Montero, and one piece of artillery, and proceeded towards the Salado. The General ordered 100 Presidiales to attack. The commander of those forces sent word that the enemy were in an advantageous position and that he required reinforcements. The answer of the General was, to send me with orders "to attack at all hazards." I obeyed; on the first charge, I lost 3 killed and 8 wounded, on the second, 7 killed and 15 wounded; I was preparing for a third charge, when Colonel Carrasco came to relieve me from my command. I returned to the side of the General, made my report, whereupon he ordered the firing to cease.

A new attack was preparing, when the attention of the General was called to some troops on our rear-guard. The aids reported them to be enemies, and near at hand. Colonel Montero was ordered, with his cavalry, to attack them. He called on them, to surrender to the Mexican Government, they answered with scoffing and bantering. Montero formed his dragoons, the Texans commenced firing, killing two soldiers; Montero dismounted his troops, also began firing, and sent for more ammunition. The General angrily sent him a message, asking, whether his dragoons had no sabres or lances. Before Montero received this answer, he had charged, sabre in hand, ending the engagement in a few minutes; only some ten or fifteen Texans survived. During this time, I remained by the side of General Woll, and was there when Montero made his report and brought in the prisoners.

At dusk, the troops received orders to return to San Antonio. In accordance with his orders, not to remain over a month on this side of the Rio Grande, General Woll begun his retreat by the road he came.

The families, who left San Antonio, were put under my charge, and, consequently, I was not in the affair of "Arroyo Hondo."

Remarks

After the expedition of General Woll, I did not return to Texas till the treaty of Guadalupe Hidalgo. During my absence nothing appeared that could stamp me as a traitor. My enemies had accomplished their object; they had killed me politically in Texas, and the less they spoke of me, the less risk they incurred of being exposed in the infamous means they had used to accomplish my ruin.

As to my reputed treason with Vasquez, when we consider that Don Antonio Navarro and I were the only Mexicans of note, in Western Texas, who had taken a prominent part in the war, the interest the Mexican General had in causing us to be distrusted, will be seen. Mr. Navarro was then a prisoner; I alone remained; and if they were able to make the Texans distrust me, they gained a point. This is proved by the fact, that, since I withdrew from the service, there was never seen a regiment of Mexico-Texans. The rumor, that I was a traitor, was seized with avidity by my enemies in San Antonio. Some envied my military position, as held by a *Mexican*; others found in me an obstacle to the accomplishment of their villainous plans. The number of land suits which still encumbers the docket of Bexar county, would indicate the nature of these plans, and any one, who has listened to the evidence elicited in cases of this description, will readily discover the base means adopted to deprive rightful owners of their property.

But, returning again to the charge of treason, if I had sold myself to Mexico, the bargain would have been naturally with the Government; it would have been the interest of Mexico to keep the secret, and not allow inferior officers to know it. Whilst I enjoyed the confidence of the Texans, I might have been useful in imparting secrets, &c., but as soon as my fellow-citizens distrusted me, I was absolutely useless. And is it not strange that the Mexican officers should have been so anxious to inform the Texans of my treason? General Vasquez merely took out a paper from his pocket, and observed to Chevallie that that was from me; and when the latter desired to see the letter, Vasquez refused to shew [*sic*] it to him.

But I take the expedition of Vasquez to be my best defence. What did Vasquez accomplish in that expedition? The coming into and going out of San Antonio, without taking any further steps. Undoubtedly, if I had been confederated with him, I would have tried to make his expedition something more than a mere military promenade. Far from doing this, however,

I presented the letter, which I received from Vasquez, to the corporation of San Antonio; I predicted the expedition, and counselled such steps as I thought should be taken.

And, why, if my treason were so clear, did the patriotic and brave Burleson refuse to subject me to a Court of Enquiry? Undoubtedly, he knew it to be his duty to put me on trial, if the slightest suspicion existed as to my character. He refused; and this proved that Burleson and the superior officers were convinced of the shallowness of the charges against me.

During the electoral campaign, of August, 1855, I was frequently attacked in newspapers, and was styled in some "the murderer of the Salado." As for some time previously I had proposed to publish my memoirs, I thought it useless to enter into a newspaper war, more particularly as the attacks against me were anonymous, and were directed with a venom which made me conclude that I owed them to the malevolence of a personal enemy.

I have related my participation in Woll's expedition and have only to say, that neither I nor any of my posterity will ever have reason to blush for it.

During my military career, I can proudly assert, that I never deviated from the line of duty; that I never shed, or caused to be shed, human blood unnecessarily; that I never insulted, by word or deed, a prisoner; and that, in the fulfilment of my duty, I always drew a distinction between my obligations, as a soldier on the battle-field, and, as a civilized man after it.

I have finished my memoirs; I neither have the capacity nor the desire to adorn my acts with literary phrases. I have attempted a short and clear narrative of my public life, in relation to Texas. I give it publicity, without omiting or suppressing anything that I thought of the least interest, and confidently I submit to the public verdict.

Several of those who witnessed the facts which I have related, are still alive and amongst us; they can state whether I have in any way falsified the record.

{2}

From Juan Seguín
To the Customs Administrator of Béxar
Béxar, May 11, 1833

Mr. Administrator:
  Please be served to issue the appropriate license for the effects that I have bought in this town and I take with me to sell in the districts of Rio Grande and Monclova; which are as follows:

No. 1.	1	chest containing the following
	1	length manta [in Mexico a coarse cotton cloth]
	16	lengths of linen
	3	lengths of northern manta
	20	cuts of dyed English chintz
	3	yards of heavy lining cloth
2.	1	chest containing the following
	1	length of manta
	4	dozen colored pocket handkerchiefs
	4	id.
	6	lengths of imperial
	7	lengths of taffeta
	2	lengths of manta
	2	dozen colored handerchiefs
	1-7/8	yards of hemp cloth for coats
3.	1	case containing the following
	1	length northern manta
	25	cuts of English cotton prints
	4	lengths of French cotton prints
	4	pounds of cotton thread
	4	packages of pins
	82	cotton handkerchiefs
	2	lengths of northern manta
	2	yards of hemp cloth for coats
4.	1	case containing the following
	1	length northern manta
	15	lengths of fine English cotton prints
	3	lengths of superfine id.
	4	pounds of cotton thread
	29	lengths of blue nankeen [coletilla]
	2	lengths of cotton print for bedspreads
	1	length light nankeen [coletilla]
	16	six yard lengths of id.

5.	1	case containing the following
	3	lengths manta
	7	lengths linen
	5	dozen pairs of cotton stockings
	9	pairs of large scissors
	1	dozen small id.
	20	pairs of small scissors
	23	pairs of belt buckles
	18	silk women's belts
	2	lengths muslin
	1	length damask
	1	dozen knitted silk stockings
	13	lengths superfine lace edging
	2	lengths manta
6.	1	case containing the following
	2	lengths manta
	33	yards canvas
	1	length semi-fine linen
	6	dozen fans
	21	red-trimmed black silk handkerchiefs
	5	pairs stone earrings
	3	of the same, lower quality
	14	lengths black ribbon
	1	dozen chambray linen handkerchiefs
	1	length semi-fine linen
	6	lengths manta

Juan Nepno. Seguin

{3}

From Juan Seguín
To the Ayuntamiento of Béxar
Béxar, December 20, 1833

By way of a communication of 17th instant from your lordships, I am informed that according to the total count of votes taken in this municipality's [electoral] assemblies, celebrated on the 8th and 9th days of this month, I was constitutionally elected as alcalde for the coming year of 1834.

Accordingly, I will present myself in the hall of that illustrious corporation at nine in the morning, on the 1st day of January next, to take possession of the charge conferred upon me after taking the required oath, as your lordships inform me in the said communication. In having the honor to reply, I take the opportunity to offer your lordships my highest consideration and profound respect.

God and liberty
Juan Nepno. Seguin

{4}

From Juan Seguín
To Political Chief José Miguel Arciniega
Béxar, January 1, 1834

I have just taken charge of the office of alcalde of this municipality, and have at this moment received Your Lordship's communication of this date. Informed of its contents, I am satisfied that Your Lordship ceases to perform the duties of that chieftainship according to law, and that I am to take charge of it. I will, consequently, assume that office today, leaving the administration of justice to First Councilman Citizen Francisco Xavier Bustillo. With which, I answer your said communication and take the opportunity to extend to you my consideration and particular esteem.

God and liberty
Juan Nepno. Seguin

{5}

From Juan Seguín
To José Antonio Navarro
Béxar, January 17, 1834

It has come to my attention that you have news that somewhere in the interior of the republic Citizen Stephen F. Austin has been arrested. And, as this chieftainship has orders for the arrest of the person of the said individual, I expect that you will be served to communicate to me the news

you may have regarding the imprisonment of the said Austin, detailing
them as much as possible in regard to this matter, and indicating the degree
of confidence merited by the person from whom you received the news.

God and liberty
Juan Nepno. Seguin

{6}

From Stephen F. Austin
To the Ayuntamiento of Bexar, transmitted by Seguín
Monterrey, January 17, 1834

I include for you a copy of the answer that the Lord Governor gave me,
dated 7th ultimo, concerning the petitions from Texas so that Your
Lordship may be served to publish and circulate it in order that the
inhabitants may be informed of the Lord Governor's favorable disposition
toward favoring them in everything that may relate to the development of
that country, and that he will unreservedly support [Texas's] efforts to form
a state or territory of the Federation, with the understanding that legal
means be used, in conformity with the constitution and laws.

I suppose that Your Lordship is already informed of my arrest by order
of His Excellency the Minister of War, and that I am to return to Mexico
City in order to answer an accusation made, as I understand it, for having
written to the ayuntamientos of Texas on October 2, recommending that
they consult among themselves in order to organize a local government *in
case* nothing was done to remove the evils that menaced that country with
ruin.

I do not blame the government in any way for this move. It should be
kept in mind that I went to Mexico City as a public agent and that as such
it was my duty to comply with my instructions. Because at the time I left
Texas in April the majority opinion expressed was decidedly in favor of
separation from Coahuila, and that Texas should be set up as a state of the
Federation; because there was no determination on the part of the majority
for organizing a local government at all costs if no relief was found; it is
clear that it was my sacred duty to work *as a public agent* in conformity
with this public will of my constituency and, consequently, it was also my
duty to inform them of the state of their affairs.

In October I lost hope of obtaining any remedies, and believing that the
towns would organize themselves, I knew very well that it would have been

better for Coahuila, for Texas, and for the Federation if the said organization was made by the local authorities rather than by way of a popular uprising convoking another convention. That is how I fulfilled my duty as a public agent, and as a Mexican citizen. On its part, the government has also fulfilled its duty in arresting me in order to determine my motives. It should also be noted that as soon as circumstances and the prospects for Texas took on a favorable aspect, I made it known to the ayuntamientos, believing that with this step I revoked the October recommendation, which was entirely temporary and subject to future events.

I hope there will not be any disturbance in Texas as a result of my arrest, and toward avoiding one, I have written a letter to the ayuntamiento of [San Felipe de] Austin, which copy I include.

I am reaching the end of my years, my strength, and health for serving those settlements and to wrest them from the wilderness and from the power of the barbarous Indians. I entered Texas in 1821 in the flower of my life, a philanthropic enthusiast, and now at the age of 40 years, I find myself at misanthropy's door, alienated from men and their business.

I wish Your Lordship to circulate this communication and the enclosed copies to all the ayuntamientos of Texas and to the state and federal governments.

God and liberty
Juan Nepno. Seguin

{7}

From Juan Seguín
To the Ayuntamiento of Béxar
Béxar, February 27, 1834

On the first day of the coming month of March I will hand over to the incumbent political chief, Ramón Músquiz, the political charge that has provisionally been in my charge according to law.

And I have the satisfaction to communicate it Your Lordships for your knowledge, and that I will soon have the honor to rejoin that very illustrious corporation.

God and liberty
Juan Nepno. Seguin

{8}

From Juan Seguín
To Political Chief Ramón Músquiz
Béxar, March 12, 1834

This very day I have handed over to the gentleman alderman, Don Francisco X. Bustillo, the magistracy, informing him of all pending matters, and according to the formalities that Your Lordship advises in your order of the 10th instant, thereby leaving matters in order upon my leaving for my commission, which I do on this day.

God and liberty
Juan Nepno. Seguin

{9}

From Juan Seguín
To Political Chief Ramón Músquiz
Béxar, July 7, 1834

In accordance with what Your Lordship requires of me in yesterday's communication, I convened the Illustrious Town Council in extraordinary session with the object of approving the transfer of the *alcaldía* to the senior alderman in turn, as required by the law on the matter.

By virtue of this, Citizen Ignacio Chaves is appointed, [and] tomorrow I shall proceed to take charge of the chieftanship that has been in your charge, by succession to it under article 80 of the regulations for the economic and political government of the towns. I give Your Lordship the required notice for your knowledge.

God and liberty
Juan Nepno. Seguin

{10}

From Commandant General Pedro Lemus
To Juan Seguín
Monclova, August 31, 1834

The disturbances against the authorities in some of this state's towns have brought me to this city with the goal of mediating the matter and thus prevent Coahuiltexans from being torn to pieces by the horrors of civil war, and the efforts directed at defending the nation and private property from the continual aggressions of the barbarous [Indians] from coming to naught.

The state's authorities, peacefully listening to the voices of their constituents, have not vacillated in adopting those measures which, while simultaneously carrying out public opinion, offer sufficient guarantees to those individuals and the various towns who have taken part in the various and partisan pronouncements. These measures will be apparent to Your Lordship in the decree that I enclose, a copy of which I have no doubt you will immediately publish. At the same time, you will use your influence so that, with a uniformity of opinion, all the ayuntamientos of the Department under your charge will pay deference to the newly appointed governor, and cooperate in this manner to restore to the state the peace so required for its prosperity.

I have not doubted for a moment in being able to count on the enlightenment and patriotism of Your Lordship in order to carry out such a laudable goal. In directing myself to you with this motive, I proclaim in the sincerest way my consideration and respect for your person.

God and liberty
Pedro Lemus

{11}

From Juan Seguín
To Commandant General Pedro Lemus
Béxar, September 22, 1834

{Draft}
By Your Lordship's esteemed note dated August 31, ultimo, I am informed that the disturbances between some of the state's towns and the authorities have brought you to that capital city with the goal of peacefully mediating the matter and avoiding both that we Coahuiltexans should be torn to pieces by the horrors of the civil war and that those efforts should come to naught which need to be directed toward defending the national independence and our properties from the continual attacks by the barbarous [Indians].

Along with Your Lordship's note, I have received, and by order of the governor circulated to the ayuntamientos of the department under my charge, the decree issued by the permanent deputation, council of government, and the gentlemen deputies present in the capital, dated August 30 ultimo. Furthermore, carrying out the charge given to me by Your Lordship, I have used my influence so that, with a unity of opinion, the authorities of the department should show the proper deference to the newly named governor, and cooperate in this manner toward restoring the state to that peace that it so much requires for its prosperity.

For my part, Your Lordship may rest assured that I will put in practice all that may be within my reach to achieve the accomplishment of the proposed goal. In having the honor of replying to your already cited note, I have the satisfaction to repeat to Your Lordship those tokens of my surest consideration and respect toward your person.

God and liberty
Juan Nepno. Seguin

{12}

From Commandant General Martín Perfecto de Cos
To Juan Seguín
Matamoros, October 12, 1834

Having been named Commandant General of these states by the Supreme Government, I arrived at this place within the last week and received the command held by General Don Pedro Lemus. Under this circumstance there came to hand Your Lordship's communication dated September 22 ultimo, which I have found very satisfying. In answer, I have the honor to say to you that I expect that with your creditable patriotism and truly liberal ideas, and without making those citizens of your department feel the afflictions of persecution, you will be able to restrain the excesses of the uprisings, and champion peace by whatever means you may.

Confident, above all, in the good esteem that Your Lordship merits from me, and satisfied of the peacefulness and good customs of those inhabitants, it pleases me that restraint shall provide an example of love and prudence to those towns which have not been as reflective. At the same time, I limit myself to offering Your Lordship my cooperation in achieving so glorious an end, as well as my faithful friendship and respectful consideration.

God and liberty
Martin Perfto. de Cos

{13}

From Juan Seguín
To the Ayuntamiento of Béxar
Béxar, October 13, 1834

I enclose to Your Lordships a copy of the resolution enacted by the citizenry of this city on the 7th instant. Which, having received my approval, Your Lordships will require that the ayuntamientos under your charge be convoked by means of an ordinance or by the customary means, on the first Sunday and following day of November next, and proceed to name in the same manner as the ayuntamiento members, the three commissioners who are to come to this city.

On the third day, your illustrious corporation shall meet and, in the company of the citizen electoral examiner and secretaries of the respective assemblies, shall open the registers. You shall write up a certificate in which the corporation shall make known the names of the commissioners who have been popularly elected, and by the assembly competently authorized, so that in passing to this capital, where they will present themselves on the fifteenth day of November next, they may work in union with the other commissioners of their class on matters of the greatest interest for the general good of Texas. With this end, Your Lordships please receive the tokens of my distinguished appreciation.

God, Mexico, and Federal System
Juan Nepno. Seguin

{14}

From Juan Seguín
To Political Chiefs of Brazos and Nacogdoches
Béxar, October 14, 1834

I have the honor to forward to Your Lordship the enclosed resolution enacted by this citizenry on the 7th instant, by which Your Lordship and the worthy citizens subordinate to you will be informed of the chaotic circumstances in which the State of Coahuila y Texas finds itself, and of the complete anarchy that reins in almost all its towns.

In order for us to free ourselves from the grave evils that are a consequence of such events, this citizenry agreed, as I have stated, that it is convenient for an assembly to meet in this capital composed of three commissioners from each of the capital ayuntamientos of the departments and two from each of the ayuntamientos that make up the territory of Texas. The said commissioners should come competently authorized by their respective ayuntamientos to legally and without restraint treat all matters that may relate to our security and the interests of the inhabitants. And, all of this having met with my complete approval, I have the satisfaction of communicating it to Your Lordship, satisfied that moved by your patriotism and love for the general good of Texans, you will be served to adopt this measure and determine that it is put into effect by the indicated means, at the same time advising you that the date designated for the meeting of the commissioners in this city is November 15 next.

In communicating this to Your Lordship, I take the pleasure of offering you all my esteem and consideration.

God, Mexico, and Federal System
J.N.S.

{15}

From Commandant General Martín Perfecto de Cos
To Juan Seguín
Matamoros, October 22, 1834

I have received certain news that an upheaval is being prepared in the department of Texas, or better said, that there is an intention to carry out audacious ideas that, poorly thought out by their authors, would result in incalculable evils to the fatherland. I am informed that Your Lordship, capriciously considering the state leaderless, is moving to disavow the authority of His Excellency the Governor, which officer exercises his office legally, having received it from the Council of Government and those deputies existing in the capital at the time of Mr. Vidaurry's dismissal, as well as having the needed approval of the President of the Republic.

This conduct, all the more scandalous when observed in an officer who would be better occupied in putting out the flames of revolution rather than fanning them, has caught my complete attention, as well as that of every Mexican who wonders what ideas move those who promote disturbances in Texas, and what reasons they have for doing it. Your Lordship should be persuaded that the Supreme Government of the Republic has enough power to suppress such disturbances, and we, its secondary agents, shall always work with the necessary resolution, in observance of our most sacred obligations.

I deeply hope that Your Lordship, turning your attention to your fatherland, will desist from those projects whose evils are impossible to calculate if they are carried out. Your Lordship should remain as you have been, subject to His Excellency the Governor at Monclova, to whom I send, under today's date, instructions that he may take appropriate measures.

The Supreme Government, despite having been surrounded by very grave matters, has not ignored the frontier towns. Making such provisions as have appeared convenient for the purpose of meeting their necessities and raising troops to provide for adequate security, the government shall look upon Your Lordship's actions with much disapproval. I invite you in the name of the Nation not to trespass the limits of your authority nor to make bad use of the influence that you may have, and to preserve it in order to use it in favor of your fatherland.

I repeat to Your Lordship, in the most sincere manner, my avowals of friendship.

God and liberty
Martin Perfto. de Cos

{16}

From Juan Seguín
To the Citizen Judge of First Instance of Béxar
Béxar, January 1, 1835

Today I will turn over the political chieftanship of this Department, which by superior order and the terms of the law has been temporarily in my charge, to Citizen Angel Navarro, the sole constitutional alcalde who is to serve during the coming year of 1835. And in communicating this to you, I take the opportunity to offer you my gratitude for the efficacious cooperation that you have given me in carrying out my instructions during the time you have been under my orders.

God and liberty
Juan Nepno. Seguin

{17}

Captain's Commission
Federal Army of Texas
Headquarters on the Salado, October 23, 1835

The worthy patriot, Juan Nepomuceno Seguín, is named captain of the Federal Army of Texas. As such, he is duly authorized to raize [sic] a company of patriots to operate against the centralists and military, and in defense of the Constitution of 1824 and the federal system. Given at Headquarters on the Salado, October 23, 1835.
    By order
    Warren D. C. Hall   Stephen F. Austin
    Adjutant Inspector General   General in Chief

{18}

Stephen F. Austin's Affidavit of Seguín's Services

Headquarters before Béxar, November 24, 1835

This is to certify that Juan N. Seguin of Bexar presented himself to me at the camp of the volunteer army at the Salado on the 24 of October, and offered his services as a volunteer in the defense of the rights and liberties of Texas.

I gave him the appointment of Captain of a volunteer company of native Mexicans which he raised. This company altho not a full one was very efficient in the cause. It intercepted two expresses from the interior to Genl Cos which were of the highest importance, and Cap Seguin and his men were at all times ready and willing to go on any service they were ordered. They uniformly acquitted themselves to their credit as patriots and soldiers.

I also recommend the first Lieut of said Company, Salvador Flores, and Vicente Zepeda a private. The latter discovered and took one of the expresses to Cos above mentioned.

I give this certificate for the purpose which the interested parties may deem necessary.

S.F. Austin
Comr. in chief of the
Volunteer army

{19}

From Juan Seguín
To Francisco Ruiz
Béxar, February 10, 1836

In the general count of votes made on the 3rd instant, of the elections held on the 1st instant, you received the majority of votes to represent this municipality in the general convention of all Texas that will meet on the 1st of March in the town of Washington, as mentioned in the superior decree of the provisional government of Texas, dated December 10, ultimo. By virtue of this, you will be served to present yourself on March 1, at the said town of Washington to carry out the charge that this municipality has lawfully entrusted to you. Please be served, with this motive, to receive those tokens of my singular esteem and consideration.

God and liberty
Juan Nepno. Seguin
Judge

{20}

Muster Roll of Seguín's Company at San Jacinto

NAME & RANK
Irvin N Seguin—Captain
Manuel Flores—1st Sergt
Antonio Manchaca—2nd [Sergeant]
Neph Flores—1st Corpl
Ambro Rodengues—2nd [Corporal]
Antonio Cruz
Jose Maria Mocha
Edwardo Ramarez
Lucio Enniques
Matias Curvier
Antonio Curvier
Simon Ariola
Manl. Avoca
Pedro Herrera
Manl. Turin
Thos. Maldona
Cesario Carmona (Carnonia)
Jacinto Pena
N. Navarro
Andres Varcenas

{21}

From General Vicente Filisola
To Juan Seguín
River Colorado, May 2, 1836

Sir:
   It is now 8 o'clock at night, and Mr. Jas. Wells has presented to me a passport from His Excellency, the President of the Republic, Don Antonio

López de Santa Anna, with a pass from general Houston, stating that he is the bearer of despatches [*sic*]; but had arrived without them, because Mr. Fucher, who accompanied him, remained behind. I am consequently ignorant of their contents. By the couriers, I learn that you are coming on with a force under your command; and I judge that the aforesaid despatches contain advance of this movement; as, however, I am not certain of it, I trust that until I received them, you will be pleased not to come within sight of my troops, for in this state of uncertainty, a disagreeable result might ensue; whereas, this army is repassing the Colorado, pursuant to the agreement entered into by His Excellency the President, Don Antonio López de Santa Anna, and which in good faith we wish to fulfill. In the enclosed paper, Mr. Wells requests his companion to send him the said despatches, and I hope you will forward them to me, for the purpose of complying with the instructions contained in them, and to communicate them to the different divisions under my command.

God and liberty
Vicente Filisola

{22}

From General Pedro de Ampudia
To Juan Seguín [incorrectly addressed to Erasmo Seguín, Juan's father]
Contraband Marsh, Quarter until eight in the Evening, May 2, 1836

By way of a report received from the officer charged with assisting the sick, I am informed that there is a large force in those woods, which, according to you, has as its sole objective the recovery of black slaves and such [property] as may belong to the citizens of this country. In regard to the former, I say to you that there are no slaves at this place and, with regard to the latter, that I have no knowledge of any property belonging to the individuals who accompany you.

You assert that you come in peace, his excellency the President being in negotiations, and therefore a suspension of hostilities is presently being observed. Under such circumstances, I hope you will order or persuade whomever is in command to order that your force does not advance until permission has been received from his excellency, Commanding General Don Vicente Filisola, [and be] assured that on the part of the division under my command there will be no hostile acts. However, if without that permission your force wishes to advance, I will carry out my duty.

The said commander in chief, to whom I am giving an account at this moment, is with part of the army some four leagues distant. In any case these matters, as you must understand, should be resolved exclusively between the commanding generals of the contending forces.

God and liberty
Pedro de Ampudia

{23}

From Juan Seguín
To General Pedro de Ampudia
Headquarters, Vanguard of the Army of Texas, May 3, 1836

By your communication dated a quarter before eight in the evening yesterday, I am informed that from the report given to you by the officer in charge of assisting the sick, you learned there is a force at this place which, as I stated to the said officer, has no other object than to gather the slaves and other property of these citizens. [To which] purpose my commanding general, upon ordering me and the vanguard to observe the enemy's movements in its retreat, instructed me to communicate with its leader in order to let him know that the slaves who were to be returned as a result of the negotiations (which, upon my departure from General Headquarters, were being celebrated with the President of Mexico), were to be turned over to me and not left loose in the fields, and that in the future the President of Mexico's troops were not to avail themselves of Texas property.

On the same day that Mr. Santa Anna fell prisoner to us, the first thing he requested from my general was a suspension of hostilities after which, upon being granted, he ordered General Filisola to retire toward Béxar with the army. All commanders of forces observing the movements of the enemy divisions have orders that under no circumstances are we to attack. Which order I have the satisfaction of having religiously observed, as the officer caring for your sick must have told you.

The forces under my command will not move from this place until those of the enemy have crossed the Colorado River.

I am informed that Mr. Filisola is [four] leagues from that place, and that you have given him an account of everything which has occurred. You will have the kindness of communicating to me his decision.

This occasion affords me an opportunity to offer you my singular respect and consideration.

God and independence
Juan N. Seguin

{24}

From General Pedro de Ampudia
To Juan Seguín
Camp on the Sandy Bernard, May 4, 1836

Col. John N. Seguin: Sir—
Your communication of yesterday informs us that the forces under your command, forming the vanguard of that army, will not move from your present station, until the division under my command shall have crossed the Colorado, agreeably to the armistice made between His Excellency, the President of the Mexican Republic, Don Antonio López de Santa Anna, and the commander of the army to which you belong; and have no doubt it will be complied with on your part. With Lt. Col. Don Ignacio Barragan, the bearer of the present despatch, I forward to the sick the necessary supplies, until His Excellency, Don Vicente Filisola, can take measures for their removal; and inasmuch as those sick men are on the ground occupied by your camp, I hope you will in future attend to them, as I have been informed you will. General Filisola has ordered me to preserve strict harmony, so that at no time it may be said that we proceed in bad faith; and also because it is not only conformable to the laws of war, but the orders of our President.

God and liberty
Pedro de Ampudia
Comdt of Artillery

{25}

From General Pedro de Ampudia
To Juan Seguín
Camp on the Sandy Bernard, May 4, 1836

Sir:
An officer from your camp came to me yesterday morning, acquainting me that his companies were surprised that their courier had not returned,

and wished to know the reason of it. I informed him that he passed through our camp, that the affair was a very simple one, for even the despatches of the President were not answered within one hour of their reception; nor do I believe that General Filisola will, for the sake of one man, infringe the armistice, and especially, when the honor of the chief magistrate of Mexico, that of the whole army, and of Gen. Filisola, himself, is interested in carrying into effect these treaties. I have written to the General and the courier will certainly return today.

Your attentive, obdt. servt.
Pedro de Ampudia

{26}

From General Thomas J. Rusk
To Juan Seguín
Head Quarters Army Victoria, May 30, 1836

Sir:
   You are hereby authorized to recruit for the service of Texas a Battalion of men in whom you can place confidence not to exceed in number one Hundred and twelve men rank & file for the purpose of being stationed at Bejar under the same pay emoluments and duties as other soldiers in the cause of Texas when on duty and you are particularly enjoined to be vigilant in keeping a look out upon the different roads towards the Rio Grande for the purpose of ascertaining the movements of the enemy communicating fully and frequently all the information you may collect to the commandant of the army.
   This will be a responsible arduous and important duty and I know of no one to whose hands it may be committed with more confidence than yourself and the welfare of Texas for which you have already suffered so much greatly depends upon the vigilence with which your duties are discharged in this matter.

Thomas J. Rusk
Brig. Genl. Comt.

{27}

From Juan Seguín
To General Thomas J. Rusk
Béxar Command, June 7, 1836

Sir:

On the 4th instant I took possession of this town without any opposition. By order of General Andrade, who was in command here, it was garrisoned by Lieutenant Don Francisco Castañeda and eighteen soldiers. The said officer, in replying to the communication I sent him that he evacuate the town, told me that I could enter it without opposition and that he was retiring with the few soldiers that he had, who were dispersed throughout the town. Castañeda left here on the 6th instant.

In the city the rumor circulates that the Mexican troops have stopped at the Nueces River, on the road to Matamoros, and that very soon hostilities will resume. As the said place is closer to that town [Victoria] than to this one, I have not sent out spies to observe the enemy since it may be done more easily from there.

You promised me that a garrison of at least 150 men from our army was coming here. Today it has been six days since I have been here and not one man has appeared.

I am in jeopardy. My unit is composed of only twenty-two men and these are not enough to make ourselves respected. I repeat that I am jeopardized, and the orders that I brought with me I have not put into effect because if I happen to encounter any resistence I do not have the forces with which to execute them. The majority of citizens do not want to take up arms against Mexican soldiers, they wish to remain neutral, consequently, your decision with regard to raising a battalion has not been put into effect.

On the 5th instant three merchants, who have my confidence, arrived from the other side of the Rio Grande. They told me that there is not a soldier as far as Monclova, nor do they know of any coming from the Mexican interior. I have confiscated Músquiz's property [torn] much of our [torn] if he had brought a [torn] because he still has his property.

I have detained [torn] sweet and soap of these [torn] that you tell me that if I should [torn] owners and I believe that it is the most [torn] because the population is [torn] hunger.

Many families have [torn] for Rio Grande, and I do not know [torn] or let them go. You will do me [torn] what I should do regarding [torn].

If a unit of sufficient size, such as you have at Victoria, does not come, you will do me the favor, my general, of sending me an order to retire from this town because my situation is very jeopardized.

Receive, my general, those tokens of my surest respect and esteem as your devoted servant.

Juan N. Seguin
Lieut. Col. Comdte.

{28}

From General Thomas J. Rusk
To Juan Seguín
Head Quarters, Victoria, June 12, 1836

Sir:

I have detached one Hundred and eighty men by way of San Antonio where I have directed them to remain and co-operate with you for a few days and then pass on Eastward the detachment is under Col Smith You will communicate with me frequently giving me all the information you may be able to collect whether or not I occupy Bejar depend upon the resources furnished me by the Government to whom I have written very fully on these subjects if you can obtain any correct information from the interior or any newspapers from them you will not fail to communicate it to me immediately.

I trust I shall hear from the Government soon and will be able to make permanent dispositions upon this frontier.

I have &—
Thomas J. Rusk

{29}

TO THE INHABITANTS OF BEXAR

Béxar, June 21, 1836

Fellow Citizens:

Military movements compel me to repair to Head Quarters. I have in consequence to evacuate this town, but previous to doing so, I require your aid to carry off the cattle and place them where the enemy cannot make use of them. I have no doubt that you will assist cheerfully in this measure, thereby furnishing to the supreme government of Texas a proof of your attachment to the just cause, and the beloved liberty we are contending for. If, on the contrary you fail to render this slight service, your disaffection will be manifest; and although a matter of regret to the supreme government, yet it can then no longer treat you as Texians, but, perhaps, as enemies. Be not deceived with the idea we have no forces wherewith to repel force—time will show to the contrary and will convince you that Texas must be free.

Fellow citizens your conduct on this day is going to decide your fate before the general government of Texas. If you maintain your post as mere lookers-on; if you do not abandon the city and retire [to] the interior of Texas, that its army may protect you, you will, without fail, be treated as real enemies, and will suffer accordingly. My ties of birth and the friendship I entertain towards you, cause me to desire your happiness, and I therefore address you in that spirit of truth which in me is characteristic.

Bexians: render every possible aid, and soon shall you enjoy your liberty and your property, which is the wish of your countryman and friend.

Juan N. Seguin

{30}

From Secretary of War John A. Wharton
To Juan Seguín
War Department, September 17, 1836

Order No 1
Sir,

The president has directed me to order you to proceed to Bexar de San Anto. and take possession of that town of which post for the present you will be the Commandant.

You will immediately commence the recruiting service appointing the necessary superintendent and will endeavor to obtain as many Regulars as will complete a Battalion. You will also organize the civic Militia and endeavor to bring them to such a condition that they can be brought into the field at the shortest notice.

You will take pains regularly to drill not only your own command but the Civic Militia and the Civic Militia when brought in the field will be under your command.

You will make monthly returns of the recruits and of the recruiting party accompanied with a copy of the enlistment of each recruit during the last month you will also forward muster and descriptive rolls of every company under your command when you shall have organized your command and forwarded your muster and descriptive Rolls you will make the necessary requisitions on the Quarter Master General for clothing provisions arms ammunitions &c &c

You will at all times keep out scouting partys as far West as the Rio Bravo Del Norte and all information of importance that they may obtain, you will convey with the utmost expedition to this Department and to the Head Quarters of the army You are authorized to receive as many Volunteers as will offer themselves and proceed as far West as you may consider safe observing the condition of the enemy harassing them and bringing off as many Mules Horses & Cattle as you can obtain of the result of these expeditions you will always make an immediate report

You will ever bear in mind that the Commanche Indians are friendly disposed towards us you will therefore endeavor to conciliate and by all means to avoid collision with them should you fall in with any of this tribe you will inform them that we have sent an agent to talk with them & that we desire their friendship

You are also empowered to arrest try and punish all malefactors & suspicious person (by Court Martial) provided that such punishment does not extend to loss of life or limb

You are authorized to employ an interpreter and requested to make your reports in the English language.

By order of the President
John A. Wharton
Secy. War

{31}

NOTICE

September 20, 1836

Having been authorized by the Government to raise a corps of regular Cavalry for the Army of Texas, in the county of San Antonio de Bexar, to serve during the present war, notice is hereby given to individuals desirous of enlisting for that time, to apply to the Lt. Col. of Cavalry, John N. Seguin, commandant of Bexar, and they will be received on the term prescribed by law.

Juan N. Seguin

{32}

From Juan Seguín
To D. M. Barnett
Headquarters on the La Vaca, October 22, 1836

My Dear Old Friend:

Mr. Lysander Wells, lieutenant colonel of the 1st Cavalry Regiment of the Army of Texas, is going to your town to transact some business for which he has been commissioned. And, taking advantage of the friendship that we profess, I take the liberty of recommending him to you, so that as a friend you may help him in any business that he may encounter difficulty in concluding. The proper and distinguished character of Lieutenant Colonel Wells does not leave any room for an apology regarding those distinguished moral qualities that make him commendable, and so I limit myself to telling you that he is one of the leaders who with his military skill and brilliant valor distinguished himself in the famous Battle of San

Jacinto, by which we managed to destroy Santa Anna's forces and make him a prisoner of war.

I believe it has come to your attention that I embraced the cause of Texas from the beginning. In that army I am now employed with the rank of Lieutenant Colonel, in which position I offer myself at your disposal and that of your kind family, of whom, to repeat, I remain an obedient and attentive servant.

Juan N. Seguin

{33}

From Juan Seguín
To the Judge of First Instance of the Municipality of Béxar
Béxar, November 16, 1836

The commanding general of the Army of Texas has been pleased to give me the following superior order, to wit:

Headquarters in Victoria, July 2, 1836
Don Francisco Antonio Ruíz will deliver to Colonel Juan N. Seguín the three hundred pesos from the public funds of the city of Béxar that he holds as depositary. Don Nicolás Flores will do the same with the three hundred pesos that have been loaned to him at interest. The same will be done by all other individuals who may be in Béxar with the amounts they hold at interest, as soon as Col. Seguín may request them. Colonel Seguín will repay this money from the salaries that may come to him as an officer in the permanent army of Texas, and his present and future property. Colonel Seguín will extend the corresponding receipts to the interested parties for the amounts he may take for his use.

Thomas J. Rusk, Brigadier General Commanding.

I approve the above order.
Nacogdoches, August 20, 1836.
Samuel Houston, General, Commander in Chief.

And I relate it to you for your knowledge and so that as judge of this municipality, with a view to the bonds made by the individuals who have been given money at interest from the public fund, you may be served to reclaim them and place them at my disposal in obedience to the enclosed superior order.

God and Texas
Juan N. Seguin

{34}

From Juan Seguín
To President Sam Houston
Béxar, December 6, 1836

My Dear Sir:

In accordance with an order given me by the Honorable Secretary of War, I left headquarters on November 4 ultimo for this city with seventy commanders, officers and men who, at the moment, make up the cavalry battalion under my orders. I took possession of this city without any incident and I remain in it in the same manner.

The news that I have received up until now from the Republic of Mexico informs me that throughout the frontier to Saltillo there is no unit in the field other than that which makes up the garrison of Matamoros, whose numbers I have not been able to ascertain because of the difference found in the reports of those coming from that place.

I hold prisoner a man who arrived two days ago from Presidio Río Grande after a very quick march. He has not yet made a formal declaration to me, having arrived in a very drunken state. The rumor raised in the city by this man's arrival is that within a few days a force of 200 to 500 dragoons will leave Río Grande with the goal of robbing the commercial stores of this town. My soldierly duty obliges me to maintain myself and defend at all costs this location, with which I have been entrusted. However, I would like Your Excellency to issue an order for my reinforcement from headquarters as soon as possible with two hundred men, cavalry or infantry, otherwise I believe the safety of the force under my command in this town to be in great peril.

I wish Your Excellency well, and that you dispose of the matter as you wish. Your most obedient servant w.k.y.h. [who kisses your hand]

John N. Seguin
Lieut. Col. Comandg.

{35}
Muster Roll of Seguín's Regiment[*]

Company A

ENROLLED	NAMES	RANK	PERIOD
	None	Captain	
2nd Nov	John Miller	2 Lt. Cmdg.	D. War
3 "	L.C.D. Antignac	2 Lt.	"
19 "	William Twooney	1 Sergt	
19 Oct	Christopher Walter	2 Sergt.	"
20 "	John H. Miles	3 Sergt.	"
19 "	Edward Fitzgerald	4 Sergt.	
19 "	William Johnston	1 Corpl	"
24 "	Saunders L. Nobles	2 Corpl	"
19 "	John Nolan	3 Corpl	"
1 Nov	John A. Archer	4 Corpl	
28 Oct	Samuel L. Arledge	Private	"
19 "	James Beard	"	"
24 "	John H. Bostick	"	"
25 "	Solomon W. Bull	"	"
22 "	John Cakhill	"	"
25 "	Charles Calliott	"	"
29 "	Therence Carlin	"	"
19 "	James Cooper	"	"
19 "	David Miles Cule	"	"
31 "	John Dorsey	"	"
24 "	George Francis	"	"
19 "	Andrew Gable	"	"
22 "	Peter Gass	"	"
27 "	Richard Gillom	"	"
19 "	Simeon Glenn	"	"
22 "	Thomas Handcock	"	"
29 "	Henry Howel	"	"
24 "	Charles B. Hyde	"	"
31st "	Samuel Kelly	"	"
29 "	James McBeath	"	"
22 "	Joseph McGinnis	"	"

[*]The "Remarks" column, indicating promotion dates and unit transfers, is not shown.

1 Nov	Samuel McLean	Private	D. War
4 "	Nathan R. Mallan	"	"
25 Oct	Robert Middleton	"	"
19 "	Patterson Moore	"	"
25 "	Daniel Nicodemas	"	"
5 Nov	R.D. Price	"	"
24 Oct	Thomas Price	"	"
22 "	William Roach	"	"
24 "	John Smith	"	"
27 "	Joseph Smith	"	"
21 "	William Snape	"	"
3 Nov	James Tenant	"	"
19 Oct	Edward Welsh	"	"
24 "	Charles S. Widgeon	"	"
5 Nov	Joseph Williamson	"	"
22 Oct	James Woodward	"	"
3 Nov	Thomas McClure	"	6 Mos.
7 Oct	John Boone	"	"

Regiment Head Quarters
Bexar, December 31st 1836

"Signed" John N. Seguin
Lt. Colonel Commanding 1st Regt.

John Miller
Lieut Commanding.

Company B

ENROLLED	NAMES	RANK	PERIOD
	None	Captain	
14th October	Manuel Flores	1 Lt. Cmdg.	D. War
2 Nov	John Reating	1 Lt.	"
5 "	Ambrosio Rodigues	2 "	"
5 "	Antonio Conix	1 Sergt	
" "	Lucio Ernigue	2 "	"
" "	Mathias Curvier	3 "	"
" "	Pedro Herrera	4 "	"
10 June	Agapio Gaitan	1 Corpl	"
"	Jacinto Pena	2 "	"

5 Nov	Edward Ramirez	3 Corpl	D. War
"	Andrew Barcenas	4 "	"
19 Oct	Englebert Bader	Private	"
3 Nov	Morgan Brian	"	6 Mos.
5 "	Manuel Bueno	"	D. War
10 June	Simon Contreras	"	"
3 Nov	Michael Dugan	"	6 Mos.
5 "	Joseph M. Espinosa	"	D. War
5 "	Ensebio Fanias	"	"
10 June	Manl. Ma. Flores	"	"
3 Nov	Michael Fox	"	6 Mos.
5 "	Simon Garcia	"	D. War
3 "	Thomas Hays	"	6 Mos.
5 "	John Huffman	"	"
3 "	Walter Lambert	"	"
5 "	Juan Maldonado	"	D. War
19 Oct	Lewis Mallet	"	"
26 "	Henry F. Maillard	"	"
10 June	Miguel Mata	"	"
4 Nov	Peter McRensie	"	"
5 "	Manuel Montate	"	"
3 "	Thomas O. Conner	"	6 Mos.
5 "	Antonio Pereg	"	D. War
3 "	James Quina	"	6 Mos.
3 "	Patrick Quinn	"	"
20 Oct	John Rockwell	"	D. 16
5 Nov	Antonio Sanches	"	"
5 "	Guadalupe de los Santos	"	"
10 June	Juan Vallanceon	"	"
4 Nov	Joseph L. Walker	"	"
10 Oct	John Williams	"	"
5 Nov	Jose Ma. Landera	"	"
2 Oct	Anselmo Bergara	"	"

Regiment Head Quarters, Bexar, December 31st 1836.

"Signed" John N. Seguin, Lieut Col. Comg. Regt.

"Signed" Manuel Flores,
Lt. Comg.

Company C

ENROLLED	NAMES	RANK	PERIOD
Dec 23d	Salvador Flores	Captain	D. War
2nd Nov	Arthur Thyne	2 Lt .	"
7 Nov	William G. Still	Actg. 2 Lt.	
11 "	Henry Richardson	1 Sergt. 30	
21 "	John C. Campbell	2 Serg	
t.2 Dec	William B. Smith	3 Sergt.	"
11 Nov	William Webber	4 Sergt.	"
8 Dec	Jilson P. Morton	1 Corpl.	"
8 "	Andrew J. McDonald	2 Corpl.	"
20 Nov	Mathew J. Fairchilds	3 Corpl.	"
12 "	David Anderson	Private	"
8 Dec	Richard F. Blackburn	"	"
11 "	James V. Bosley	"	"
30 Nov	Abraham Bradley	"	"
29 "	Thomas H. Brown	"	"
5 Dec	Thomas Casey	"	"
21 Nov	David Compton	"	"
7 "	Henry Danettell	"	"
5 Dec	John Footman	"	"
28 Nov	John B. Fox	"	"
12 "	William Gillmore	"	"
16 "	Edward R. Green	"	"
16 "	Henry Rattenhorn	"	"
11 "	Peter Rendall	"	"
7 Dec	Newton H. Morris	"	"
7 "	Smith Newton	"	"
29 Nov	Leroy H. Smith	"	"

December 31st, 1836
Bexar Regiment Head Quarters

"Signed" John N. Seguin
Lieut Col. Commanding Regiment

"Signed" Salvador Flores
Captain

{36}

From President Sam Houston
To Juan Seguín
Camp Independence 16th January, 1837

Sir, Your communication of the 6th Inst, is before me and I reply to it with much pleasure! I have conversed with General F Huston on the subject of his order, a copy of which he sent enclosed, and can assure you that it was not his design to supercede you in command with Lieut Col Swytzer, but for him to cooperate with you in any opportunity of promoting the public interests—

General Huston is now directed to withdraw those of the command of Bexar, who have not been able to procure cavalry, or that you have not mounted, to the *Main Army,* as it would be hazardous to footmen to remain at the post if the enemy should advance—Col Swytzer will be recalled to his command, leaving you in command of the Station of Bexar, so long as it can be maintained *with safety and advantage to the country*— Your own knowledge of facts as well as the position of the enemy, must in a great measure regulate your conduct, and you will forward reports to the General as well as to the War Department of all important information touching the movement of the enemy and the political condition of Mexico, so far as they may come to your knowledge. Your suggestion in regard to the removal of the inhabitants of Bexar, has claimed my solemn attention, and I have resolved that as great distress must be the consequence, as well as much exposure of life; *that they shall remain at their homes*, believing as I *must* that they will feel bound to return good faith and fidelity to our cause, for the humanity shown them— You may assure the Citizens who do acts of friendship to the Government and send important information to you of the enemy, which can be relied on, and proves true, or in any way give faithful support to our cause, that the greatest lenity shall be extended to them by the President and Congress tho' they may have done something heretofore improper, but no persons who commit *improper conduct hereafter shall ever receive favor or kindness from [the] Government.*

To those whom you *know to be enemies* you will *extend no favors.* Let it be known (as your discretion may suggest to you) that you will report to me the services of those who may hereafter be useful in any way to the republic—

You will render all the facilities possible to the commissioners sent to treat with the Indians, and I hope the most favorable results to our cause from the mission—

As to my having confidence in you, I solicit you to rest assured that I entertain for you a *high regard,* and repose in your honor and chivalry the most *implicit* confidence.—

I regard you as a sentinel at your present *post,* and I well know how you bore yourself in the conflict. I shall always be proud to reward your merit and requite your services.—

You will, I confidently hope, be satisfied that no intention has been entertained to wound your feelings, or to compromise your honor! You will therefore retain your command, and command of the post of Bexar—

I need not suggest to you the necessity of sleepless vigilance, and increasing caution— You know the enemy whom you have to guard against— therefore I rely upon your ability, patriotism, and watchfulness to preserve the charge confided in you!

Present my kind salutations to your relatives. Embrace your Father for me!

Sam Houston

{37}

From Juan Seguín
To the Secretary of the War Department
Béxar, January 26, 1837

Sir:

I have the honor to advise you that I have this day forwarded to Head Quarters of the Army Five Mexicans as prisoners of war apprehended by me at this place on the 24th inst. they comprise a Sergeant and four soldiers of the Presidial Companies at Laredo from which place they came direct. I have also two others (citizens) in confinement whom I retain here for the purpose of obtaining evidence against them. I have also taken the horses mules arms and accoutrements of these men for the public service and have dispatched an officer and party of men to the Ranchos a few leagues below this place to take a lot of horses said to belong to the same men; these men bring little news or rather none in relation to the movements of the main army of the Enemy.

From and undoubted sources I have collected the following information: that Genl. Nicholas Bravo is commander in chief of the army intended for the invasion of Texas. He arrived at Saltillo on the 10th of December. The whole force there amount to little over 2500 men. another section of the army of 1000 to 1500 men are at Matamoras. The Division has 14 pieces of artillery. Some say that the army has 800.000 Dollars, but others affirm probably nearer the truth, that it brought to Saltillo but 20,000 not enough to reimburse what he had borrowed there. It is stated and on good authority, that the greater part of the army is composed of recruits and a great part of them convicts. All agree that the resources of the army are scanty. It is said and thought probable by some that the campaign will open in the spring. The majority of the Mexicans are opposed to the Independence of Texas, nevertheless they know its resources and are desirous that the question should terminate in any way so that it does not too glaringly compromise their national honor.

It appears to be the intention of Genl. Bravo to march the invading army into Texas by the lower route from Matamoras, but it is the opinion of some of the best informed men that the campaign will not be realized in consequence of the scarcity of money.

With assurances of my respect and esteem

I have the honor to be
Respectfully Sir
Your obtsvr.
John N. Seguin
Lieut. Col. Commanding

{38}

From President Sam Houston
To Juan Seguín
Columbia, Texas, February 17, 1837

Sir:

I have received this morning under date of the 6th Inst. giving information that the Mexican Army consisting of 4 or 5,000 men under General Amada were shortly to march into Texas and take possession of San Antonio and Goliad, upon the taking of which commissioners were to be dispatched to the Government of Texas for the purpose of entering into a definitive treaty recognizing our independence upon certain conditions. Upon this subject I have to observe that nothing could be more unfortunate upon the end they have in view, which seems to be a reasonable adjustment of our difficulties, than the marching of their army across the Rio Grande. Their motives could never by the army, or by the people of Texas, be considered in any other light than as bearing the most hostile character, the necessary consequence of which would be in all probability a reiteration of the tragedies that were acted in the last campaign. Our men now in the field are burning to meet the enemy, and there can be no doubt that they would hail with joy and acclamation the news of their coming and fly to any point within their reach to oppose them with all their strength.

Another important consideration is that which relates to the prisoners now in our possession in the event contemplated—no one can answer for the indignation which might fall upon them or the probable consequences in moments of popular excitement produced by seeing the magnanimity they had displayed towards them returned by a violation of the engagements of their Government.

I have, therefore, to request to you, if it is in your power to send a communication to Genl. Amada as soon as possible, informing him that information had reached me (in various ways, you may say for the purpose of concealing the *real source of the information*) of the coming of the army under his command, and that I have expressed to you my views of the consequence.

You should add, too that the crossing of the Rio Grande would be an express violation of the treaty made by Genl. Santa Anna with the Government; and of the conditions upon which the Mexican prisoners here have received supplies and extraordinary conveniences to enable them to leave the country. You may, if you think proper, run suitable extracts of this letter translated to accompany your communication for the purpose of giving it additional weight.

Sam Houston

P.S. I can view the course of the enemy as a *trick of war only*, and in fact, it is but that, and to give time and bring the Indians upon us.

{39}

Juan Seguín's Address at the Burial of the Alamo Defenders

Béxar, February 25, 1837

Companions in Arms!! These remains which we have the honor of carrying on our shoulders are those of the valiant heroes who died in the Alamo. Yes, my friends, they preferred to die a thousand times rather than submit themselves to the tyrant's yoke. What a brilliant example! Deserving of being noted in the pages of history. The spirit of liberty appears to be looking out from its elevated throne with its pleasing mien and pointing to us, saying: "there are your brothers, Travis, Bowie, Crockett, and others whose valor places them in the rank of my heroes." Yes soldiers and fellow citizens, these are the worthy beings who, by the twists of fate, during the present campaign delivered their bodies to the ferocity of their enemies; who, barbarously treated as beasts, were bound by their feet and dragged to this spot, where they were reduced to ashes. The venerable remains of our worthy companions as witnesses, I invite you to declare to the entire world, "Texas shall be free and independent, or we shall perish in glorious combat."

{40}

From Juan Seguín
To President Sam Houston
Camp Vigilance, River San Antonio, March 9, 1837

Dear Sir:
Your esteemed favor of the 17th Ulto. came duly to hand contrary to your expectations therein expressed you perceive I have fallen back with my command towards Head Quarters, tho' in fact not as much on account of any serious apprehensions I entertain of the immediate approach of the enemy as the situation of the men under my command, most of them are on foot and some shoe-less at that. Very indifferently clad and last tho' not the least important consideration is that I am short of ammunition; this is owing to no oversight of my own, I sent my Quarter Master to Head Qrs. for supplies the first of last month but he returned as he went. I shall therefore continue to retire to the east bank of the Guadalupe near or about

Gonzales a central point where with the difference of a day or two I can receive news from my spies almost as soon as on the banks of this river, shall be nearer to Head Quarters to obtain supplies and be ready to return to my post at Bexar at any moment it may be deemed expedient; with this object in view I proceed in my march early tomorrow morning—I am well aware my dear general that there may be some inhabitants in this section of the country who if only stimulated to raise false reports by their contrary ideas and sordid views would wish to see me and my command far from them and therefore put rumors afloat with the design to alarm me but they have no influence over my actions or communications. I know them all and know them well, too well to be deceived by them.

I have received from Genl Johnston a peremptory order dated Camp Independence Feby 27th to fall back immediately with my command to Head Quarters which order you perceive I am executing meanwhile I have the objects in view above stated.

By a private of this corps (a Mexican by birth to whom I had given permission to go on the other side of the Nueces to catch mesteñas [mustangs]) I have learned the following information— He states that in his perambulations he went within six leagues of Matamoras and there remained some days at the Ranch of a Relative of his who is a person known to me and considered friendly to our cause. He left there on the 2d of this month and on the day previous to his departure the relative above alluded to returned to that Ranch from Matamoras and stated to my informant that there were then in that place six thousand troops under the command of Genl. Bravo with sixty pieces of artillery and an immense train of baggage including an iron bridge which has been furnished by the Gachupines in Mexico for the purpose of crossing the Rivers of Texas— That at Reynosa there were fifteen hundred troops. at Camargo another fifteen hundred. Some also at Alcantaro and Revilla and even at Laredo, and that at Saltillo there were about two thousand convicts (Cuerda) also intended for the invasion of Texas. This account of the forces, my informant further states his relative had from the lips of Colonel Bravo who also told him that the van-guard at Matamoras only awaited to be joined by Gen. Urrea who was expected immediately from the city of Mexico whither he had gone with a brigade of those troops who evacuated Texas last spring under Filisola and that upon General Urrea's joining them they were forthwith to take up the line of March.— Genl. Santa Anna was said to be still in Vera Cruz but nothing transpired within the knowledge of our informant as to his movements or intentions.

My informant further states that returning here he met at the Pintas the Lepan Chief Castro with about forty of his warriors of his tribe. they are hostile to our cause as well as the Tancahuas a number of whom were said to be adjacent to that place. that he also saw at that place twenty Cherokee Indians some mounted and others on foot accompanied by two Mexicans Jose Delgado of Bexar and one Castro of Santa Rosa. these took the route when our informant saw them depart in a northern direction to cross the Nueces high up avoid Bexar and take their eastern route through the Mountains; it is judged that they are in the pay of the Mexican government as it is known to be a fact that the Lepans and Tancahuas are.

A few Tancahuas are lurking about these environs in small marauding parties. they recently murdered two inhabitants on the opposite side of the river a little above this place. our attempts to chastise them have been fruitless.

A vague rumor spread this day reports that a considerable body of the enemy's cavalry are between Laredo and this place. I can trace it to no creditable source yet I shall send off scouts in the morning in a direction towards the point where they are said to be to ascertain facts which I shall duly communicate to you.— Major Western has received his appointment which you had the goodness to send him and expresses his regret that your occupations should have deprived him of the pleasure of a line from you. I say nothing of his merits. he is too well known in Texas to require eulogium from my feeble pen. he enjoys my entire confidence and is worthy of that of his country.

In reference to your con[fidential] communication I have to say that I have prepared a letter to Genl. Armador, commander in chief of the Mexican Army, setting forth your views of the subjects therein and have also a person in preparation as its bearer. I shall send you a copy of it I feel myself highly flattered by the discretionary power which you confide to me and being on the spot shall continue to exert my judgement and act as circumstances and necessities may require for the good of our cause and our country.

My father salutes you and highly appreciates your friendly manifestations. and

I have the Honor to subscribe your obt. Sert. and friend John N. Seguin

Confidential

*the name of the informant is Jose Ma. Arocha one of my company in the battle of San Jacinto.

The Relative alluded to is Jesus Cantun uncle to the above.

{41}

From Juan Seguín
To General Albert Sidney Johnston
Camp Vigilance, River San Antonio, March 9, 1837

Sir:

I have the honor to reply to your communication of the 27th ult. with your orders to fall back to Headquarters of the Army—previous to its receipt I had left Bexar with my command directing my line of march by the route of Gonzales as you designated to me. I have been encamped here thirty two miles below Bexar for the purpose of replenishing oxen, provisions, etc. and shall proceed on my march at an early hour tomorrow morning, but few of my men are mounted, and those indifferently, altho I have pressed all the horses and mules to be found in these neighborhoods. The troops under my command are in good health and spirits altho they are much in want of many articles of clothing, blankets, and more particularly, shoes. I am short of ammunition, of powder in particular, and shall dispatch in the course of the day tomorrow if possible an officer to Headquarters to obtain supplies of those articles of greatest necessity to meet me at Gonzales. I shall use every vigilance and precaution on my march and shall advise you of such events of importance as may occur.

By a private of this corps (a Mexican by birth to whom I had given permission to go on the other side of the Nueces to catch mesteñas) I have just received the following information. He states that in his perambulations he went within six leagues of Matamoras and there remained some days at the ranch of a relative of his who is a person known to me and considered friendly to our cause. He left there on the 2nd of this month and on the day previous to his departure the relative above alluded to returned to that ranch from Matamoras and stated to him that there were then in that place six thousand troops under the command of Genl. Bravo with sixty pieces of artillery and an immense train of baggage including an iron bridge which has been furnished by the Gachupins in Mexico for the purpose of crossing the rivers of Texas. That at Reynosa there were fifteen hundred troops, at Camargo another fifteen hundred, some also at Alcantair and Revilla and even at Laredo, and that at Saltillo there were about two thousand convicts (cuerda) also intended for the invasion of Texas. This account of the forces my informant states his relative had from Colonel Bravo who also told him that the vanguard at Matamoros only awaited to be joined by Genl. Urrea who was expected immediately from the city of Mexico wither he had gone with a brigade of those troops who evacuated Texas last spring under Filisola, and that upon Genl. Urrea's joining them they were forthwith to take up the line of march.

Genl. Santa Anna was said to be still at Vera Cruz but nothing transpired within the knowledge of our informant as to his movements or intentions.

My informant further states that returning here he met at the Pintas the Lepan Chief Castro with about forty warriors of his tribe, they are hostile to our cause as well as the Taucahuas a number of whom were said to be adjacent to that place; that he also saw at that place twenty Cherokee Indians, some mounted and others on foot, accompanied by two Mexicans, Jose Delgado of Bexar and one Castro of Santa Rosa, these took the route when our informant saw them depart in a northerly direction to cross the Nueces high up avoid Bexar, and take their eastern route through the mountains. It is judged that they are in the pay of the Mexican Government, as it is known to be a fact that the Lepans and Taucahuas are.

A few Tancahuas are lurking about these environs in small marauding parties. They recently murdered two inhabitants on the opposite side of the river a little above this place. Our attempts to chastise them have been fruitless.

A vague rumor spread this day reports that a considerable body of the enemy cavalry are between Laredo and this place. I can trace it to no creditable source yet I shall send off scouts in the morning in a direction towards the point where they are said to be to ascertain facts, which I shall duly communicate to you.

I have now on the route between here and Gonzales two hundred head of cattle destined to Headquarters of the Army. They are not as many in number nor of as good a quality as I would wish, but it is well known to be an impossibility to collect and drive prime cattle in this country without the best horsemen and the very best horses, and the want of the latter is the apology I offer you for the small drove of cattle which I send you.

In conformity with your orders I leave in Bexar an officer and ten men of this corps to keep a look-out and communicate with me.

I have the honor to be
Very respectfully your obt. sevt.
John N. Seguin
Lieut. Col. Commgt.

{42}

From Juan Seguín
To General Albert Sidney Johnston
Camp Houston, Cibolo, Paso del Nogal, March 13, 1837

The bearer of this is John A. Zambrano Adjutant of this corps, whom I despatch to those Head Quarters for the purpose of obtaining supplies for my command according to the requisition with which he is furnished. In accordance with your orders and the tenor of my communication of the 9th inst. I have proceeded thus far on my retreat, a point defensible and comparatively safe until I may be advised by my scouts in Bexar and westward of it of the probable immediate approach of the enemy. I am well aware that commander as I am of a corps, being an integral part of the army of Texas the whole of which is under your command I am bound to obey all your orders to the very letter. finding myself nevertheless at a point so distant from you, and having discretionary powers not only of a former but of a very recent date from his Excellency Sam Houston Prest. of this Repc. and being in a section of our country where I must in all human probability obtain the earliest information of the movements of the enemy and my only object being the purest of motives to render the greatest service to my country in whatever situation I may be placed to these considerations be pleased to add that of my men being chiefly on foot, naked and barefoot and the probability there is of mounting them, here I hope you will not take offence [*sic*] nor charge me with the remotest intention of disobeying your, orders should I remain yet awhile on this side of the River Guadalupe, that is should it meet your entire approbation after taking into consideration the reasons for my delay as I have just set them forth. Should these reasons however not have sufficient weight with you and should you still wish me to effect an immediate retreat with my command [upon] the slightest intimation from you the subject shall be instantly obeyed, and I beg leave to reiterate my assurances of my great esteem for you as my General and as a friend and of my highest respect for yourself and the orders you may be pleased to communicate.

I crave of you to have the goodness to cause the Quarter Master at Hd Quarters to furnish transportation for the supplies I now require as far as Gonzales, I shall either meet them there or have means to transport them to my camp wherever it may be.

In conformity with the orders from Genl. Felix Huston dated some time back, I caused the honors of war to be paid to the remains of the Heroes of Alamo on the 25th of Feby last. The ashes were found in three heaps. I caused a coffin to be prepared neatly covered with black, the ashes from the two smallest heaps were placed therein and with a view to attach additional solemnity to the occasion were carried to the Parish Church in Bexar whence it moved with the procession at 4 O'Clock on the afternoon of the day above mentioned. The Procession passed through the principal street of the city, crossed the River and passing through the principal avenue arrived at the spot whence part of the ashes had been collected, the procession halted, the coffin was placed upon the spot, and three volleys of musquetry wer [sic] discharged over it by one of the companies, proceeding onwards to the second spot from whence the ashes were taken where the same honors were done and thence to the principal spot and place of interment [*sic*], the coffin was then placed upon the large heap of ashes when I addressed a few words to the Battallion [*sic*] and assemblage present in honor of the occasion in the Castillian language as I do not possess the English. Major Western then addressed the concourse in the latter tongue, the coffin and all the ashes were then interred and three volleys of musquetry were fired over the grave by the whole Battallion [*sic*] with an accuracy that would do honor to the best disciplined troops. We then marched back to quarter in the city with music and colors flying. Half hour guns were not fired because I had no powder for the purpose, but every honor was done within the reach of my scanty means. I hope as a whole my efforts may meet your approbation.

The cattle I alluded to in my former respects are on the march and you may expect them shortly and more shall be collected as soon as possible circumstances permitting.

I have the honor to be
Very Respecty. yr. obt. Sert.
John N. Seguin
Lieut. Col. Commg.

{43}

From Juan Seguín
To Captain Thomas Pratt
Camp Houston, March 26, 1837

Sir:

You are ordered to proceed with the detachment of this corps under your command to the ranches below and about Bexar and collect and press for the Public service and use of this Regt. all the horses and mules you can find without excepting any, except those belonging to members of this corps, You will give receipts to their owners for all you so press which receipt of yours shall be redeem'd by my own so soon as presented.

Capt. Manchaca accompanies you and is subject to your order altho as he is acquainted with the Country and Language you may find it eligeable [*sic*] to consult with him on such points as may be necessary to carry into due effect the object of your mission.

You will permit no individual whatever under your command to seperate [*sic*] from the detachment and you will not remain in Bexar more than 24 hours.

Should the Alcalde of Bexar deliver to you Salt Tobacco or other Articles for the use of this Regt. you will receive and cause them to be convey'd to this camp with your command and all the horses and mules you can obtain with the greatest posible [*sic*] brevity

Your most obt. Servt.
John N. Seguin
Lieut Col. Commd.

The above is a copy of the order in possession of Capt. Pratt in english [*sic*] sign'd by Seguin, Bexar 28 March 1837.

Jno. W. Smith
Clerk P.C.C.

{44}

From Nicolás Flores
To Juan Seguín
Béxar, March 28, 1837

Citizen Nicolás Flores, alcalde in turn of this city, with the greatest respect represents to you that the sad and lamentable state in which the few and miserable residents of this settlement find themselves demand, for humanity's sake, the most just compassion, which will not be denied by any man who is an eyewitness, as you are, of the residents of Béxar and their misfortunes. Supposing this, and remembering the recommendation of them made by His Excellency the President, regarding protection of their properties and lives, I have determined to present to you the following: This morning the whole population of Béxar presented itself to me reporting that individuals from your regiment were going about rounding up all the horses they found outside the city, those found inside being removed at gun point. The resulting evil is almost the same as taking their lives, for those who own beasts base their livelihood and the maintenance of their families on it—and even the safety of their lives while working in the fields during the present state of hostilities against the barbarous Indians. For these just and powerful reasons I have reached an agreement with the commander of the detachment, Captain Pratt (who showed me an order written in English and signed by you to carry out what I have stated) in which we agreed to await an answer on my petition to you because he did not have the power to accede to any request.

This, Colonel, is the anguished state of these residents, in whose name, and my own, I implore you to revoke the said order, if not completely at least in part. That is, beasts should be returned to those who only own one, and one returned to those who own two, and in this way help the poor [military] in its time of need while the owners attend to their many needs. Otherwise, their desperation will climax and the petitions and claims of the residents shall be taken to the supreme government for its remedy to the innumerable ills that afflict us.

Nicolas Flores

{45}

From Juan Seguín
To Nicolás Flores
[Headquarters, March 29, 1837]

Sir:

At 8:45 p.m. yesterday, there came into my hands your note dated Béxar, March 28, 1837, by which I am informed (despite being previously knowledgable) of the sad situation in which the residents of that city find themselves. Granted this, as well as the merit that you place in His Excellency the President's recommendation with respect to some residents, I have determined to totally suspend execution of the superior order of the general commander of the Army of Texas (the date of which I do not cite, it not being in my presence), which orders that all the horses and mules of the residents of Béxar, without exception of any person, be gathered. Until the general disposes of the matter otherwise, I will limit myself to the following: the alcalde of Béxar will raise, on his own responsibility, an exact account of the beasts that may exist within his jurisdiction, he will collect them all, and from them he will take twenty-five for the protection and assistance to the residents, and the rest he will send to me, either by Captain Pratt, if he is there, or with residents you find convenient to send to this place. Do not think that the step I take is because I was mistaken in how I proceeded earlier in this matter. No sir, the general in his superior order tells me to take all the beasts belonging to the residents of Béxar, not that I request them, and all those who understand Castilian will know the great difference there is between take and request. Yet leaving aside all these reflections, you will do, if you think it wise for the population, what I have said with respect to the said petition, and you will send me a list of all the individuals to whom the beasts that you send me belong, as well as those taken from the beginning, that receipts may be issued to them.

Tomorrow the mail leaves for the Army, and by it I will send the petition dated yesterday, made on behalf of the citizenry that you sent me, and I will be very pleased if has a good effect.

With all due respect, I am your obedient servant
Juan N. Seguin
Col. Commanding

{46}

From Juan Seguín
To General Albert Sidney Johnston
Camp Houston, Cibolo, April 10, 1837

Sir.

I have the honor to acknowledge the receipt of the communication you are pleased to make me through the adjutant general, dated 24th Ult. and am gratified to find by it that the funeral honors paid to the remains of the illustrious defenders of Alamo merit your approbation.

Your order to remove my camp to the vicinity of Bexar shall be obeyed forthwith, the spot I have selected for it is the Mission of San Jose situation upon the right bank of the San Antonio about 5 miles below the City. As I have now well grounded expectations of immediately mounting the balance of my command and as you are pleased to grant me discretionary powers in the case, I do not now send to head quarters any of those who remain on foot for the reason that I shall be very soon able to mount them all. The force of the companies of this corps and the horses they have, here as follows

Company	A	aggregate	48	horses and mules	28
	B		55		49
	C		28		13
			131		90

The field and staff are well mounted & I have also some fast running horses for the purpose of Catching "mesteñes" The expectation I have of mounting the balance of my command is grounded upon the wild horses which are taken and taking by a party I have out for the purpose, upon also the probability of a number of gentle horses & mules which I hope will be brought in from the environs of Rio Grande by a party I intend to send out there shortly with that effect.

Immediately after the establishing of my new Camp I will in conformity with your orders place a guard in Bexar under the command of an officer. At present I have out to the west of it a scouting party of 15 men. I shall also pay strict attention to the dicipline and instruction & drill of my command and all the duties of a camp shall be strictly attended to and the rules & regulations of the Army rigidly inforced.

The rights of Citizens have been duly respected in all cases during the permanance of my command in Bejar, but after my departure, some depredations it will appear were committed. I have obtained sufficient information to designate the perpetrators of the acts of outrage whom I remit to you under charge of Lieut. Keating with the necessary documents & witnesses to substantiate the charge. I also remit to these Hd. Quarters Sergeant Fitzgerald with a copy of his sentence by General Court Martial. Agreeably with your order I herewith send you duplicate requistions of the Articles needed by this Command.

The man you mention disposed of a horse at Hd. Quarters is under guard awaiting trial, and you may be assured that exemplary punishment shall be inflicted upon him.

The Muster Rolls, returned & due from this corps at the Adjutant General's office are now forwarded to that office. the reason of their delay was that the Regt. was in continual movement & the writer for the Regt. was parts of the time under arrest.

I have the honor to inform you that I have had the good fortune to leave two Indians (Tancahuas) dead on the field on the 23d Ult. The circumstances of the case were these. I left camp on the 19th previous accompanied by a Lieut. & 5 of my men for the purpose of exploring the country around and ascertaining the resort of the best droves of wild horses and the situation of the Pens in which they are taken. On the morning of the day first above mentioned we met seven Indians of the above tribe and in the encounter we killed two of them took two of their horses and wounded another Indian who escaped with the balance without any loss on our side. From appearances I have good reason to believe that they had been in among the American settlements & have no doubt committed depredations there as they had American horses with them, no arrows left in the quivers, and from other certain signs on those whom we killed I drew this conclusion.

The Comanches have commited recent depredations in the environs of Bejar since I left that place, six or eight of this tribe did go on the 18th ult. to the Ranches of Francis Ruiz and with professions of friendship towards the inhabitants there, said they were going to Laredo to rob the Mexicans our enemies. They inquired for tobacco powder &c. and upon being told that none could be had at the Ranche but that it might be obtained in Bejar they invited a young man Fernando Ruiz nephew of Francis Ruiz to accompany them thither, calling him brother and reminding him of their friendship for his Uncle he alledged that he had no horse they loaned him one of their own and proceeded with one Indian on the road towards Bejar, a few minutes afterwards the report of a gun was heard the rest of the Indians who had remained at the ranche flew to the spot and they afterwards disappeared the young man Ruiz had been killed by his treacherous companion about a half a mile from the house his body was found horribly mangled and mutilated. Two days previous another young man was missing from one of the missions and upon search being made his remains were found hanging to a tree the mere skeleton which had been stripped of the flesh by these savages.

Upon communication dated Camp Preston 1st inst. is received and in compliance with the order therein expressed I have ordered Major Western to report in person to the Secretary of War by order of the President and he will depart forthwith.

I have the honor to be with highest respect and Esteem Your Obdt Sert.

John N. Seguin
Lieut. Col. Commg.

{47}

From Juan Seguín
To General Albert Sidney Johnston
Camp Houston (Cibolo) April 13, 1837

Sir,
    As there is no probability now of the Enemy invading us until next fall, if then, and matters of importance to me requiring my presence at the Seat of Government, I pray you to grant me a furlough for one month, as the major of the Regt. is now proceeding to Columbia by order of the President, the officer next in command is Captain Pratt a prudent & efficient officer upon whom the temporary command of the Regiment will devolve and be safely intrusted during my absence.

I have the honor to be very Respectfully,
Your Obdt. Sert.
John N. Seguin
Lieut. Col. of T.A.

{48}

From Juan Seguín
To General Albert Sidney Johnston
Camp Travis, April 18, 1837

Sir.

I have the honor to inform you that on the morning of the 17th Inst. about 3 O.clock the Taguacana Indians stole 32 of our horses. Lieut. Arreola & sixteen men were ordered immediately to pursue them, they did so and overtook them at a place called las Cuevas about 36 miles from our camp they had a small skirmish with them without either party being injured retook the horses and arrived in camp with them about 12 O.clock the same day. There were about one hundred Indians.

There has been no news from the Enemy's troops.
I am very Respectfully
Your Obdt. Servt.
John N. Seguin
Lieut. Col. Commg.

{49}

From Juan Seguín
To President Sam Houston
Béxar, June 21, 1837

My Dear General and Friend:

Don José Casiano, an old resident of this city [Houston], is going to that city with the object of disabusing the government of some false accusations that some persons have gratuitously made against him.

I have known the said Don José Casiano since 1827, and since that time he has maintained in this city a conduct worthy of a gentleman, and I have seen him interested only in his own private business, that is commerce, which is the only industry he has exercised. In 1835, when we began the struggle for Texas that now occupies us, he was the only resident of the many I visited at this municipality's ranches, who spoke decisively in favor of our cause. After we took this place, he volunteered whatever help we requested of him until immediately before the arrival of Santa Anna and his troops, and according to my information, he has consequently maintained the same conduct in our favor as before.

For these reasons that I have set down, I believe that you will have no doubt that Casiano is a true friend of Texas, and as such I recommend him to you, so that you may do me the favor of attending to him as a good Texan with a native family and as one whose interests have suffered not a little in the present conflict.

Please be served to receive the friendliest regards from my father, who has lately arrived from New Orleans. I remain, as always with the deepest respect, your obedient servant

John N. Seguin

{50}

From Juan Seguín
To President Mirabeau B. Lamar
New Orleans, January 2, 1838

My Dear General.

You will be informed of the latest news of this republic and that of Mexico from the gazettes I here send you. I am of the opinion that we are again going to have war in Texas.

An ailment which struck me during the journey and from which I still suffer has prevented my return to that capital as quickly as I would have liked, but now being much recovered, I will do so as soon as possible.

I am, with due respect, your obedient servant

John N. Seguin

{51}

From Juan Seguín
To Thomas J. Green
Velasco, February 4, 1834[*]

My Dear Friend:

Your brother spoke to me in New Orleans and told me that I should make an effort to see you, that you had an interesting business proposal for me respecting land. Moreover, he told me that you were determined that together we should take the salt lakes on the other side of the Nueces River. If this is so, I hope you will make a considerable effort to go to Columbia, where we shall see each other six or seven days from now.

I am not taking any land in this port because the people who came to see me from Béxar are waiting for me in Houston, where I will land. I hope we shall see each other in Columbia at the time I have said.

I am your sincere friend
W.K.Y.H.
John N. Seguin

*The year should be 1838. Seguín wrote this letter at midnight, and it bears the sign of fatigue. Moreover, Seguin did not visit New Orleans in 1834, but from late 1837 to early 1838.

{52}

From Juan Seguín
To President Sam Houston
Béxar, June 25, 1838

My Dear General:
    The bearer of this is Captain Don Salvador Flores, a great lover of the cause of Texas, to which cause he has rendered important services from the beginning of the Revolution. For these reasons, and because he deserves all my esteem, I take the liberty of introducing him to you, that you may be served to attend to him as a friend during the visit he is making to your city.

    I hope my words on this matter will not prove fruitless, and that enjoying the best of health, you dispose as you wish of your obedient servant and friend

John N. Seguin

{53}

Affidavit on Parish Priests of Béxar and La Bahía

Houston, January 5, 1839

Report on the religious and moral lives that the ecclesiastical bachelors Refugio de la Garza, elected priest of San Fernando de Béxar Parish, and José Antonio Valdéz, priest of La Bahía del Espíritu Santo, have observed in Texas.

D. Refugio de la Garza

This gentleman is a native of the City of San Fernando de Béxar for which he was elected priest in a competition of curates in 1820 and authorized to function as priest by the See of Monterrey; he took possession of his office that same year. At the beginning he carried out his duties with great care and decency, and much zeal and dedication to the divine cult. He made notable repairs and improvements to the parish church, for which he gained the appreciation and respect of all the residents. In 1824, when he returned from Mexico City, where his parishioners sent him as a deputy to the General Congress, he began to abandon the obligations of his post almost entirely. It is shameful to see how filthy the temple remains after it caught fire because of his carelessness in leaving it in charge of a too young, careless, and licentious boy. As far as his religious and moral life, he has done it with so little discretion that almost no one in Béxar is ignorant of his having lived during his entire tenure as priest with various lovers, by whom he has had the following illegitimate children; Concepción, José de Jesús, and Dorotea. He is an enlightened and cultured man.

D. José Antonio Valdéz

I know that he is the priest of La Bahía del Espíritu Santo, by authority of the bishopric of Monterrey. He is a man of an entirely depraved conduct; who has lost the public's faith in his private contracts; whose behavior is so scandalous that he takes his two illegitimate daughters (whom he had by a young maiden he seduced) hanging from his arms down the middle of his parish church, and who enters the sacristy by the altar to change in order to say mass. He has been prosecuted various times by the justices for his scandalous life.

Juan N. Seguin

{54}

From Nathaniel C. Amory
To Juan Seguín
Department of State, Houston, March 16, 1839

Sir:

In compliance with my promise made at the adjournment of the last Congress, to keep you informed of the progress made in publishing the laws in Spanish, I have to state that we have waited for laws of last session to be printed, that the Attorney General might select those contemplated in the act in order to send the whole to New Orleans to be translated and published & with the utmost dispatch, a course which our present Secretary of State Judge Webb considers the best.

The delay in printing was unexpected had it been anticipated those of former sessions would have been forwarded long since, to have enabled the contractor to have made a commencement.

On the attorney Generals return from Galveston tomorrow the selection will be completed and all be forwarded by next packet.

and accept my assurances of esteem
N. Amory, C. Clerk
Deprt. of State

{55}

From Juan Seguín
To Mirabeau B. Lamar
[November 1839]

My Dear General and Friend:

Mr. Navarro, who was elected as one of the representatives from the county for the current consitutional term, has been forced by a serious illness to tender his resignation, which he forwards by the present mail. And, since the absence of a member of Congress may, without a doubt, result in one or more prejudices to the west, I hope that you will do the inhabitants of this part of the republic the favor and justice of giving, as quickly as possible, an order to the county judge here to hold an election to fill the said Navarro's vacant seat.

I wish my General health and good judgment in his government, and I offer myself as your humble servant and friend

Juan N. Seguin

{56}

Juan Seguín's Address in Senate

[February 1840]

Mr. President: With the permission of the honorable Senate, I beg leave to make a few remarks in regard to the last estimate of the honorable Secretary of the Treasury, originated in the Second Auditor's office. I wish, sir, to know upon what data the Second Auditor founded his estimate of the cost of translating and printing the Laws to be enacted by the present Congress, to the amount of $15,000. I wish to know, Mr. President, what the cost of translating the laws, encacted [*sic*] by the former Legislative bodies of Texas is, laws which in virtue of the existing laws upon that subject, ought to have been translated, and printed; also, what laws have been translated, and where do they exist? My constituents have, as yet, not seen a single law translated and printed; neither do we know when we shall receive them: Mr. President, the dearest rights of my constituents as Mexico-Texians are guaranteed by the Constitution and the Laws of the Republic of Texas; and at the formation of the social compact between the Mexicans and the Texians, they had rights guaranteed to them; they also contracted certain legal obligations—of all of which they are ignorant, and in consequence of their ignorance of the language in which the Laws and the Constitution of the land are written. The Mexico-Texians were among the first who sacrificed their all in our glorious Revolution, and the disasters of war weighed heavy upon them, to achieve those blessings which, it appears, are destined to be the last to enjoy, and as a representative from Bexar, I never shall cease to raise my voice in effecting this object. But, in order not to detain this honorable body, at this time, any longer, I will conclude these cursory remarks, leaving my detailed observations upon the subject to a more proper occasion.

{57}

From Juan Seguín
To Mirabeau B. Lamar
San Antonio, April 20, 1840

My Dear General and Friend:

The presenter of this letter will be General Licentiate Antonio Canales, who goes to your city on important business. For this reason, I take the liberty of introducing him to your knowledge and friendship, so that you may be served to attend to him in all you may be able, for which favor I will be forever grateful.

In regard to the qualities which adorn and distinguish the said General Canales, I omit mentioning them to you because in dealing with him you will be satisfied of his merits.

With all due respect, I am your obedient and faithful servant, w.k.y.h.

Juan N. Seguin

{58}

From Joseph Waples
To Juan Seguín
Department of State, Austin, July, 1, 1840

Sir:

Yours of 21st June is at hand, making enquiries relative to the publication of the Spanish translation of the laws of the Republic; I regret to have to inform you that they are not yet completed, but the Department has been informed that they are now in a good way of publishing and will soon be done, and as soon as they are, a number of them shall be forwarded to your county. The reason of the delay has been occasioned by the want of paper, which could not be obtained in New Orleans until recently; the laws and Journals of last session are not yet printed from the same cause.

With much respect, I am
Your Obdt Servt.
Joseph Waples
Chief Clerk & acting Sec. of St.

{59}

From Juan Seguín
To the President of the Republic
San Antonio, October 14, 1840

Sir:

The poor state of health in which I find myself and the proximity of the coming sessions of Congress force me, with considerable regret, to take the unavoidable step of resigning the office of senator, which I hold by the confidence I have merited from my constituents. I make this known to Your Excellency that you may be served to proceed according to law in the matter, and that the county that I would represent does not suffer some setback in the coming sessions for want of the senator to which the law entitles them.

In making this communication to Your Excellency, I have the honor to offer myself to Your Excellency, your most avowed and obedient servant, who K.Y.H.

Juan N. Seguin

{60}

From Juan Seguín
To the President of the Republic
Austin, December 26, 1840

Sir:

I received with pleasure your Exly.s note of yesterday & proceed to reply to it.

After the conclusion of an amicable convention between the Generals Canales and Reyes, which contained stipulations for the payment of the services of the Texian auxiliaries, as well as for the debts contracted in the fitting out of those auxiliaries.— The Regiment under my command commissioned me to proceed to the town of Mier, where Generals Canales and Reyes were, for the purpose of recovering the amt. due it.— The security guaranteed by the convention to the members of the Federal Army and the desire to recover a sum of more than $3000 that I expended in fitting out the volunteers that enlisted for the Federal Service, induced me to pass to Mier, where I was well received and treated by Genl. Reyes. During the three or four days that I was in that town I heard frequent conversations relative to the approaching campaign against Texas. The chiefs officers and soldiers are all enthusiastic and anxiously desire the moment for undertaking the march to Texas.— Genl. Reyes made many enquiries of me relative to the feelings of the old Colonists and their disposition to return to their former state of obedience to the Mexican government under certain guaranteed privileges.

On the second day after my arrival at Mier Genl. Vasquez entered with his Brigade of seven hundred men, and three pieces of artillery— Being present at the meeting between him and Genl. Reyes, the former expressed his gratification at the union of forces to enter Texas, to which Genl. Reyes replied, that they were ready to march for that destination.

Genl. Canales having left Mier previous to my arrival, I was obliged to proceed to Monterrey to see him— Upon reaching that city I visited Genl. Arista, in the company of a number of my former friends. He stated that he wished to converse with me alone. In the course of a private conversation had at his request, after enquiring relative to certain information which Genl. Canales had given him he remarked.— It is impossible that those men can continue much longer as a nation or Republic— without means to meet the public expenses, without credit abroad, their paper worth only 18 cents pr. dollar, and even their agent in England has been unable to obtain any money—- My Government has obtained a loan of three millions, one third of which has been appropriated for the purchase of steam vessels of war. & the balance is for the forces destined to operate by land against Texas. I have also received from the House of the Rulios an order on Tampico for $80,000 and their agent in Matamoras has placed at my command in New York and New Orleans each $60,000— with these means and six thousand men, now ready to move at my order, out of 15,000 which the Government has destined for the campaign, I shall march upon my return from Saltillo to take possession of San Antonio and Goliad, from which places I shall offer the following terms to the old colonists—Lands to all who have not obtained it— their ports free for 10 or 15 years— and a state legislaure and government—Should these propositions have no efffect, I will continue the War until the country is subdued. I have already given orders to my light troops to advance and commence hostile operations on the frontier.

The different sections composing the Army of the North are all in movement, some for Mier and others for Laredo.— The Cavalry are well mounted and as well as the Infantry and artillery are well clothed and paid. Gen. Arista has with him ten pieces of Artillery, and Gen. Vasquez four & there are in Matamoras some sixty pieces of all sizes ready for the field. Col. Rodriguez was ordered to Cadareta for seven hundred mules and five hundred horses for the Army. I should have required more information from Gen. Arista, but as soon as he observed that I did not coincide with his ideas, (for he had been induced to believe I was a friend of the Mexican cause) he withdrew from the conversation.

The campaign against Texas is most certain and I am sure we shall be attacked very soon. I have never witnessed such enthusiasm as that which exists amongst all classes of Mexicans against Texas. Your Ex'y may have seen in the note I handed to Mr. Van Ness that Genl. Andrade was moving on from San Luis de Potosi with 6,000 men to this frontier. I also stated that Gen. Vasquez was under orders to take immediate possession of San Patricio, where he would be joined by Col. Bradburn, with forces from Matamoros. I am with the highest resp. &

Your most obt. Sevt.
J.N. Seguin

{61}

From George W. Hockley
To Juan Seguín
Department of War and N[avy], Austin, February 3, 1[842]

Sir:
Your letter to His Exce[llency] the President, dated 30th January has been received [and] referred to this Department.— I regret exceedingly that [the] impoverished condition of our country renders it almo[st] helpless, and that we must depend upon the patrio[tism] of those who are willing to defend it.— I hope that [you] will be enabled to rally a few about you upon [whom] you can depend, in case the threatened advance [should be made] and rest assured that all assitance [will] be given by this Deparment, which its limited me[ans] will allow.

Very Respectfully
Sir
Your Mo. Obdt. Servt.
Geo. W. Hockley
Secy. of War & Navy

{62}

From Juan Seguín
To the Bexar County Judge
San Antonio, April 18, 1842

Sir:

The turbulent state in which this unfortunate county finds itself at present obliges me to present to Your Honor my resignation as president of the corporation of the City of San Antonio.

Your obedient servant
Juan N. Seguin
President

{63}

From Juan Seguín
To General Adrián Woll
Camp at Cibolo Creek, September 14, 1842

The scouts on the left flank, under the command of Don Manuel Carbajal, lieutenant of the first company of the Defenders Regiment discovered on Cibolo Creek two leagues from this road three Texans and a Mexican who, having been ordered to place themselves in obedience to the supreme government, instead of doing so grabbed their weapons and attacked the detachment. The scouting party, giving battle, killed the three Texans, excepting the Mexican who from the first placed himself at the disposal of the Supreme Government and remains with the detachment.

I have the honor to tell Your Lordship that two thirds of the horse herd belonging to Captain Francisco Herrera's squadron has arrived here tired. The same is true of the greater part of mounts belonging to the Defenders under my command. Despite this great obstacle, we continue our march in order to carry out, as well as may be possible, Your Lordship's superior order. In making this communication to Your Lordship, we have the honor to offer our consideration and respect.

God and liberty
Juan Nepomuceno Seguín

{64}

From Juan Seguín
To Anson Jones
Rio Grande, July 24, 1845

My Dear Friend and Brother:

Despite being separated by a long absence, which has produced a suspension of our friendly communications, I find myself today with the obligation of writing to my friends, and I would do a great wrong to my heart and to the loyal friendship that we have always professed if I did not address you a few words on this occasion. I know that you are a true Texan, a lover of your country and, therefore, very interested in the common good. Under these principles, I know that the true happiness of Texas, according to the general direction its question has taken, consists in preserving its independence from any other power other than Mexico. The latter, which has also come to know the truth, understands that it behooves it to avoid a war that would bring upon itself great devastation. Mexico is, therefore, resolved to recognize the independence of Texas by way of treaties to which (as you may know) England and France have offered themselves as guarantors. So fortunately, if Texas sends its commissioners with its proposals to this government, I am sure that they would be heard, and our difficulties would be over in a manner greatly beneficial to both countries.

I know the great influence that you enjoy there, and satisfied of your good judgment, I have not hesitated to write you that you might make an effort to get those inhabitants to decide in favor of the ideas that I have here expressed.

Wishing you the best of health and placing myself at your disposal, I am your obedient and faithful friend and servant, who K.Y.H.

Juan N. Seguin

[*Endorsement.*—Col. Seguin fought as well at San Jacinto as any man there; but has been forced by bad usage to quit the country, and, as is said, has turned traitor; but I am unwilling to believe it. I think this letter expresses his *true* sentiments, but it is unnecessary for me to reply.—A.J.]

{65}

From Juan Seguín
To Samuel Houston
Saltillo, April 17, 1848

My Dear Sir and Friend:

After many losses and toils which I have suffered in this fated campaign, I have in this city rejoined my numerous family, who have also suffered much, and have resolved to retire with them to my native place (Bexar) and to remain for the rest of my days peacefully occupied as a laborious citizen.

To secure the object I have designated I believe you will agree with me that it is indispensable for me to obtain your weighty and important recommendation to my former fellow citizens, as also a protection from the President of your Republic. Both those documents I hope to obtain through the friendship with which of old you favored me, as also that you will be pleased to send them to me at San Antonio de Bexar, whither I am about to proceed with my family, and where I will await your honored commands.

You are I think acquainted with the causes which obliged me to leave my country, and as the explanation of them would be long, I defer it till I have the gratification of seeing you.

I have had the great pleasure of meeting in this city with my old and gentlemanly friend major G.T. Howard to whom I and my family are indebted for generous and important favors, which indeed I had expected from him. This worthy friend has conversed with me in very satisfactory terms respecting you, insomuch that I have no doubt of his being our sincere well wisher and personally attached to yourself. In consideration of this, and as I know he would be much more useful to us in Bexar where we could count on all his influence and cooperation in the popular elections, I have proposed to him to go thither; and he is only deterred from doing it by his duties at this place as major and Quarter Master in the U.S. Army, since he would incur great injury to his personal interests by not attending to those duties in person. To obviate this difficulty I make bold to suggest that by obtaining for him from your government the same employment in San Antonio which he exercises here (which I entreat you to do) we would secure the advantage of having so good a friend in that place, one who has always been well disposed towards me, and who I consequently believe would be of service to me there, for which I would be eternally grateful.

I have also met in this city with our old and constant friend Mr. Thomas
H.O. Addicks, from whom I have received kind and courteous attentions,
and who has offered in many ways to serve me.

This good friend sends you his particular regards.

My wife and family send a cordial salutation to you and your lady; and
with great desire to see you again, I offer myself to you as your affectionate,
true and attentive friend and servant.

Juan N. Seguin

{66}

Seguín's Company at the Siege of Béxar

Office of the Commissioner of Claims, February 10, 1858
List of the individuals of the volunteer company of the municipality of
Bexar who participated in the taking of the city of Bexar:

Captain: Juan N. Seguin
1st Lieutenant: Placido Venavides
2nd Lieutenant: Salvador Flores
Sergeant: Manuel Flores

Soldiers
Mateo Cacillas
Ciriaco Conti
Estivan Villarreal
Ramon Rubio
Antonio Ruiz
Toribio Herrera
Jose Zuñiga
Esmirigildo Ruiz
Ygnacio Espinosa
Vicente Ramos
Pablo Cacillas
Juan Jose Palacios
Paulin de la Garza
Julian Conti
Carlos Chacon
Domingo Diaz
Jesus Garcia
Agapito Cervantes

Clemente Bustillo
Luis Castañon
Francisco Diaz
Pablo Mansolo
Eduardo Hernandez
Agapito Tejada
Vicente Zepeda
Juan Jose Arrocha
Jesus Gomez
Margil Salinas
Miguel Cilva
Manuel Escalera
Francisco Gomez
Francisco Salinas
Jose Maria de la Garza
Francisco Valdez
Antonio Hernandez
Fernando Curvier
Clemente Garcia
Miguel Mata
Nepomuceno Navarro
Ambrosio Rodriguez
Jose Alemeda
Domingo Losoyo
Pedro Herrera
Pablo Salinas
Guadalupe Garcia
Pedro Gaona
Manuel Bueno
Francisco Miranda
Juan Gimenes
Marcelino de la Garza
Manuel Gallardo
Eduardo Ramires
Graviel [*sic*] Gonzales
Gregorio Hernandez

[I,] Juan N. Seguin, Captain of the volunteer company of the municipality of Bexar,

Certify that the individuals who appear on the preceding list are the same as those who I listed for [fragment]

Office of the Comr. of Claims
Feby 10th 1858

Before the undersigned Commissioner of Claims for the State of Texas personally came and appeared Juan N. Seguin who is known to me and being duly sworn on his oath deposes—

That the above list of names of the company of Juan N. Seguin as being at the Storming of Bexar in 1835 under the command of Genl. Burleson, is a true copy of a list which was filed in the Adjutant General's office of the State of Texas before the burning of the same, upon which the said Adjutant General proceeded to issue certificates, with the exception that the said list had attached to it the certificates of Juan N. Seguin, Manuel Flores & Salvador Flores, a certificate of Col F. W. Johnson and Col. W. T. Austin stating that the company of said Seguin to about that number was in the storming of Bexar and performed good and valuable service—

This affiant further states that all the persons above named were members of the said company of which he was in command at Bexar in 1835, that they entered the said company about 13 October 1835, and they all entered Bexar from December 5th 1835 to the 10th of the same month and actually took part in the reduction of the said place and that they remained at their posts assisting the army in the reduction of Bexar till the surrender of General Cos.

That said parties were honorably discharged from his said company, a portion of them leaving about the 22nd Feby following and a portion joining the Texas Army & serving on through the following year.

Juan N. Seguin

Sworn to & subscribed before
me this 10th day of Feby 1858
Edward Clark
Comm of Claims

{67}

Seguín's Company for the 1839 Indian Campaign

San Antonio, September 28, 1860
the State of Texas}
County of Bexar }

Personally Before me the undersigned a Notary Public in and for said County. Appeared Col John N. Seguin, who duly sworn on his oath says

That in the summer of 1839 two companies of volunteers were raised in San Antonio Bexar County, one being composed of Mexicans, and the other of Americans. that the deponent was elected Captain of Mexicans composed of fifty four or fifty five men and L B. Franks was elected captain of the American company also composed of 54 or 55 men and Henry W. Karnes was elected Colonel Commanding said companies that said two companies were raised for the purpose of fighting the Comanche Indians (then hostile) and actually went into this country. north west and west of San Antonio hunting the Indians on the headwaters of the Medina, Hondo Seco and Cañon de Ubalde that said companies returned to San Antonio and were disbanded after an absence or campaign of three weeks. that said companies with the assistance of the citizens who did not go furnished themselves with horses provisions etc. and were never paid either by the Republic or State of Texas to his knowledge.

That the deponent has no list of the men composing his company from the time of service. the same having been lost or mislaid, never expecting to receive pay for said service.

That as far as he recalls, the following is a correct list of the officers and men composing his company

1   John N. Seguin Captain
2   Salvador Flores 1st Lieutenant
3   Leandro Arreola 2d do.
4   Franco. A. Ruiz
5   Gregorio Soto
6   Jose Luis Carabajal
7   Marcos A. Veramendi
8   Agustin Chaves
9   Manuel Lopez
10   Ignacio Espinosa
11   Antonio G. Navarro
12   Polonio Dias
13   Pedro Flores Morales, Killed on the campaign
14   Luciano Navarro
15   Damacio Galban
16   Eusebio Almaguez
17   Vicente Garza
18   Francisco Morales
19   Manuel Leal
20   Gabriel Martinez
21   Nepomuceno Flores
22   Antonio Hernandez Zavala

23 Jose Maria Valdez
24 Felipe Jaimes
25 Nemecio de la Cerda
26 Juan Sombraña
27 Nicolas de los Santos
28 Antonio Benites
29 Nicolas Delgado
30 Cristobal Rubio
31 Jesus Zavala
32 Trinidad Coy
33 Ramon Treviño
34 Francisco Rodriguez
35 Leandro Garza
36 Cayetano Lerma
37 Cayetano Rivas
38 Francisco Ruiz
39 Xavier Lazo
40 Jose Maria Rios
41 Ambrosio Rodriguez
42 Mariano Romano
43 Agapito Servantes
44 Miguel Arsiniega Jr.
45 Ignacio Castillo
46 Manuel Martinez
47 Antonio Sombraño
48 Antonio Estrada
49 Manuel Montalvo
50 Pedro Camarillo
51 Juan Rodriguez
52 Manuel Estrada
53 Antonio Ruiz
54 Manuel Hernandez

Further deponent says that the companies herein mentioned were raised and organized by virtue of a Proclamation of M. B. Lamar, then President of the Republic of Texas.

To certify all which I hereto sign my name and affix my oficial seal at San Antonio this 28th day of Sept. A.D. 1860

P.L.Buquet
Not Pub B C

The State of Texas}
County of Bexar   }

Personally appeared John James & F.L. Paschal who under oath say that the facts and statements as set forth herein by Col John N. Seguin are correct and true. F. L. Paschal

Sworn and subscribed
Before me this 12th day of April A.D. 1861 To certify which I hereto sign my name and affix my official seal at San Antonio the day and date hereof

/s/RL Buquet
Not Pub B C

{68}

Application for Pension

San Antonio, October 2, 1874
The State of Texas}
County of Bexar   }

On this, 2d day of October One Thousand Eight hundred and Seventy-four, before me Saml. S. Smith Clerk of the District Court in and for said County and State, personally appeared Col. Juan Nepomuceno Seguin, to me personally known from 1837 up the present time, who being duly sworn according to Law, deposes and says, that he is Sixty Seven years of age, and was born in the City of San Antonio Bexar, Texas; that he is the identical, Juan Nepomuceno Seguin: who participated in the Revolution for the Independence of Texas in the struggle against Mexico: and further says: that he was a Captain of a mounted volunteer Company at the taking of Bexar between the 5th and the morning of the 10th of December A.D. 1835, and remained therein until after the surrender of Genl. Cos. That he remained in the service of Texas and was at the battle of San Jacinto in April 1836, in command of a part of his company, the remainder of his company under command of Lieut. Salvador Flores, having been sent out from Gonzales by Genl. Sam Houston, to guard and protect the fleeing Texan families. That he was commissioned in the Regular Army of the Republic of Texas as Lieutenant Colonel, was commander of the army of the West with headquarters at San Antonio de Bexar in 1836, [and in 183]7, up to April or May in 1838, that he was a Senator from Bexar County in the Session of Congress of 1838 and 1839, that he has always been a citizen of Texas, but has been temporarily absent at different times in the Republic of Mexico, on business. The said Col. Juan N. Seguin makes these declarations for the purpose of obtaining the benefits which may arise to him under the Laws of the Legislature of the State of Texas, under the Act Granting Pensions to the Veterans of Texas, and in proof of his Services would refer to the Public Archives at the City of Austin, and to many old citizens and companions here, as to his identity. He hereby appoints Edward Miles of San Antonio, to represent his said claim:

His home is, at his Ranche, Wilson County, State of Texas: and his Post Office address is: Floresville

Juan N. Seguin
Witnesses
H.P. Brewster
Antonio Menchaca

Sworn to and subscribed before me this 2d day of October A.D. 1874. To certify to which I have hereunto signed my name and affixed the Seal of the District Court of Bexar County, at office, in San Antonio, this 2d day of October A.D. 1874.

Sam S. Smith
Clk D.C.B.Co.

:Also, before me, personally appeared this day; Henry P. Brewster and: Antonio Menchaca who were in the battle of San Jacinto in 1836: his credible witnesses, and to me well known, who being by me duly sworn, upon their oaths depose and say, that they are well acquainted with Colonel Juan Nepomuceno Seguin: the applicant above named, and have known him since, the first named since March 1836 and the latter ever since he was born and that he participated in the battle of San Jacinto: and know him to be the identical person he represents himself to be, and that they, said witnesses, have no interest whatever in this application:

H P Brewster
Antonio Menchaca

Sworn to and Subscribed before me, this 2d day of October A.D. 1874:
Witness my hand and official Seal, at office in San Antonio, the day and
year above written;

Sam S. Smith
Clk D.C.B.Co.

{69}

From Edward Miles
To Juan Seguín
Austin, October 6, 1874

My Dear Sir:

I have through the hand of our friend Mr. Sam S. Smith received your
application for pension, and it meets the case and soon will receive attention
and I will obtain your Bonds.

In behalf of the Veterans Association of Texas, it has become my duty
to ask for contributions for the "Log Cabin History of Texas," and I wish
you to aid us in the good work, by penning some of your earliest recollections in other words to add a leaf to the page of its History.

Please be simple and brief in your statements, and if possible something
that has never before appeared in print with reliable data.

This work if properly gotten up will meet with a ready sale, the proceeds
of which it is intended shall relieve the veterans who may be in need.

Yours Truly,
Edward Miles,
"Committeeman" 29 sen. Dis. T.V.

P.S. Please direct your communications to Col. Moses Austin Bryan,
Secy. T.V.A.
Independence
Texas

{70}

From Juan Seguín
To the Comptroller of the State
San Antonio Dec. 5 1874

My Dear Sir:

In the year 1856, if my memory serves me right, I was called upon by several of my comrades in arms to make up a list of those persons who with me had aided, proclaimed, and sustained the Texan cause from the beginning of the year 1835 up to 1838, when a few who had remained in the service up to that time withdrew to their homes, their services being no longer required. Recognizing the justice of their request I concluded to make out a list, including the names of those members of my company who were with me at the battle of San Jacinto; of those who at that time made the request and of some who I could then remember.

You will admit me, Comptroller, that the long lapse of 21 years intervening between 35 and 56, in which the request was made by those who had served in the cause, rendered it impossible to retain the names of all in my memory, consequently many were omitted in the list and now that the surviving veterans have been pensioned, the news has spread, and they came from a great distance to proove up their services and perfect their claims by presenting themselves in person and proving their identity by the testimony of two of their comrades.

While we were beseiging Bexar no muster rolls were made. My company was made up of men from this city. And as this was their home, [and] being familiar with the country, [they] were detailed to accompany the different expeditions of Americans that went out.

You should not think it strange that of so large company, containing over one hundred men, only over twenty were at the battle of San Jacinto, because Genl. Sam Houston sent Lieutenant Salvador Flores from Gonzales with over forty men to escort the families that were on the farms exposed to the attacks of Indians and which Santa Ana considered as enemies, and that many previous to our being surrounded at the Alamo had received furloughs from Bowie and Travis in order to look after their families who were exposed to the same dangers.

When I submitted the list referred to above to Generals Houston, Rusk and Austin, they certified that they could not identify the names of the persons in the list but that they were satisfied that it did not contain the names of all those that were in the company because when it was being made up at Gonzales it was the largest one in the army. An escort from my company also left this city in charge of the Mexican families that left for Nacogdoches fleeing before Santa Ana.

I make this statement, Mr. Comptroller, in behalf of my comrades, believing their claims to be just under the circumstances. You can, however, attach such weight to it as you may deem proper.

Respectfully yrs c.
Juan N. Seguin

{71}

Colonel Juan N. Seguin

A representative of the Times called on the venerable Col. Juan N. Seguin, sole surviving Captain of the Texan army participating in the battle of San Jacinto. Col. Seguin was born in San Antonio, October 29th, 1806, and is consequently 80 years of age. He comes of pure Castilian descent, his ancestors being of the first colony that came from the Canaries to San Fernando, as San Antonio was first called. He would easily pass now for a man of 60, so gently has time indented its furrows upon his brow and face, although his hair is snow white. In personal appearance Col. Seguin is about five feet eight inches tall, and rather heavy, doubtless weighing 170 or 180 pounds. His complexion is fair, his features regular, and the general expression of the countenance indicating gentleness of heart and firmness. As a commander his force must have been rather in persuasion, and the love of his men, rather than in the exercise of stern power, as was largely the case with Gen. Ross. His manner is dignified yet kindly and confidential, and tears came to his eyes as he dwelt upon the stirring scenes of 1836, and he inquired of his friends of that period, and their descendants. Of those known to the writer, only one survives: Mr. Thomas O'Connor, of Refugio; and as the old veteran inquired of John J. Linn, Edward Linn, John S. Menefee, and others, the answer was "Dead!" In many respects Col. Seguin was an unique figure in the Texas revolution, siding as he did against the majority of his countrymen. That he was actuated by the purest of motives there can be no doubt. And equally as true is it that he contributed his full share in achieving the independence of Texas. He was shut up in the Alamo by the encircling lines of Santa Anna's army, and was the fourth, and the last, messenger sent out by Travis for aid, Major Red being the only one so sent whose name he could recall. The message was verbal, directing Col. Fannin, at La Bahia, Goliad to us, to march to his

rescue. His egress from the beleagured Alamo was under the friendly cover
of darkness, and was accompanied by great danger, as the Fort was entirely
surrounded. Bombs were bursting all around. However, he made his way
stealthily through the Mexican lines on foot, and often upon all fours. A
horse was provided at a ranch, and he rode night and day until La Bahia
was reached, and faithfully delivered, the message to Col. Fannin. Col.
Seguin says Fannin said it would be impossible for him to comply, as
General Urrea was then near his position. Being unable to reenter the
Alamo, and fortunately for him, Col. Seguin went to Gonzales, where was
General Houston and the Texan army. Here he organized his company, a
brave and gallant band of Mexicans who did their whole duty at San
Jacinto. The old veteran recalled with evidences of pride and pleasure the
fact of Houston's friendship, and even partiality, for him, saying that "Old
Sam" was wont to call him his son. Col. Seguin was twice elected mayor
of San Antonio, and served four years in the Congress of Texas, being
chairman of the Senate committee on military affairs. In May 1836 he was
made colonel of the first regiment of cavalry, and assigned to the command
of the fourth department of the west. He was one of the joint committee
of the Texas Senate and House of Representatives empowered to select the
cite for the capital of the republic, and recalled the names of Menefee,
Morehouse, Westover and Holmes as of the number. During their encamp-
ment upon the ground now occupied by the city of Austin they killed a
number of buffalo, and subsisted wholly upon game. He accounts for the
naming of the town of Seguin for him from the fact that he caused the first
post office to be established there. The place had been called Nogales
before. The old gentleman speaks some English, but the conversation was
mainly carried on through the medium of his grandson, Mr. Guillermo M.
Seguin, a young gentleman of thorough education and polished manners,
who will yet shed additional honors upon the name of Seguin. The
Colonel's son, ex-mayor Santiago Seguin, is on a visit to the City of Mexico.
He has lately become involved in political troubles, which swept away his
splendid estate, and the family are now far removed from affluent circumstances. He hopes, however, to recover some of this, as he is a warm
friend of President Diaz, having engaged actively in the revolution which
drove President Lerdo de Tejada from power. The old gentleman was
much interested in the descendants of his old compatriots, and inquired
especially of the Bryan brothers, Moses Austin [Bryan] and Guy M.
[Bryan]. When told that John J. Linn's son, E.D. Linn, was a prominent
man in State politics, and had a brilliant future, and that a son of General
Houston was now in the Senate, he felt gratified, and said it was right to

keep the sons of the old patriots to the front. Col. Seguin has never received any material recognition of his services to Texas, though no one is more deserving than he. He will go back to Austin as soon as his son comes back from Mexico, and the good citizens of the capitol city should extend to him the freedom of the same, and accord him all the distinguished honors so manifestly due a venerable and illustrious patriot of the Texas revolution.— Laredo Times.

{72}

From Juan Seguín
To Hamilton P. Bee
Laredo de Tamaulipas, March 28, 1889

My Dear Sir and Friend:

I now answer your kind letter of 9th instant, which I had not done for lack of health.

The remains of those who died in the Alamo were burned by order of General Santa Anna, and the few fragments I ordered deposited in an urn. I ordered a sepulcher opened in San Antonio's cathedral next to the altar, that is, in front of the two railings but very near the steps.

This is all that I can say to you relating to this matter.

I repeat myself your friend and servant
Juan N. Seguin

[P.S.] If you are the son of he who was secretary of war during the time of the Republic of Texas, I will never forget him and I offer you my friendship.

{73}

From Juan Seguín
To William Winston Fontaine
Nuevo Laredo, June 7, 1890

My Dear Sir:

Your favor of the 26th May ult. to hand and contents carefully noted. In answer, I beg to state, that I am glad to be able to be of service to you, in the recollection of those days of glory long past, but not forgotten. Santana's army was drawn up before Bexar on the 22nd day of Feby. 1836.

Col. Travis had no idea that Santa ana with his army would venture to approach the city of Bexar (now San Antonio) and for this reason, only a watch was kept on the church tower that existed where today stands the cathedral of San Antonio; this watchman was an American whose name I do not now remember. About three o'clock in the afternoon he sent a messenger stating that on the road to Leon, he saw a moving body which appeared like a line of troops raising the dust of the road. Upon the receipt of this notice John W. Smith, a carpenter (alias "el colorado") was sent to reconoiter, and returned in the evening, about five o'clock saying "there comes the Mexican army composed of cavalry, infantry and artillery!" In the act of the moment Col. Travis resolved to concentrate all his forces within the Alamo, which was immediately done. As we marched "Potrero Street" (now called "Commerce") the ladies exclaimed "poor fellows, you will all be killed, what shall we do?" Santa ana occupied the city of Bexar at about seven o'clock in the afternoon of that same day and immediately established the siege of the Alamo, which at first was not rigurosly kept as the sons of a widow named Pacheco, one of whom was named Esteban, took me my meals, and by them we were enabled to communicate with those external to the Alamo.

The day following the arrival of Santa Ana, the bombardment was vigorously commenced and lasted three days. Finding ourselves in such a desperate situation, Col. Travis resolved to name a messenger to proceed to the town of Gonzalez and ask for help, thinking that Sam Houston was then at that place. But, as to leave the fortification at such a critical moment was the same as to enounter death, Santana having drawn as it were a complete circle of iron around the Alamo, no one would consent to run the risk, making it necessary to decide the question by putting it to a vote; I was the one elected. Col. Travis opposed my taking this commission, stating that as I was the only one that possessed the Spanish language and understood Mexican customs better, my presence in the Alamo might become necessary in case of having to treat with Santana. But the rest could not be persuaded and I must go. I was permitted to take my orderly Antonio Cruz and we left eight o'clock at night after having bid good bye to all my comrades, expecting certain death. I arrived safely at the town of Gonzalez, and obtained at once a reinforcement of thirty men, who were sent to the Alamo, and I proceeded to meet Sam Houston.

When the notice of the arrival of the thirty men was given to Santana, it is said, he gave orders to allow them entrance stating that he would only have that many more to kill.

In the city of Bexar at the time of which we speak, there were no others by the name of Seguin than my father Don Erasmo Seguin and myself. My father was the Judge of the Probate Court and I was commander of the 4th department of the West, with headquarters in Bexar.

Even though there may have been a misunderstanding between Bowie and my father, the forces of Col. Travis did not reah [*sic*] the Medina then.

Col. Bougham [Bonham] was about six feet in height, thin, fair complexion, brown hair, gray eyes, he was not vicious and of very honorable conduct as I knew.

I have an oil painting of my likeness presented to me by Gen. Houston in the year 1838, and as we have no photographer in town and my pecuniary resources are very limited, I cannot afford to have the painting sent somewhere else, to have a picture taken from it. This picture to which I refer, and the one you may now see in the House of Congress there were taken at the same time.

Any other data you may desire in reference to those days long past, I will gladly endeavor to give you to the full extent that my old age will permit me.

Believe me dear sir
Yours respect.
Juan N. Seguin

Sources for Appendices

Unless otherwise stated, all documents written by Juan Seguín are translations from Spanish by the editor.

No.	Location
1	TSL.
2	BA.
3	BA.
4	BA.
5	BA.
6	BA.
7	BA.
8	BA.
9	BA.
10	BA.
11	BA.
12	BA.
13	BA. This document is followed by an identical draft with the following list attached: Béxar, Goliad, San Patricio, Refugio, Guadalupe, Victoria.
14	BA.
15	BA.
16	Bexar Land Papers, Spanish Collection, GLO. Original incorrectly dated December 1, 1835.
17	BA.
18	BA. Original in English.
19	Election Returns, Secretary of State Records, TSL.
20	Col. Sherman's Command 2nd Regt. Texas Volunteers, contd., Muster Roll Book, GLO, 39.
21	*Telegraph and Texas Register*, September 21, 1836. English language copy.
22	Ampudia (Pedro de) Item, BHC.
23	Ampudia (Pedro de) Item, BHC.
24	*Telegraph and Texas Register*, September 21, 1836. English language copy.

25   *Telegraph and Texas Register*, September 21, 1836. English
        language copy.
26   Army Papers, Adjutant General Records, TSL.
27   Thomas Jefferson Rusk Papers, BHC.
28   Rusk Papers, BHC.
29   *Telegraph and Texas Register*, September 21, 1836. English
        language copy.
30   Audited Military Claims, Treasury Records, TSL.
31   *Telegraph and Texas Register*, September 21, 1836.
32   John W. Smith Collection, DRT. Reprinted by permission of the
        Daughters of the Republic of Texas History Research Library, The
        Alamo.
33   Folder, "Payment of certain monies," Juan N. Seguín Papers, DRT.
        Reprinted by permission of the Daughters of the Republic of Texas
        History Research Library, The Alamo.
34   Madge W. Hearne Collection, BHC.
35   Muster Roll Book, GLO, 166-69.
36   A. J. Houston Collection, TSL.
37   Albert Sidney Johnston Papers, TU. This was a copy forwarded by
        the War Department to Johnston for his information. English
        language copy.
38   A. J. Houston Collection, TSL.
39   *Telegraph and Texas Register*, April 4, 1837. The March 28, 1837,
        edition of the *Telegraph* carried a poor transcription accompanied by
        a poor translation, which was then corrected in the April 4 edition.
40   Sam Houston Hearne Collection, BHC. English language copy.
41   Johnston Papers, TU. English language original.
42   Johnston Papers, TU. English language original.
43   A. J. Houston Collection, TSL. English language copy.
44   A. J. Houston Collection, TSL.
45   A. J. Houston Collection, TSL.
46   Johnston Papers, TU. English language original.
47   Johnston Papers, TU. English language original.
48   Johnston Papers, TU. English language original.
49   Correspondence relating to domestic affairs, Secretary of State
        Records, TSL.
50   Lamar Papers, TSL.
51   Thomas Jefferson Green Papers, Southern Historical Collection,
        University of North Carolina Library, Chapel Hill.
52   Photostat, Houston Collection, Catholic Archives of Texas, Austin.

53   Enclosure in: John Fitzgerald to Bishop Blanc, February 1[7], 1839,
      Archives of the Archdiocese of New Orleans.
54   Domestic Correspondence, Letter Book No. 1, Secretary of State
      Records, TSL, 78.
55   Correspondence relating to domestic affairs, Secretary of State
      Records, TSL.
56   Austin *City Gazette*, February 5, 1840.
57   Mirabeau B. Lamar Papers, TSL.
58   Domestic Correspondence, Letter Book No. 1, Secretary of State
      Records, TSL, 181.
59   Folder: "Tentative Resignations," Election Returns, Secretary of
      State Records, TSL. English language original.
60   Domestic Correspondence, Secretary of State Records, TSL.
      This is a certified copy of a copy then in the secretary of state's
      office. English language copy.
61   Seguín Papers, TSL.
62   Journal A, Records of the City of San Antonio from 1837 to 1849,
      transcription, vol. 815, Material from Various Sources, BHC.
63   Communication contained within a letter from Woll to Santa
      Anna, printed in *Expedición hecha en Tejas, por una parte de la
      división del Cuerpo de Egército del Norte* (Monterrey, 1842), 31.
64   *Memoranda and Official Correspondence Relating to the Republic*
      of Texas, Its History and Annexation, Anson Jones, comp., New
      York,1859.
65   A. J. Houston Collection, TSL. English language original, improperly
      cataloged under April 17, 1846.
66   Muster roll of Seguín's company during the Siege of Bexar, Office of
      the Commissioner of Claims, Feby. 10th 1858, Republic of Texas
      Collection, GA36, Special Collections Division, University of Texas at
      Arlington Libraries.
67   Unpaid Claims, Comptroller of Public Accounts Records, TSL.
      English language original.
68   Republic Pension Applications, Comptroller of Public Accounts
      Records, TSL.
69   Casiano-Pérez Collection, DRT. Reprinted by permission of the
      Daughters of the Republic of Texas History Research Library, The
      Alamo.
70   Draft copy of a translation, Business Regarding the Spanish
      Collection, GLO.
71   *Northern Standard* (Clarksville), February 25, 1887.

72   Juan N. Seguín letter, TSL.
73   W.W. Fontaine Collection, BHC. English language original.

Bibliography
Archival Collections

Eugene C. Barker Texas History Center, The University of Texas at Austin:
Ampudia, (Pedro de) Item
Austin Papers
Valentine Bennet Papers
Bexar Archives
Robert Bruce Blake Research Collection
W. W. Fontaine Collection
Madge W. Hearne Collection
Maverick Family Papers
Andrew Neill Papers
Records of the City of San Antonio, 1837-1849
Sam Houston Hearne Collection
Texas Veterans Association Collection
Thomas and Mary F. Howard Papers
Nacogdoches Archives Transcriptions
Thomas Jefferson Rusk Papers

Nettie Lee Benson Latin American Collection, The University of Texas at Austin:
Archivo General de la Nación de México, microfilm
Valentín Gómez Fárias Archives
Mariano Riva Palacios Archives

Archives and Library Divisions, Texas State Library, Austin, Texas:
A. J. Houston Collection
Army Papers
Comptroller of Public Accounts Records
Laredo Archives
Mirabeau B. Lamar Papers
Secretary of State Records
Juan N. Seguín Papers
Treasury Records
United States Census Records

Archives and Records Division, Texas General Land Office, Austin, Texas:
  Business Regarding the Spanish Collection
  Court of Claims Collection
  Muster Roll Book
  Original Land Grant Collection
  Spanish Collection

Bexar County Clerk's Office, San Antonio, Texas:
  Bexar County Deed Records
  Bexar County Probate Records
  Family Genealogy Files
  Spanish Archives of Bexar County

Daughters of the Republic of Texas Research Library, San Antonio, Texas:
  Casiano-Pérez Collection
  Juan N. Seguín Papers
  John W. Smith Collection

Archivo General de Indias, Audiencia de Guadalajara, microfilm.

Mrs. Mason Barret Collection of Albert Sidney Johnston and William Preston Johnston Papers, Manuscripts Department, Howard Tilton Memorial Library, Tulane University, New Orleans, Louisiana.

Thomas Jefferson Green Papers, Southern Historical Collection, University of North Carolina Library, Chapel Hill, North Carolina.

Houston Collection, Catholic Archives of Texas, Austin, Texas.

Library of Congress, Historic Buildings Collection, Division of Prints and Photographs, Washington, D.C.

Republic of Texas Collection, GA36, Special Collections Division, University of Texas at Arlington Libraries, Arlington, Texas.

Samuel May Williams Papers, Rosenberg Library, Galveston, Texas.

Newspapers

Austin *City Gazette,* Austin, Texas, 1840.

Northern Standard, Clarksville, Texas, 1843-87.

Morning News, Dallas, Texas, 1975.

Weekly Herald, Dallas, Texas, 1884.

Telegraph and Texas Register, Houston, Texas, 1836-45.

El Bejareño, San Antonio, Texas, 1855-56.

Daily Express, San Antonio, Texas, 1907.

Express News, San Antonio, Texas, 1973.

La voz de Zaragoza, Monterrey, Mexico, 1961.

Ledger, San Antonio, Texas, 1857.

San Antonio *Light,* San Antonio, Texas, 1882-1974

Enterprise, Seguin, Texas, 1974

Printed Documents and Compilations

Barker, Eugene C., ed. *Austin Papers.* 3 vols. Vol. I and II, Washington, D.C.: Government Printing Office, 1924, 1928; Vol. III, Austin: University of Texas Press, 1927.

Benavides, Adán, ed. *The Bexar Archives (1717-1836): A Name Guide.* Austin: University of Texas Press, 1989.

Chabot, Frederick C., ed. *Texas in 1811: The Las Casas and Sambrano Revolutions.* San Antonio: Yanaguana Press, 1941.

Corner, William, ed. *San Antonio de Bexar: A Guide and History.* San Antonio, 1890.

Archivo del General Porfirio Díaz. Prologue and notes by Alberto María Carreño. 30 vols. Mexico: Editorial Elede, 1947-61.

Expedición hecha en Tejas, por una parte de la División del Cuerpo de Egército del Norte. Monterrey, Mexico, 1842.

Gammel, Hans Peter Nielson, ed. *The Laws of Texas, 1822-1897.* 10 vols. Austin, 1898.

Jenkins III, John J., ed. *The Papers of the Texas Revolution.* 10 vols. Austin: Jenkins Publishing Company, 1973.

Jones, Anson, comp. *Memoranda and Official Correspondence Relating to the Republic of Texas, Its History and Annexation.* New York, 1859.

Journals of the Fourth Congress of the Republic of Texas, 1839-1840. Volume I, The Senate Journal. Austin: Texas Library and Historical Commission State Library, 1929.

Lauter, Paul, et al., eds. *The Heath Anthology of American Literature: Volume 1.* Lexington, Mass.: Heath, 1990.

Leal, John O., trans. Sacramental registers of the Archdiocese of San Antonio for San Fernando Church and the San Antonio Missions. Unpublished, copies available at the Daughters of the Republic of Texas Research Library and the Institute of Texan Cultures, San Antonio.

Miller, Thomas L. *Bounty and Donation Land Grants of Texas, 1835-1888.* Austin: University of Texas Press, 1967.

McLean, Malcolm D., ed. *Papers Concerning Robertson's Colony in Texas.* 16 vols. Fort Worth and Arlington: University of Texas at Arlington Press, 1974-1990.

Spanish Archives, Bexar County Clerk's Office, San Antonio, Texas. Church of Jesus Christ of the Latter Day Saints microfilm.

Weber, David J., ed. *Northern Mexico on the Eve of the United States Invasion: Rare Imprints Concerning California, Arizona, New Mexico and Texas 1821-1846.* New York: Arno, 1976.

White, Gifford, ed. *The 1840 Census of the Republic of Texas.* Austin: Pemberton Press, 1966.

Williams, Amelia W. and Eugene C. Barker, eds. *The Writings of Sam Houston, 1813-1863.* 10 vols. Austin: University of Texas Press, 1938-1943.

Diaries, Journals, and Memoirs

Castañeda, Carlos E., ed. and trans. *The Mexican Side of the Texas Revolution, 1836, by the Chief Mexican Participants.* 1928. 2d ed. Austin: Graphic Ideas, 1970.

Gray, William F. *From Virginia to Texas.* Houston: Gray, Dillaye & Company, 1909.

Green, Thomas J. *Journal of the Texian Expedition Against Mier; Subsequent Imprisonment of the Author; His Sufferings, and Final Escape from the Castle of Perote.* New York, 1845.

Jenkins, John Holmes III, ed. *Recollections of Early Texas: The Memoirs of John Holland Jenkins.* Austin: University of Texas Press, 1987.

Labadie, N. D. "Narrative of the Anahuac, or Opening Campaign of the Texas Revolution," *Texas Almanac,* 1859.

Maverick, Mary A. *Memoirs of Mary A. Maverick.* ed. Rena Maverick Green. San Antonio: Alamo Printing Company, 1921.

Menchaca, Antonio. *Memoirs.* San Antonio: Yanaguana Press, 1937.

Muir, Andrew Forest, ed. *Texas in 1837: An Anonymous, Contemporary Narrative.* Reprint. Austin: University of Texas Press, 1988.

Olmsted, Frederick Law. *A Journey Through Texas: Or, A Saddle-Trip on the Southwestern Frontier.* Reprint. Austin: University of Texas Press, 1978.

Peña, José Enrique de la. *With Santa Anna in Texas: A Personal Narrative of the Revolution.* College Station: Texas A&M University Press, 1975.

Rodríguez, José María. *Rodriguez Memoirs of Early Texas.* 2d ed. San Antonio: Standard Printing Company, 1961.

Smither, Harriet, ed. "Diary of Adolphus Sterne," Part XV, *Southwestern Historical Quarterly* 33 (April 1930): 5.

Smithwick, Noah. *The Evolution of a State, or: Recollections of Old Texas Days.* Reprint. Austin: University of Texas Press, 1983.

Monographs and Reference Works

Almaráz, Félix D., Jr. *Governor Antonio Martínez and Mexican Independence in Texas: An Orderly Transition.* Reprint, San Antonio: Bexar County Historical Commission, 1979.

_____. *Tragic Cavalier: Governor Manuel Salcedo of Texas, 1808-1813.* Austin: University of Texas Press, 1971.

Alessio Robles, Vito. *Coahuila y Texas desde la consumación de la independencia hasta el Tratado de Paz de Guadalupe Hidalgo.* 2nd ed. Mexico: Editorial Porrúa, 1979.

_____. *Coahuila y Texas en la época colonial.* 2nd ed. Mexico: Editorial Porrúa, 1978.

Barker, Eugene C. *The Life of Stephen F. Austin: Founder of Texas, 1793-1836.* Reprint. Austin: University of Texas Press, 1969.

_____. *Mexico and Texas, 1821-1835.* Dallas: P.L. Turner, 1928.

Benson, Nettie Lee. *La diputación provincial y el federalismo mexicano.* Mexico: El Colegio de México, 1955.

Berrueto Ramón, Federico. *Ignacio Zaragoza.* Mexico: Secretaría de Gobernación,, 1962.

Binkley, William C. *The Texas Revolution.* Reprint. Austin: Texas State Historical Association, 1979.

Broussard, Ray F. *San Antonio During the Texas Republic: A City in Transition.* El Paso: Texas Western Press, 1967.

Castañeda, Carlos E. *Our Catholic Heritage in Texas, 1519-1936.* 7 vols. Reprint. New York: Arno, 1976.

_____. *A Report on the Spanish Archives in San Antonio, Texas.* San Antonio: Yanaguana Press, 1937.

Chabot, Frederick C. *With the Makers of San Antonio.* San Antonio: Artes Gráficas, 1937.

Colin Sánchez, Guillermo. *Ignacio Zaragoza: Evocación de un héroe.* Mexico: Editorial Porrúa, 1963.

Diccionario Porrúa de historia, biografía, y geografía de México. 3 vols. 5th ed. Mexico City: Editorial Porrúa, 1986.

Dixon, Sam Houston and Louis Wiltz Kemp. *The Heroes of San Jacinto.* Houston: Anson Jones Press, 1932.

Drossaerts, Arthur J. *The Truth About the Burial of the Remains of the Alamo Heroes.* Private printing. San Antonio, 1938.

Friend, Llerena B. *Sam Houston: The Great Designer.* Reprint. Austin. University of Texas Press, 1969.

Gambrell, Herbert. *Anson Jones: The Last President of Texas.* 2nd ed. Austin: University of Texas Press, 1964.

Garrett, Julia Kathryn. *Green Flag Over Texas: A Study of the Last Years of Spain in Texas.* Reprint. Austin: Pemberton Press, 1969.

Gracy, David B., II. *Moses Austin: His Life.* San Antonio: Trinity University Press, 1987.

Gutiérrez Ibarra, Celia. *Cómo México perdió Texas: Análisis y transcripción del Informe secreto (1834) de Juan Nepomuceno Almonte.* Mexico City: Instituto Nacional de Antropología y Historia, 1987.

The Handbook of Texas. 3 vols. Austin: Texas State Historical Association, vols. 1 and 2 1952, vol. 3 1976.

Henson, Margaret Swett. *Juan Davis Bradburn: A Reappraisal of the Mexican Commander of Anahuac.* College Station: Texas A&M University Press, 1982.

_____. *Samuel May Williams: Early Texas Entrepreneur.* College Station: Texas A&M University Press, 1976.

Hogan, William R. *The Texas Republic: A Social and Economic History.* Reprint. Austin: University of Texas Press, 1980.

Holley, Mary Austin. *Texas.* Reprint. Austin: Texas State Historical Association, 1985.

Jackson, Jack. *Los Mesteños: Spanish Ranching in Texas, 1721-1821.* College Station: Texas A&M University Press, 1986.

_____. *Los Tejanos: The True Story of Juan N. Seguín and the Texas-Mexicans During the Rising of the Lone Star.* Stamford, Conn.: Fantagraphics Press, 1982.

James, Marquis. *The Raven: A Biography of Sam Houston.* Indianapolis: Bobbs-Merrill Company, 1929.

Kennedy, William. *Texas: The Rise, Progress, and Prospects of the Republic of Texas.* Reprint. Clifton, New Jersey: Augustus M. Kelley, 1974.

Lowrie, Samuel H. *Culture Conflict in Texas, 1821-1835.* New York: Columbia University Press, 1932.

Lozano, Rubén Rendón, *Viva Tejas: The Story of the Mexican-born Patriots of the Republic of Texas.* San Antonio: Southern Literary Institute, 1936.

Montejano, David. *Anglos and Mexicans in the Making of Texas, 1836-1986.* Austin: University of Texas Press, 1987.

Nance, Joseph M. *After San Jacinto: The Texas-Mexican Frontier, 1836-1841.* Austin: University of Texas Press, 1963.

_____ . *Attack and Counterattack: The Texas-Mexican Frontier, 1842.* Austin: University of Texas Press, 1964.

Reichstein, Andreas V. *Rise of the Lone Star: The Making of Texas.* College Station: Texas A&M University Press, 1989.

Rogers, L. Randall. *Two Particular Friends of Stephen F. Austin.* Private printing, 1990.

Taylor, Virginia H. *The Spanish Archives of the General Land Office of Texas.* Reprint. St. Louis: Ingmire Publications, 1983.

Valadés, José C. *México, Santa Anna y la guerra de Texas.* Mexico: Editorial Diana, 1979.

Vigness, David M. *The Revolutionary Decades 1810-1836.* Austin: Steck-Vaughn, 1965.

Warren, Harris Gaylord. *The Sword Was Their Passport: A History of American Filibustering in the Mexican Revolution.* Baton Rouge: Louisiana State University Press, 1943.

Weber, David J. *The Mexican Frontier, 1821-1846: The American Southwest Under Mexico.* Albuquerque: University of New Mexico Press, 1982.

Yoakum, H. *History of Texas from its First Settlement in 1685 to its Annexation to the United States in 1846.* 2 vols. Reprint. Austin: Steck, 1935.

Articles

Bacarisse, Charles A. "The Union of Coahuila and Texas," *Southwestern Historical Quarterly* 61 (1958): 341-49.

Benson, Nettie Lee. "Texas as Viewed from Mexico, 1820-1834," *Southwestern Historical Quarterly* 90 (1987): 219-91.

Davenport, Harbert. "Captain Jesus Cuellar, Texas Cavalry, Otherwise Comanche," *Southwestern Historical Quarterly* 30 (1926): 56-62.

De la Teja, Jesús F. and John Wheat. "Bexar: Profile of a Tejano Community, 1820-1832," *Southwestern Historical Quarterly* 89 (1985): 7-34.

De León, Arnoldo. "Tejanos and the Texas War for Independence: Historiography's Judgement," *New Mexico Historical Review* 61 (1986): 137-146.

Foley, Patrick. "Jean-Marie Odin, C.M., Missionary Bishop Extraordinaire of Texas," *Journal of Texas Catholic History and Culture* 1 (1990): 42-60.

Graham, Don. "Remembering the Alamo: The Story of the Texas Revolution in Popular Culture," *Southwestern Historical Quarterly* 89 (1985): 35-66.

Machado, Mauro M. "El Coronel Don Juan Nepomuceno Seguín," *Lulac News* 5 (1938): 1-8.

Santos, Richard. "Juan Nepomuceno Seguín, espía tejano en la comandancia del noreste de México," *Humanitas: Anuario del Centro de Estudios Humanísticos de la Universidad Autónoma de Nuevo León* 17 (1976): 551-567.

Stuart, Ben C. "Hamilton Stuart: Pioneer Editor," *Southwestern Historical Quarterly* 21 (1918): 381-88.

Vázquez, Josefina Zoraida. "The Texas Question in Mexican Politics, 1836-1845," *Southwestern Historical Quarterly* 89 (1986): 309-44.

Vernon, Ida. "Activities of the Seguins in Early Texas History," *West Texas Historical Association Year Book* 25 (1949): 11-38.

Williams, Amelia. "A Critical Study of the Siege of the Alamo and of the Personnel of Its Defenders," *Southwestern Historical Quarterly* 36-37 (1936-1937).

Manuscripts

Benavides, Adán, Jr. "Spanish and Mexican Letters on the Texas Frontier, 1795-1835." Paper presented at the Annual Meeting of the Texas State Historical Association, Dallas, March 1991.

Butterfield, Jack C. "Juan N. Seguin: A Vindication." Manuscript in Daughters of the Republic of Texas Research Library, San Antonio, Texas.

Lack, Paul D. "Los Tejanos: Texas Mexicans in the Revolution." Chapter in forthcoming book on the Texas War of Independence.

Robbins, Jerry D. "Juan Seguin." Master's thesis, Southwest Texas State University, 1962.

Index

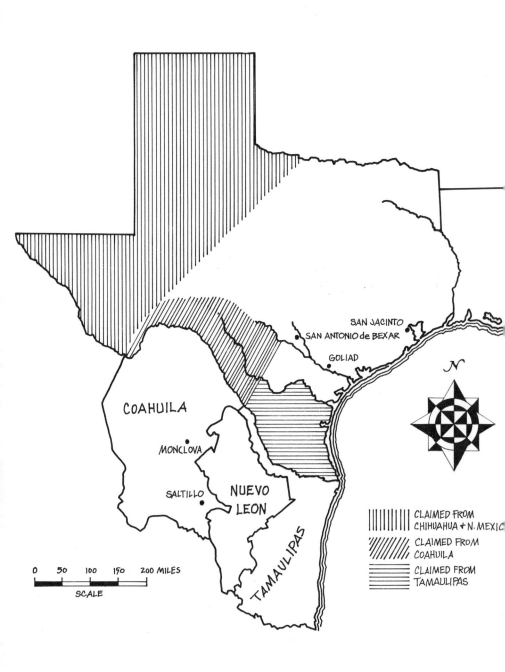

SAN JACINTO

SAN ANTONIO de BEXAR

GOLIAD

COAHUILA

MONCLOVA

SALTILLO

NUEVO LEON

TAMAULIPAS

N

CLAIMED FROM
CHIHUAHUA + N. MEXICO

CLAIMED FROM
COAHUILA

CLAIMED FROM
TAMAULIPAS

0   50   100   150   200 MILES

SCALE